SEX, LIES & POLITICS

THE NAKED TRUTH

LARRY FLYNT

SEX, LIES & POLITICS
The Naked Truth

KENSINGTON BOOKS
www.kensingtonbooks.com

KENSINGTON BOOKS are published by
Kensington Publishing Corp.
850 Third Avenue
New York, NY 10022

All Kensington titles, imprints, and distributed lines are available at special quantity discounts for bulk purchases for sales promotions, premiums, fund-raising, educational, or institutional use.

Special book excerpts or customized printings can also be created to fit specific needs. For details, write or phone the office of the Kensington special sales manager: Kensington Publishing Corp., 850 Third Avenue, New York, NY 10022, attn: Special Sales Department; phone 1-800-221-2647.

Kensington and the K logo are Reg. U.S. Pat. & TM Off.

Library of Congress Control Number: 2003116199

ISBN 0-7582-0483-3

Designed by Lenny Telesca

First printing: July 2004

10   9   8   7   6   5   4   3   2   1

Printed in the United States of America

This book is dedicated to my father, Larry Claxton Flynt.

ACKNOWLEDGMENTS

I want to thank Kim Dower, William Patrick, and Jeremie Ruby-Strauss. Without their patience, support, and dedication, this book would never have been possible.

CONTENTS

FOREWORD
by Robert Scheer

This is a tough, provocative, and informative book, well docu-
mented and logically thought out, which might come as a shock to
people who have known Flynt as a more outrageous and raunchy
personality. I wasn't surprised by the book because in recent years
I've come to know another Larry Flynt: the one who has appeared
as a guest lecturer in my Media and Society class at the University
of Southern California every semester for the past three years. I
am familiar with just how on-target his message has become.

I always begin by screening Milos Forman's classic movie *The
People vs. Larry Flynt*, which is the chronicle of a wild man put
into a straitjacket by the system. Woody Harrelson captures the
madness of a man trying to make a buck off sex who runs smack
into the hypocritical standards we live by. Courtney Love is brilliant as the symbol of the chaos into which Flynt's life degener-
ated.

But that was then, many trials and travails ago, and suddenly the
curtain parts and in rolls the real life Larry Flynt—the charming, at-
peace-with-himself, super-rich and carefully groomed businessman
in his gold-plated wheelchair. It is instantly obvious that the ad-

versity that ripped his gut has also produced an incredibly different man.

I know he's been a pig in his day—objectifying women, as they say, and blowing away the pretense that highbrow *erotica* is different than down and dirty *porn*. Nope, said Flynt, it's just a matter of taste, and mine is decidedly low class. Of course they're not just reading the articles or admiring the beautiful stylized airbrushed pictures, Flynt proclaimed. This has always been material for wankers, and what's wrong with letting the little guy in on some safe sex?

But over the years, there came to be much more to Flynt than his original goal of turning auto-eroticism into a guilt-free national pastime and a terrific profit center. What he's become is a truth-seeker who takes no prisoners. I know it's hard to adjust and think of this self-described "smut peddler" as the Tom Paine of our time, issuing broadsides that skewer the pompous asses who dare to presume that they know what's best for us. But that's Larry these days. In particular, he has George W. Bush's number, debunking, as he does in a good part of this book, the "just a Texas country boy" con of the President, who screws ordinary folks while living to fatten the wallets of the country club set who are his real base.

Bush plays at being a redneck who made good on his own, which steams Flynt, who is the real thing. Bush was raised in the lap of luxury, was pushed through the best schools, then failed at every business venture until bailed out by his old man's money and contacts. Flynt never had a break from family, class, or influence, but he made big-time money on his own. The strength of this book lies in Flynt's anger over Bush's coming on as a hardworking everyman.

There is no real George W. Bush other than the one that highly paid campaign hucksters have conjured up to fool ordinary folks while he picks their pockets. Flynt, on the other hand is genuine— an American Horatio Alger, warts and all, a hustler's hustler who snatched from the rich and powerful what they never wanted to give. Along the way of cons and schemes, of sex and sales, Flynt became something he never set out to be—a fighter for truth and justice—and he seems more amazed by that outcome than anyone around him.

As when he says, "I never thought about the First Amendment and civil liberties until I was facing a judge who was set on putting me away for twenty years." After all those arrests, trials, incarceration, and finally being sentenced to a wheelchair by a mad would-be assassin's bullets, Flynt was born again as a human being. This is the accidental warrior who survived the battlefield to settle scores with those who wanted to steal his freedom. In the process, he became an uncompromising brawler for the freedom of all.

Flynt delights in calling himself a smut peddler and studiously affects an "aw shucks" trailer-trash style, but that's just an act to mask a shrewd capitalist entrepreneur who has made a great deal of money through thirty-three magazines and the adroit use of the Internet and a variety of other electronic outlets. Porn may be the most lucrative, but it is not the entirety of his marketing, which ranges from naked shots of what are purportedly the girl next door to the intricacies of skateboarding.

This guy has crawled up from the bottom depths of American life to become an untutored but brilliant analyst of how the system works. As he put it when he saved President Clinton's job by exposing the sexual peccadilloes of the president's puritanical right-wing accusers in the Congress: "They call me a bottom feeder, and it's true, but look what I found down at the bottom." What he found was that a host of uptight, prudish Republican congressmen were living lives of such debauchery as to make Clinton seem like a Boy Scout in comparison.

That story, one of many revealed here in fresh detail, captures the recent impact of Flynt on the culture wars that have roiled our politics of late. The right-wing thrives on hypocrisy, blasting everyone else as weird. Newt Gingrich liked to refer to the "normal Americans" who supported him and his branch of the

Republican party. The rest of us who don't see things his way are not just wrong, we are *abnormal*—so far out of the mainstream that our opinions are not worthy of note.

How refreshing, then, to discover with the help of hypocrisy busters like Flynt that the so-called "normal" ones are as weird as one could imagine. In the case of Gingrich, he visits his wife who's suffering in the hospital from cancer to tell her he's leaving her for another woman. Then he leaves the next wife for the secretary that he's secretly shacking up with during the very months that he's leading the charge for Clinton's impeachment.

I hardly need to tell you that Flynt is no prude. As he told my class on more than one occasion in discussing his views on homosexuality: "I don't care if you screw trees, it's not my or the government's business." His credo is: "The best thing any government can do for you is leave you alone." Personally, I believe the government should do a great deal more, such as providing good schools and a strong safety net, but Flynt's genuine passion is that of the consistent libertarian, and we need more of them at a time when, thanks to the hysteria over terrorism, liberty is at grave risk.

What Flynt lacks in formal education, he more than makes up for with the world's most finely honed bullshit detector. His singular enemy is hypocrisy, and while that doesn't make him a saint, it sure turns him into a helluva perceptive social commentator. Sorry, Larry—hate to break the news to you, but pornography is no longer your main game. Honesty is.

ROBERT SCHEER is co-author of *The Five Biggest Lies Bush Told Us About Iraq,* and a nationally syndicated columnist based at the *Los Angeles Times,* clinical professor of communications at USC's Annenberg School, and visiting lecturer at the UC Berkeley Graduate School of Journalism.

INTRODUCTION: "I'VE BEEN 'FLYNTED'!"

Sooner or later, any notable person with an unseemly past and a friend who owns a camera, can expect their dirty pictures to turn up on my desk.

In the summer of 2003, I was approached by a couple of soldiers from the 507 Maintenance Company who wanted to sell me pictures of Jessica Lynch, poster girl for the war in Iraq, bare breasted and in sexual situations. From the look of the images, they had been taken with a cheap camera in an army barracks. The soldiers said they had done their little photo shoot at Fort Bliss (you couldn't even make this stuff up) just before they shipped out to Iraq.

I had a forensic photo expert examine the images to prove that the girl in the pictures was indeed Jessica, and that the photographs were legitimate. Then I gave the boys the money they wanted, and put the photos in a drawer. It cost me a bundle in lost circulation for *Hustler,* but I decided not to run them. (In fact, I wouldn't be saying any of this if the *New York Daily News* hadn't got wind of the photo deal and run a story on it.)

My feeling was that if Private Lynch wanted to have a good time, more power to her. I'm all for healthy sex among America's fighting men and women. And I couldn't see exploiting the girl any further than she was already being exploited by the Bush administration, the people who were using her as a stage prop to sell their war in Iraq.

I'm an opponent of hypocrisy, not sex. In 1998, after I exposed certain details about Republican Congressman Bob Livingston's private life, he did an interview with the *New York Times.* Sputtering and fuming about having his dirty laundry brought to light, he said, "I've been Flynted!" But I didn't "Flynt" Congressman Livingston, the man designated to replace Newt Gingrich as speaker of the House, for immorality. I Flynted him for saying one thing in public (expressing shock and outrage at Clinton for having an affair, going on and on about the sanctity of marriage) and then doing quite another in private (having a number of affairs of his own).

He and his conservative colleagues had been trying for years to bring down President Clinton any way they could. Unable to get any of their other accusations to stick, they found pay dirt with Monica Lewinsky, and then they began to howl about the shame of it. Week after week they made long-winded speeches about the threat to the nation posed by Clinton's sex drive—and all the while many of them were getting it down and dirty on the side themselves.

Jessica Lynch, on the other hand, was no hypocrite. She never claimed to be a hero, or a saint. When she got a chance to tell her own story, she set the record straight and gave credit where credit was due, and I admire her for that. It was the Bush administration's media experts who had played fast and loose with the truth about her supposed exploits. A soldier captured behind enemy lines, young, good looking, brutalized while defenseless—and female! It was the perfect image to rile public opinion on the evening news. She could be Snow White to her own Prince Charming; Rambo and the leading lady too. In the hands of Bush's spin-doctors, she was Joan of Arc with an M-16.

So the defense department made up a cock and bull story about how she fired her weapon until her ammo ran out, how she was wounded by enemy fire, and how she was mistreated by her captors in the hospital. They even went so far as to set up the perfect Hollywood rescue, complete with camera crew rolling the video, as the Special Operations boys stormed the hospital to extract her.

Of course, we all know now that none of it was true. She has told her story in her book and in interviews. She was injured in the wreck of her Humvee. Her weapon jammed and she never fired a shot. She was taken in and given good medical care by the Iraqis, who tried several times to return her to U.S. authorities. But the most ridiculous part is how the mainstream media, who'll follow any parade as long as it boosts their ratings, played along with the Rambo version dished out by the Defense Department. The joke is the *New York Times,* the "newspaper of record" in this country, ran a piece by Jayson Blair, the cub reporter they later found out was making up articles right and left! The assignment was tailor made for this young man. He described visiting Lynch's family home in West Virginia and got all the physical details wrong—because he was never there.

Think about all the sorry circumstances that were necessary for this article to see print. The compliant media gives us a make-believe story about make-believe heroism in a war fought for make-believe reasons—declared by a president whose election was pure make-believe. Well, I'm all about the naked truth, and I'm going to expose it, starting right at the top with Bush, his administration, and his cronies.

I'm all about the naked truth, and I'm going to expose it, starting right at the top with Bush, his administration, and his cronies.

The Bush administration has sold a bundle of lies to the American people, and the Jessica Lynch story is only one of them. Fortunately, a number of critics have called our attention to George W. Bush's arms-length relationship with the truth throughout his career. David Corn wrote *The Lies of George W. Bush*. Joe Conason wrote *Big Lies,* expanding his look at lying to include the whole right-wing movement. Al Franken did a funny take on the same subject with *Lies and the Lying Liars Who Tell Them*.

In *Sex, Lies & Politics,* I want to expose an issue larger than Bush's smear tactics, or his habits of ignoring uncomfortable facts or bending the truth when it's convenient. The deception we see in the Bush administration is the end result of a campaign of hypocrisy that's been gathering steam in conservative circles for thirty years.

John F. Kennedy once said, "The great enemy of the truth is very often not the lie—deliberate, contrived, and dishonest; but the myth—persistent, persuasive, and unrealistic." For the radical conservatives who brought Bush to power, lying isn't enough. Lying is useful when someone gets caught in a squeeze and has to weasel out of it. But when you have something as bogus to sell as an elective war or tax cuts for the rich (or *both*), you need a myth—a whole view of the world that's basically horse manure—in order to close the deal.

Ever since the so-called "Reagan Revolution" of the 1980s, the radical conservatives have been creating the myth that liberals are to blame for all our troubles. They've lied about who liberals are and what they stand for, and worse, they've lied about who they—the conservatives—are and what *they* stand for. Those who stand to gain from the myth—the president and his administration, the radical conservatives, the corporate cronies, and the compliant press (which is of course *owned* by the corporations)—repeat distorted "facts" and deliberate lies so often that they settle over our nation like the L.A. smog outside my window. Eventually, people begin to confuse them with truth. What makes us vulnerable to this myth? It's our own hypocrisy about sex and religion—what we've been brainwashed to call "family values," even though they don't reflect the values of most American families.

More than a generation ago, unable to sell their "no millionaire left behind" agenda in an honest and straightforward way, conservatives figured out something they could sell instead—self-righteousness and solid "American values." It all started back in 1968, when the Republican Party adopted "more-patriotic-than-thou" flag waving in order to hustle blue collar and middle class Americans, especially Southerners, into voting against their own economic interest. Richard Nixon and his vice-president, Spiro T. Agnew, hyped what they called the "silent majority." But after those two disgraced themselves and had to resign—the president because of Watergate, the vice-president because of outright graft—the right-wingers needed to retool.

That's when the evangelical Christians came on board, and holier-than-thou, sexually repressed religion, along with hypocritical moralizing, became the one hand that distracts you while they pick your pocket with the other. The followers get "family values" and flag decals while the fat cats get tax cuts.

The radical conservatives talk about ending abortion and restoring school prayer to get the average Joe into the Republican camp. Then, while average Joe holds a prayer vigil outside, the fat cats close the door and pass around the subsidies, exemptions, and sweetheart deals. This is why the rich have made out like bandits ever since Reagan was elected more than twenty years ago, and why, unless you're a millionaire, you're getting screwed. In this book, I'm going to expose the manipulations that have average Americans out cheering for the conservative reverse Robin Hoods who rob from the poor to give to the rich.

I'm also going to Flynt the fundamental hypocrisy of the American voter who nods along to "family values," supports "just say no" sex education for our kids, and allows a policy of denying advice on birth control to women in Third World countries while at the same time spending *$10 billion* a year on pornography. Obviously, Americans are conflicted about sex, and we need a reality check.

In general, people who have a nice, healthy connection to their crotch have a better connection between their head and their heart. In their politics, they don't find so much to be mad-dog angry about. They're happy to make a buck, but they're not so greedy that it makes them mean, or so frustrated that it makes them blind to the cruelty they might inflict on others.

Their inability to be honest and open about sex has twisted conservatives' priorities and warped their minds. The right-wing of the Republican party is not so much a political agenda as it is a plea for help. I just wish we could get these people some therapy so they'd leave the rest of us alone.

With the election cycle rolling around again, we need to clear the air and refresh our memories. People are busy trying to make a living, and we tend to forget the details. A lot of the news is so dismal that we prefer to pop open a beer and watch sitcoms. And there are plenty of young people voting now who don't remember much about the Clinton administration, much less about the Reagan years or Nixon. They're forced to accept what they see on the surface as the whole story, because they don't know how we got here. They don't have any context. Yet those who are unable to learn from history are destined to have George W. Bush around for a second term.

But maybe you're wondering who elected me to set the record straight?

Nobody. I've run for president and I've run for governor of California, and both times I lost fair and square. For sure, I did not win the 2000 presidential election any more than George W. Bush did, so as I write this book, I do it not as any high official, but as a lowly smut peddler. I am, however, a smut peddler who cares.

I am a smut peddler who cares.

There are advantages to having a perspective that many people already look down on. No one is ever going to find anything in my past to hold over my head. If there are any compromising photographs, you can bet I paid someone to take them myself. I have nothing to gain by lying to you, because I've already made my money, and I'm not up for re-election. I own my company out-right, and I don't answer to anyone, least of all the religious right.

As for my credentials, I have spent millions of dollars and years of my life in various courtrooms defending every American's right to privacy and to free speech. Every month I travel the country lecturing in defense of our Bill of Rights. Over the last few years I've spoken to students at Harvard, Yale, Penn State, Berkeley, the University of Southern California, Oxford, and Cambridge—to name a few—in front of standing-room-only crowds. A recent poll at Cornell chose me as the speaker students most wanted to hear. Frankly, that shocked me. I used to think people wanted to hear my opinions because they were outlandish. Now I'm convinced it's because I'm one of the few people speaking out who does not censor what's on his mind. The youth of America have never been afraid of the truth.

In *Falwell v. Flynt,* the landmark 1988 case in which I was sued for running a parody of the leader of the Moral Majority, I won what has been called the most important First Amendment case to appear before the Supreme Court in the twentieth century. During the Clinton years, I did the work the media failed to do in exposing hypocritical right-wing congressmen. My *Flynt Report*—a special-edition magazine that detailed this exposure—was the essential counterweight to the *Starr Report* in providing an accurate view of the Ging-

> **I have been shot and paralyzed; sued for millions; indicted, convicted, and incarcerated numerous times; and it has never stopped me from speaking my mind.**

rich era in the 1990s, the golden age of right-wing character assassination and political mud slinging. I have been shot and paralyzed; sued for millions; indicted, convicted, and incarcerated numerous times; and it has never stopped me from speaking my mind.

For anyone who finds it odd that a smut peddler would presume to speak on political matters, let me say that I am not a pornographer trying to rise to the level of politics. As I will demonstrate, it is the attack-dog politics of the radical conservatives that has descended to the level of porn.

In Congressman Livingston's famous interview about being outed as a hypocrite, the one in which he turned my name into a verb, he also said that I was a bottom-feeder. When reporters called me and asked for a comment, I said, "Yeah, that's right, but look what I found when I got down there!"

I'm no policy wonk. I'm a common sense, common man. I also used to sell Bibles door to door, so I know a hustle when I see one, and the Republican agenda is one big hustle. I may be just the kind of guy needed to connect the dots about the Big Hustle, especially when connecting the dots means connecting the dirt.

SEX, LIES & POLITICS

THE NAKED TRUTH

I never gave them hell. I just tell the truth
and they think it's hell.
—Harry Truman

1

A Smut Peddler
Who Cares

When I was born in 1942 in Eastern Kentucky's Magoffin County, my family's annual income was $600. I grew up in a place called Lakeville, near Lickskillet Holler. There, in the poorest county in America—bootlegging and jury duty were the two biggest industries—the twentieth century didn't really hit us until around 1950. Nobody had television or household appliances. I was nearly ten years old before any of the roads were paved. And then all we heard were the grimy coal trucks groaning down the steep mountain roads.

Hard drinking was common in Lickskillet Holler, as was sexual exploration that would be frowned upon in the suburbs. At the age of nine, I did it with a chicken, but I had already determined that I liked girls better. (I had sex for the first time when I was seven, with a thirteen-year-old from down the road.)

George Bush, the president's son, who was born in Connecticut, the wealthiest state in the Union, who went to Andover and Yale and "summered" in Kennebunkport, talks like a cattle drover and makes a big deal out of cutting brush on his ranch to show what a regular guy he is. But in our part of Kentucky, people talked like hicks because they really were hicks, and hard work was not a photo-op. In Magoffin County, we "summered" where we "wintered," and our main extracurricular activity was plowing fields while looking up a mule's butt. So about the time I should have been finishing ninth grade, I ran away. (Going off to boarding school at Andover was definitely not an option.)

I made it as far as Indiana, but owing to an empty belly, I decided I could do better in the army. I contacted my mother and got her to sign the consent form, and in the summer of 1958, at age fifteen, I was sworn in and sent to Camp Gordon, Georgia. Basic training was the first time in my entire life that I didn't have to think about where my next meal was coming from, or whether I had clean clothes or holes in my shoes. I completed basic with above-average scores, but within the year there was a general cutback in personnel and I was discharged.

> **Basic training was the first time in my entire life that I didn't have to think about where my next meal was coming from.**

I went to Dayton, Ohio, where my mother was living, and I started washing dishes. Then I worked at the Dayton Mattress Factory for $1.15 an hour. My next job was with the Inland Manufacturing Company, but the pay and the conditions were so bad I decided to become an entrepreneur—a bootlegger. I went back home and began running liquor into Lakeville from nearby Mount Sterling, which was "wet," meaning that liquor could be bought legally. The county sheriff did not approve, and before long I was digging out my old, fake birth certificate and heading back to the military, only this time I visited the navy recruiting station. I passed the tests, and soon I was on a bus to the Great Lakes Naval Air Station for navy boot camp.

I owe a lot to the navy. To the extent that I ever became civilized, you might say it civilized me. Even though I was the youngest recruit in my company, I was the only one who had been through basic before (in the army), so I had an edge. Before long I was mas-ter-at-arms for my company, with the acting rank of petty officer.

The pay was still not great, so that's when I teamed up with a buddy to sell Bibles during our off-duty hours. We hit the suburbs near the base, my buddy in a wheelchair pretending to be de-mented. He did such a good job of slobbering and jabbering that the ladies were always anxious to get us off their porch, which meant that we sold lots of two-dollar Bibles, often for more than list price!

I think I was a typical American in that I always had my sights set on bigger things, and for me, being in the navy, that meant technology. I came out of Radar A school as an eighteen-year-old petty officer, second class, and in 1962, I was assigned to the *USS Enterprise,* a brand-new nuclear-powered carrier.

At a time when most boys were entering their senior year in high school, I had ninety-five men under my command, most of them older than me. I was an E-5, equivalent to a sergeant—the youngest second-class petty officer in the navy. I was sent to the Officers' CIC (Combat Information Center) school in Brunswick, Georgia, where all the buildings on the base are mock-ups of what the inside of ships look like in the navy, and people do mock demonstrations and drills. I was one of the people who manned those facilities for the officers. I got some training early on, and I was able to take my advancement course and pass it after I had been there for just a few months.

I was the absolute best at what I did. When we went to sea, I al-ways had eight to twelve weeks of starched, pressed dungarees, shirts, and white hats to wear, when everyone else was wearing the old crumpled up ones straight out of the laundry. I set an example for the men who worked for me, and I made sure that I knew each and every one of their jobs better than they knew it themselves. That's why, when President John F. Kennedy came aboard the *Enterprise* in the fall of '62, they wanted me to work on the bridge, because they knew that's where the president would come to view the ship.

When I met him I had on headphones and I was monitoring a tote board for CIC, and Kennedy put his hand on my shoulder and asked what I was doing. I'll never forget the exchange. I started explaining to him the technicalities of what I was up to, and then the captain of the ship came up behind the president and was making faces at me to make sure I wouldn't say the wrong thing. It was a thrill for me to meet Kennedy in that way—while I was doing my job. At that moment, I never could have imagined that fifteen years later, I would be publishing nude photos of his wife.

> **It was a thrill for me to meet Kennedy in that way—while I was doing my job. At that moment, I never could have imagined that fifteen years later, I would be publishing nude photos of his wife.**

I'd begun supplementing my earnings with poker, and life in the navy was great. When my enlistment was up in 1964, I went back to Dayton and Inland Manufacturing, but I knew that mind-numbing routine would kill me. I needed capital to get something going, so I worked all the overtime I could get. Sometimes, when my shift ended, I'd simply crawl under one of the machines and try to nap till the next shift began. I even took a second job working at Chrysler Airtemp on the other side of town.

My mother owned a bar called the Keewee, and as soon as I managed to scrape together $6,000, I bought it from her. This was 1965, and I was twenty-two. I didn't have any Yale College, and I didn't have any Harvard Business School, but even then I knew that everybody needs a gimmick, so I immediately changed the name of the bar to Hillbilly Haven and turned it into a knock-down, drag-out country joint for all the working-class people like myself, especially the hillbillies from Kentucky, Tennessee, and West Virginia. I set up horseshoe stakes out back, picnic tables, and put a fence around the yard so people could take a beer outside. We brought in country music, and before long we were selling six hundred cases of beer on Sundays alone. I went from wages of $200 a week from working two jobs to earning more than $1,000 a week owning my own business. Finally, I was part of the American Dream.

Birth of a Hustler

Growth is the name of the game for entrepreneurs, so I bought a second bar on the east side of Dayton and called it Larry's Hangover Tavern. Before long, I bought another near a bunch of factories and called it—The Factory.

By now, the "sixties" lifestyle was getting into full swing, and my next investment was the big one. I called it The Hustler Club, and it came not just with booze but go-go girls. This was still the Midwest, though, so I ran the place like a nunnery and sold only the *hope* of hanky-panky. The way I've always seen it, my business succeeded because I was willing to bypass the sexual hypocrisy of my competitors and cater to the erotic imaginations of real people. We didn't try to be better than anybody. We gave 'em what they wanted.

From 1968 to 1971 I expanded to Cincinnati, Columbus, Cleveland, Toledo, and Akron. By 1973, I had eight Hustler Clubs, with three hundred people on my payroll. I started giving out memberships to traveling businessmen. Then I came up with the idea of a newsletter to introduce my new dancers and let members know if a certain girl had moved to a different location.

In November 1973, I began to publish *Hustler* magazine. A year later, we went with what we'll call a slightly more explicit photo policy, and by April of 1975, I was grossing over $500,000 an issue. And that's when I made the smartest investment of my life, and bought those nudes of Jackie Kennedy Onassis, which I ran in the August 1975 issue. The rest, as they say, is history.

But that's also when I began to learn about politics, and about the hypocrisy that comes with the territory. In our bicentennial issue for July 1976, we ran a cartoon of Henry Kissinger, Gerald Ford, and Nelson Rockefeller gang-raping the Statue of Liberty.

At *Hustler,* we were being outrageously vulgar by design. We *wanted* to offend people. We felt that the First Amendment afforded us the right to be offensive. In July 1976, in Cincinnati, we got our wish and more—we were indicted not just for pandering and obscenity, but for organized crime. The indictment was thrown out due to selective proscecution. This dismayed Bruce Taylor, who was at that time the prosecutor, and who is now the loser who is heading up Ashcroft's obscenity taskforce.

> **We were being outrageously vulgar by design. We *wanted* to offend people.**

Cincinnati was the home of a bluenose group called Citizens for Decency Through Law (CDL). The CDL had been founded and funded by Charles H. Keating, a dyed-in-the-wool Catholic zealot. He had a number of lawyers on the payroll viewing pornographic magazines and films in order to keep Ohio's newsstands pure. Ironically, Keating's moral purity did not prevent him from committing fraudulent financial dealings that became known in the late 1980s as the infamous "Savings and Loan scandal," a fiasco of 1980s Republican deregulation mania that cost the American taxpayer $1.4 trillion in bailouts. The FDIC puts the cost of cleaning up Keating's mess at Lincoln Savings and Loan at $2 billion. As I've said many times, I'd rather have an honest pornographer than a crooked preacher any day of the week.

Keating's brother, Bill, was president of the *Cincinnati Enquirer.* Keating's partner in purity was another Catholic inquisitor, Hamilton County Prosecutor Simon Leis, Jr. Not satisfied with the charges they already had filed, Leis trumped up an unrelated accusation, kept me in jail for twenty-seven days before allowing me to post bail, and then charged me with perjury for pleading not guilty. I couldn't believe it.

To combat these devoutly religious protectors of Ohio's virtue,

I formed an organization called Ohioans for a Free Press. I tried to run an ad with a quote from Adolf Hitler: "The reorganization of our press has truly been a success. . . . Divergences of opinions between members of the government are no longer an occasion for public exhibitions and are not the newspaper's business. We've eliminated that conception of political freedom which holds that everybody has the right to say whatever comes into his head." Nobody would touch it. I called up the *Cincinnati Post* and asked if they would let me run the opening of the U.S. Constitution as an ad, and they still said no. The folks in Ohio were out to get me because of who I was and the threat I represented to their narrow little world.

Unfortunately, in 1973, the Supreme Court had already shirked their responsibility and turned the whole question of obscenity over to thoroughly hung-up, middle-class, local prosecutors. They had ruled in *Miller v. California* that defining obscenity was best left to local courts relying on "community standards." This meant that national publications had to avoid offending the most conservative community in the country, or take a chance on being sent to jail for as long as (in some states) sixty-five years.

We don't take any conventional advertising in *Hustler,* so we were free to run ads on the back cover—which we did, showing the effects of smoking, including pictures of a cancer-ravaged human lung and tongue. My point was that cigarettes kill people, and yet, at that time, you could still promote and display them openly. Hell, you could give them out on street corners and at rock concerts. Where was there any evidence that pornography had ever harmed anyone?

The difference was that death-for-profit in the form of cigarettes didn't threaten the world view of uptight Ohioans—but sex did. Sex profoundly offended them because it shook their uptight little lives to the

Sex profoundly offended them because it shook their uptight little lives to the very foundation.

very foundation. So while they were big on freedom to make money as the American way, they didn't quite understand the other freedoms written into our Constitution, including the number-one item in our Bill of Rights—freedom of speech.

As my attorney said at my trial in Cincinnati, "Freedom doesn't mean anything if it's not offensive. Freedom is putting up with an awful lot in society that is distasteful. Freedom is only meaningful if it includes *all* speech, no matter who is offended by it. . . . The freedom guaranteed in the First Amendment is indivisible."

What I saw as the real issue was: Are Americans afraid to be free? Is real freedom too scary and too threatening? And why do so many people have to be so two-faced about it?

I have paid dearly for my fight against hypocrisy. I have been sent to prison a couple of times, and I have spent so much time in court that it has become my second home. Along the way, I've learned that it's not enough to fight the battle one lawsuit at a time. Anyone who believes strongly in anything has to be willing to take the fight into the political arena, and that's where Flynting the hypocrites comes in.

My longest stint in the slammer was back in the 1980s, the result of refusing to give up my source in the John DeLorean cocaine trafficking trial. DeLorean was a flashy engineer who had been the king of the muscle cars at General Motors, then spun off his own company, which then went into the toilet. I had received tapes that showed FBI agents actually "setting up" the financially strapped automaker. It showed the guys who are supposed to be *fighting* crime committing entrapment, meaning that they *created* a crime for DeLorean to be guilty of. They supplied both the cocaine and the dumb idea that selling drugs was the answer to DeLorean's cash-flow problems. There was even an audio tape that captured DeLorean's voice pleading to be let out of the cocaine deal, and then the agent threatening to harm his daughter if he pulled out.

As a journalist, I couldn't reveal my source to the courts, and when I refused, the judge started fining me $10,000 a day. I paid it for a few days, then decided there wasn't any future in that, and when I stopped paying, he sent me to prison. I knew he was going to do it, especially after I said something to suggest that the judge had had conjugal relations with his mother—something that every American should say to a high government official at least once in his life. I also had an orange I was eating in the courtroom, and I threw it at him and almost hit him smack between the eyes. He changed the sentence from six months to fifteen months, and I said, "Is that the best you can do?" And he said, "Take him away." Luckily for me, the judge ignored an important law, which states that you cannot put someone away for more than six months for contempt of court without holding a hearing. He didn't have a hearing, so his case was reversed on appeal, and I was released.

If you can imagine that prison is bad, try being there in a wheelchair. It wasn't as bad for me as it was for a lot of people, because I was a celebrity. Everybody locked up in that prison saw me as a big shot, which definitely made it a little more bearable. But I think they kept me segregated from the general population because they were afraid I might cause a riot.

The fact is, I had to hang in there, because freedom gets chipped away each time we make a compromise, each time we do something contrary to what we believe. Making what we say, do, and believe all the same thing is how we avoid becoming hypocrites ourselves.

By 1986, I was even getting crap thrown at me from the other side. The girlfriend of *Penthouse* publisher Bob Guccione sued me because of a cartoon we ran in *Hustler* insinuating that Guccione might have given her a venereal disease. It was a completely frivolous lawsuit, but because of certain loopholes and circumstances, it was allowed to proceed, and we had to fight it all the way. In fact, this was first case we took to the Supreme Court.

I wanted to argue the case myself. This is allowable on the trial level in both federal and state court, but not before the Supremes, so at the last minute, they appointed some lawyer from Chicago to argue for me. When the arguments were finished, and the justices all started to get up out of their chairs, I said, "You nine assholes and one token cunt! You denied me my Constitutional right to defend myself!" Whereupon Justice Warren Burger said, "Arrest that man!" The Supreme Court police came and got me, took me down the hallway, and put me in an anteroom. I looked up at the Supreme Court policeman, who was grinning, and I said, "What are you smiling at?"

> When the justices all started to get up out of their chairs, I said, "You nine assholes and one token cunt! You denied me my Constitutional right to defend myself!"

"I've been working here for eighteen years," he said to me, "and this is the most fun I've ever had." I thought that was interesting. Here was a cop, a member of the establishment, and even *he* got a thrill out of seeing somebody stand up to authority.

Eventually, the justices sent the case back to the lower court. Ultimately, we paid the woman some money to get rid of her, but the suit had an added twist.

One right every American still has is that, when we go on trial, we are entitled to face our accusers. It was Chief Justice Warren Burger who had ordered my arrest. He was my accuser, so I wanted him subpoenaed at my trial. I wanted to get him on the witness stand and ask him what so offended him about his asshole that he would have me arrested. Soon the U.S. attorneys in Washington were calling my attorneys in California saying, "Let's make a deal." They didn't want me to bring the chief justice to my trial. They either had to drop the charges or serve Warren Burger with a subpoena. No justice in the history of this country has ever had to testify like that.

The Pornographer and the Preacher

Without question, my most important battle was the 1988 *Hustler Magazine, Inc., v. Jerry Falwell* case, in which the Supreme Court unanimously ruled in my favor. This was the landmark decision that made parody protected speech. This decision altered both the legal world and the communications/entertainment business forever. It put an end to the notion that you could win damages against someone for hurting your feelings. When it concerns a public figure like Falwell, only if someone makes a false statement of fact that they know to be untrue or recklessly disregards whether it's true, and only if it causes him harm, can you prove libel.

The story is well known by now, but in brief: We ran a parody ad in *Hustler*—a take-off on the Campari ads that showed someone describing "their first time," that is, their first experience sipping Campari. We depicted Jerry Falwell's "first time" as having been with his mother in an outhouse. He sued us for libel in Federal Court in Virginia claiming we inflicted emotional stress on him.

It wasn't an easy battle. The one thing I always knew was that we had to go through with the trial. Even if I lost, it was the principle.

A few weeks after Falwell sued, he stupidly printed 750,000 copies of the ad and mailed it to members of his flock, seeking pity—and contributions to help pay for his legal costs. That's when I counter-sued him for copyright infringement and the legal battle between the pornographer and the preacher went full steam ahead.

I lost the first round at the trial level, but I had to convince myself and my attorneys that it was not over. I was not doing this just for me. I had to take the fight to the bloody end.

> **I was not doing this just for me. I had to take the fight to the bloody end.**

Falwell had asked for $50 million, and the jury had awarded him $200,000.

My attorneys said it would cost me $2 million to take this case all the way through the appeals process. Everyone's advice to me was just settle and be done. But I said, "No way." I wasn't going to pay Falwell $200,000 for "intentional infliction of emotional distress."

I appealed to the Fourth Circuit and I lost again. Now everyone was certain that this was the end of it. We felt doomed, because we thought the Supreme Court would never hear this case. But the court surprised us. Even then, after they agreed to hear it, all my advisors still felt the judgment would go against me.

I was depressed and paranoid throughout the whole process because I really believed, every step of the way, that we were going to lose. Even while I was in court, listening to the arguments, knowing that our side was right, I felt that we were going to lose. It wasn't until after I won the case and read the judges' unanimous decision in my favor that I realized the significance of what I had won, and the real reason I never gave up going through with it. I needed to be in that courtroom, and listening carefully to every second of testimony, and living through the whole process to understand.

Those nine justices reasoned that if they supported Falwell's lower court victory, no one would ever have to prove something was actually libelous to win a judgment. All anyone would have to prove is that "some bastard hurt my feelings." "He upset me." "He made my mama cry." "He made my dog bark." The lawsuits would be endless, and that would be the end of free speech.

In the years following the Supreme Court's decision, I noticed how the skits and monologues on Leno and Letterman, and even those on "Saturday Night Live" and "The Howard Stern Show," were much more on the cutting-edge than they ever could have been before 1988. Celebrities, politicians—anyone in the news is made fun of all the time. It's a main staple of these programs. These shows can imitate, impersonate, put words in people's mouths. There is virtually no limit as long as they don't knowingly and maliciously make a false and hurtful statement, offered as fact.

When Johnny Carson used to host "The Tonight Show," he was good—funny and timely—but he was very limited in what he could get away with in terms of making fun of people. He always kept it light. His show reflected simpler, more innocent times, and his humor was on the gentler side. But, it's also true that the attorneys were standing in the background, constantly worrying about whether or not Carson was going too far and if the show would get sued. Now producers don't have to worry so much, and writers don't have to pull their punches.

Comedians, writers, and television hosts constantly thank me for changing the law, but interestingly, most of the letters of gratitude I receive come from law students who have studied the case and are fascinated by it. Ironically, the content of my own magazine hasn't changed that much as a result of the Supreme Court decision, because we were pushing that envelope of taste from the beginning.

The Million-Dollar Ad

In the 1990s, my run-ins with the government became more overtly political, and they were argued in the court of public opinion.

During the time of President Clinton's impeachment proceedings in the Senate in 1999, every night when I would go home, no matter was else was happening, no matter what channel I turned the television to, it was Bash Clinton Night. Everybody wanted his head on a platter and I thought it was grossly unfair. He hadn't robbed the country's treasury. He hadn't

No matter was else was happening, no matter what channel I turned the television to, it was Bash Clinton Night.

committed treason. At worst, he got a blow job in the Oval Office, and like any married man caught under those circumstances, he lied to cover his ass. Why was the media so fixated on his sex life? Why were they so consumed with his zipper problem that they lost track of how he balanced the budget, reformed welfare, and oversaw the biggest economic boom in American history? How did the political debate lose sight of all Clinton's accomplishments and sink down to the level of a bimbo getting diddled with a cigar? Well, as I will show in the chapters that follow, it was not by accident.

Certainly Washington had heard about sex before. I remember back in 1976, when *Hustler* was only three years old, Congressman Wilbur Mills, head of the House Ways and Means Committee, and Congressman Wayne Hayes from Ohio were both involved in extramarital affairs. Mills was involved with a stripper named Fannie Fox. The two of them got drunk and plunged into Washington's Tidal Basin. The cops got them and there was a huge scandal. In the meantime, Congressman Hayes had a babe named Elizabeth Ray on his congressional payroll, a woman who had no office skills whatsoever, but who knew how to please. The Republicans were already thumping the Bible and family values as their platform, and to expose their hypocrisy, I decided to take out an ad in *The Washington Post* offering a reward for dirt on other politicians.

I submitted the ad and it was turned down cold. I had a friend, Rudy Maxa, who wrote for the paper at that time, and I asked him if he'd talk to *Post* Editor Ben Bradley and get the ad in that way. Ben threw Rudy out of his office, saying he "didn't want anything to do with Larry Flynt."

At that point I decided to forget about Bradley and just write to his boss, the publisher, Katharine Graham. In my letter I said, "How can you, as publisher of a newspaper that epitomizes what the First Amendment is all about, that published the Pentagon Papers, that uncovered the Watergate scandal, resulting in the resignation of one of the most corrupt presidents we ever had, how can you, in good conscience, refuse to run my ad?"

I got a handwritten note back from Mrs. Graham, saying, "Mr. Flynt, please resubmit your ad." We did get some information in response to that first ad in 1976, but nothing as great and immediate as we were about to get with the second one in 1998.

The fact that Mrs. Graham had approved my ad back then was very much on my mind twenty-five years later when I decided to offer a million-dollar reward for dirt on the Republican hypocrites of the 1990s, and to announce it in an ad in the *Post*. My attorney, my friends, everybody told me, "They're never gonna publish that ad!" I just said, "You guys are going to be surprised." I submitted it to the advertising department, and it sailed right through for placement we had requested in the Sunday edition. Clearly, there were people at the *Post* who had been there in 1976 and remembered what Mrs. Graham had done the first time.

The day the ad ran, October 4, 1998, was the day the media started to see the world differently, and the day the media started to see me differently as well.

I woke up that Sunday morning, turned on the TV, and there was Tim Russert on "Meet the Press" holding up the ad. The next day, *Hustler*'s voice-mail system broke down and we needed an expert to come in and retrieve our messages. My publicist—I hadn't even told her about the ad—found over 200 messages on her answering service.

> **At least for that week, we had the government's attention.**

At least for that week, we had the government's attention. So I put out this statement to the press:

FLYNT STATEMENT REGARDING MILLION-DOLLAR AD

I want to expose the hypocrisy going on in Washington. Many of the people sitting in judgment of the president of the United States have engaged in similar illicit encounters, and they have not told the truth. We'd be more than happy to pay a million dollars to anyone who can document hav-

ing had such an affair with a key player such as Gingrich,
Lott, Armey, etc. Of course, these people would be worth
the million dollars, as opposed to some freshman congressman from a remote part of the country.

We received some very colorful leads that we ended up not pur-
suing, because our interest was exclusively in finding and exposing
the hypocrites. I wasn't interested in trashing somebody's sex life
just because they were having an affair or they were into something kinky. I only wanted to expose people who were taking a
public position contrary to the way they were living their private
lives, and who were crucifying Clinton for doing the same thing
they were.

When the Capitol Hill newspaper *Roll Call* got word that we
had the scoop on Bob Livingston, Congressman from the First
District of Louisiana, they published the story. At this point, he
had already been selected to replace Newt Gingrich as speaker of
the House. So Livingston shared his little problem with the Republican caucus the night before the Clinton impeachment hearings were about to begin. He got a standing ovation from his
colleagues, some of whom later cited his "character" for telling
the truth. I guess the idea was that if they give you lemons, make
lemonade. When he admitted on CNN that, as he said, "I had occasionally strayed from my marriage," he described it as a "simple
adulterous affair," as if hypocrites get points for going with plain
vanilla sex. Then he tried to gain more points by saying that it was
never with anyone who worked for him, or anyone who worked
as a lobbyist. But we knew better. We knew that one of the women
he was screwing was a judge in his home state of Louisiana, one
was a lobbyist on Capitol Hill, and another was a member of his
staff. And those were just the three we could document. When
that hit the fan, he resigned rather than answer questions under
oath.

There were plenty of juicy details we could have published
about Livingston's sex life and his particular fetishes, but because

his wife called me a day after he resigned and asked me to let it go, we did. "There have been a lot of people hurt in this, people you don't even know," she said. "Myself, the children. He's resigned. I see no reason to publish any more details of the investigation." I really saw no reason to humiliate him further. It took a lot of courage for her to call me, and my plan of exposing hypocrites had been accomplished. I'm certain that the resignation of Bob Livingston helped defuse the whole Clinton impeachment process.

Among the others that I Flynted during the Clinton impeachment were:

Henry Hyde

Congressman from the Sixth District of Illinois, Hyde once led the Republican House members in giving Kenneth Starr a standing ovation. He was the "mad dog" investigator who was chairman of the House Judiciary Committee during the Iran-Contra Affair, the Reagan era scandal that had high administration officials secretly selling arms to Iran and then diverting some of the profits to the "Contra" rebels in Nicaragua. When Hyde asked White House aide Colonel Oliver North if the allegations were true, North said they weren't, and that was the end of Hyde's investigation. Then, when an airplane illegally bringing arms to the Contras crashed and burned and the whole Reagan scam went public, it was Hyde who railed against what he called "destructive politics" in trying to embarrass the conservative president.

Hyde was a director of the Clyde Savings and Loan, which, when it went bust, cost the U.S. taxpayers $67 million in bailouts. In his forties, this bastion of the Moral Majority carried on a five-year affair with a married mother of three. This, too, came to light while he was grandstanding in his accusations of Clinton. When we presented the evidence against Hyde, Tom DeLay called it an "attack on the U.S. Congress!" Well, gosh. Is that anything like an attack on the U.S. president?

Bob Barr

Congressman from Georgia's Seventh District, Barr was house manager for the effort to impeach Bill Clinton. When this crusader for morality was first confronted about being seen licking whipped cream off a stripper's nipple, he dismissed it by saying that it was at a charity function and all for a good cause. (We've all contributed to that fund-raiser a time or two, I guess.) A twice-divorced advocate for the family, Barr dumped his second wife, Gail, just before Thanksgiving, 1985. The year before, he had refused to stop campaigning for the statehouse despite his wife's request—she had cancer and needed his help. After his defeat, he left his wife and two sons and moved into the same apartment complex as Jeri Dobbin, the woman he would marry just one month after his divorce became final. While Gail worked at her husband's office in 1985, she used to make luncheon appointments for Mr. Barr and Ms. Dobbin. "Obviously, at the time," she told us, "I did not realize Bob was having a romantic relationship with this woman." Prince that he is, Bob thoughtfully tried to save Gail some trouble and expense by drawing up their divorce papers himself. In the *Flynt Report*, we provided clear, documentary evidence that he condoned and paid for his wife's abortion, and also committed adultery and then lied about it under oath—the same crime of perjury for which he was trying to railroad the president.

> **Confronted about being seen licking whipped cream off a stripper's nipple, he dismissed it by saying that it was at a charity function and all for a good cause.**

In his arguments on behalf of the Defense of Marriage Act, July 12, 1996, Barr had waxed eloquent about the evils of narcissism and the threats coming from the "flames of hedonism." He accused me of trying to "drive a wedge" between him and his wife and family. Then he tried to accuse Clinton of outing him to us, when in fact, it was a disgruntled constituent, fed up with the man's shameless baloney.

After we got the dirt on Bob Barr and exposed him, we received a call from the attorney who represented his ex-wife. She was one of the sources we paid to get information on him. I had even more disdain for Barr than I did for Livingston. Barr would stand up on the floor of Congress and say "Abortion is the equivalent to murder!" But then, when his wife was pregnant, he took her to the hospital for an abortion and paid for it with his own personal check. The press conference we held regarding what we had on Barr and the subsequent publicity he received added up to his being defeated and ultimately getting him out of Congress.

Dan Burton

It was this gentleman, chairman of the House Government Reform and Oversight Committee, who called Clinton a "scumbag," at the same time that Burton was being investigated for fund-raising irregularities. It was also Burton who hounded the president with the accusation that Vincent Foster's suicide was a murder. Then in September of 1998, moral crusader Burton was forced to admit that he had fathered an illegitimate child during an affair in the 1980s. He cried foul, said it was all political mudslinging and—you guessed it—blamed Clinton. Burton also was known to have his girlfriend, Claudia Keller, on his payroll. Former gambling lobbyist John Domi also cites junkets that Burton made to Las Vegas with various women.

Porn Starr

And then there was the bluest bluenose of them all, Kenneth Starr. We never were able to blow any whistles on him, but then again, he did such a fine job of exposing his own prurient nature that maybe we didn't have to.

Starr, you will recall, was the independent counsel who led the investigation during President Clinton's impeachment hearings. It seemed fitting that Starr—whose investigation, a witch hunt as well as an embarrassment to the entire country, included wiretapping and bullying a mother to coerce the testimony of her daughter—had years before been a law clerk to former Chief Justice Warren Burger, the very same judge who had ordered my arrest for using profanity in the Supreme Court.

The *Starr Report*, as it was called, is a compilation of his findings during the investigation, and was in itself more depraved and scandalous than anything Clinton did. Starr ignored all national polls, which month after month said that the majority of Americans were not concerned with the president's private life, but with his performance as president. But still, Starr pressed on, consumed and driven by his own sick obsession, fueled by his fundamentalist religious background and his attachment to the political far right, and used his investigative privilege to undercut the legitimacy of the president of the United States.

> **The *Starr Report* was in itself more depraved and scandalous than anything Clinton did.**

The *Starr Report* was so filthy, in fact, that I felt compelled to invite Mr. Starr to put his skills to better use.

Here is the letter I sent to him:

September 22, 1998

The Honorable Judge Kenneth Starr
Office of Independent Counsel
1001 Pennsylvania Ave N.W.
Washington, D.C. 20004

Dear Judge Starr:

Let me take this opportunity to thank you on behalf of all the employees at *Hustler* magazine and LFP, Inc., for your tireless work in producing the *Starr Report*. I have been impressed by the salacious and voyeuristic materials in your work. The quality and quantity of material you have assembled in your report contains more pornographic references than those provided by Hustler Online services this month. I have included a chart in this letter that confirms this fact.

Given your exemplary work, I would like to enter into negotiations with you regarding full-time employment for *Hustler* magazine and related services offered by LFP, Inc., when you conclude your work at the Office of Independent Counsel.

You have broken historic ground in disseminating pornographic materials to a broader and more diverse community of Americans. In this context you have helped to shape and alter long-held community standards regarding the acceptance of pornographic material.

I congratulate you for having opened the doors of libraries and schools to pornographic literature. Those of us at *Hustler* need your assistance in extending the parameters of pornography to a wider community of adults. You have opened a new era in promoting explicit sexual materials. Your keen aptitude and relentless focus on disseminating pornographic materials is an inspiration to every employee at *Hustler.*

Please let me know when you or any of your representatives can sit down with me and discuss if you are interested in making a valuable contribution to promoting the First Amendment through *Hustler* magazine. As far as compensation and relocation issues are concerned, please do not be concerned. You are a valuable asset who needs to be well compensated.

> Respectfully yours,
> Larry Flynt

In its September 18, 1998, issue, The *Los Angeles Weekly* showed that it got the joke:

STARR REPORT MORE PORNOGRAPHIC
THAN HUSTLER ONLINE MAGAZINE

*Yet It's Rated "G" and Has Been Released
By the United States Congress*

We then sent out a press release based on the *Weekly*'s article:

> According to a chart in the September 18–24 issue of *L.A. Weekly,* the number of graphic references to genitalia in Hustler Online Magazine is 44; the number of graphic references to genitalia in the "Starr Report" is 69.
>
> Number of graphic references to genitalia coming into contact with tobacco products in Hustler Online Magazine is zero; in the "Starr Report," 9.
>
> Access restrictions to Hustler is adults only—membership fee; to the "Starr Report," no age verification or implied restrictions—free download.
>
> Links: Hustler has link to "Starr Report;" "Starr Report" does not have a link to Hustler Online. LFP, Inc., releases Hustler Online; The Congress of the United States of America released the "Starr Report."
>
> Hustler Online Magazine is rated XXX for adult content; "Starr Report" is rated G for adult content.

We published "The Flynt Report" as an answer to Starr's ridiculous waste of time, energy, and money, and to show him what a *real* investigative report could come up with. The key people involved were Dan Moldea, an investigative reporter from Washington, D.C., and Alan McDonnell, who was the editor of *Hustler* at the time. We were not out to expose anyone's expression of his or her sexual nature. Our purpose was to show how full of crap these guys were, and to expose the Big Hustle of their holier-than-thou hypocrisy. Shortly after our report came out, I was informed that Michael Moore, the producer and political activist, had been a guest at the White House and he and some others, including

President Bill Clinton, were passing around a copy of my letter to Starr, laughing hysterically.

Even when impeachment hearings were going hot and heavy, and we were seeing all those talking heads fuming about Clinton on TV, polls showed that 75 percent of the people believed the president should not be impeached. That's what made the whole thing so idiotic. Yet even though the public wanted Clinton to remain in office, the Republicans and even some Democrats were still asking for Clinton's head on a platter. But as soon as Livingston bit the dust, the whole tone of the Senate, and the trial in the Senate, changed. Livingston's demise had a profound effect on those proceedings, I think, because the rank and file started questioning their own motives for wanting to trash Clinton. It wasn't just partisanship—it was revenge of the nerds. Clinton was too slick, too successful, and they wanted to bring him down.

Clinton was too slick, too successful, and they wanted to bring him down.

And I don't even want to know all that was going on inside them to drive their hatred of Hillary. But clearly these guys are not comfortable with the idea of a woman on top.

Prior to my response to Clinton's impeachment trial, my supporters were mostly people in their thirties. But after the impeachment, when Clinton was acquitted, I couldn't go down the street, no matter what the city, without little old ladies in their seventies and eighties coming up to me and saying, "I want to thank you for what you did for the president."

My research team had dozens more investigations going on and many where we had almost enough proof, but not quite enough to go to press with. There were other times where we had the dirt but the people were asking for over a million dollars to let us have it. We had proof that one of the top people in the Republican National Committee was having phone sex with a girl. She mentioned to him the fact that what they were doing was wrong and immoral, and his comment to her was, "I don't have any moral values, I just talk about them on television!" When we heard that, we thought we'd just been handed a sound bite that was going to go around the world. But when our attorneys checked it out, they discovered that the tape recording was done in Pennsylvania, and Pennsylvania is a state that has two-party consent, so therefore, we couldn't use the tape because we would open ourselves up for a libel suit.

The million-dollar ad changed millions of lives, and it changed my life without a doubt. No matter who I call in this country, they will take my call, or return it as soon as they get the message. Maybe it's because they think I might have another story. I don't know. But any of the top media people around will talk to me anytime I want to talk about anything. The face of news changed the day the million-dollar ad ran and the media saw the results. Five months later, but still before I'd published my full report, *The New Yorker* wrote, "What incriminating photographs or videotapes does Flynt have left? What is he planning to release in the 'Flynt Report?' It almost doesn't matter. He has made a point that damaging information exists and can be bought and sold and disseminated."

Whenever a public figure says one thing and does another, it is a public service to bring that hypocrisy to light. The right to privacy is one of the precious rights I believe in defending. But start trampling on other peoples' rights, start pontificating about how pure you are and how low down everyone else is, and watch out— you might just find yourself on "Candid Camera."

In my thirty years of publishing *Hustler,* I've never done one single story where someone has questioned my credibility. And no one could question the information we got in our investigations of Livingston or Barr. Whether the press agreed with what I was doing or not was be-

> **We made politicians think twice before proselytizing about issues they don't really believe in.**

side the point. I followed the rules, and I conducted the investigations in the same way that a mainstream news organization would have done. We were thorough. And for a while there, what we did made politicians think twice before proselytizing about issues they don't really believe in.

Obviously, with the passage of time, we can see that the job is far from over. A new president has redefined the standards of hypocrisy, and as Americans, we need to call him on it.

2

The Hypocrite in the White House

You can hear it from me, or you can hear it from Helen Thomas, the most senior White House correspondent. She's the woman who had seen it all from Kennedy to Clinton, and who, because of her seniority, was the one to end every press conference with the words, "Thank you, Mr. President." She told the Torrance, California, *Daily Breeze* in January 2003 that George W. Bush is "the worst president ever . . . the worst president in all of American history."

That's quite a claim, and it demands a lot of supporting facts. Many of these facts come to us bit by bit over time, in various books and newspaper and magazine articles. Most of us don't have time to connect all the dots and all the dirt and really look at the big picture. I'm lucky enough to have the staff and resources needed to pull together all the information for you—to demonstrate that George W. Bush's whole life has been a series of hypocrisies, lies, and delusions. I can expose all the the fancy footwork that has arguably kept him one step ahead of the sheriff all along—whether to cover up alleged drug use, drunken driving, insider trading back at Harken Oil, or scamming the people of

Arlington, Texas, with his deal for his baseball stadium; or to have himself installed as president of the United States; or deliberately misleading the public to launch the first purely elective war in American history.

I want to link his actions today with what we've seen of the man over time. In describing Bush senior, Molly Ivins said, "He was born on third base and thinks he hit a triple." Compared to his son, though, the first President Bush is a hardscrabble, self-made man. As George W ably demonstrates, being the ne'er-do-well, duty shirking, substance-abusing son of a rich man influential enough to open every door and get you out of every scrape does not exactly build character, nor does growing up in a family where cronyism and a sense of entitlement come with the monogrammed bedroom slippers.

George W. Bush, with his claims of Christian piety, of being a "compassionate conservative," of setting out to "restore honor and integrity to the White House," is the most accomplished, bold-faced hypocrite ever to have come down Pennsylvania Avenue. He has gotten away with it because, in his words, we have "misunderestimated him." The American public and the media simply thought he was a little stupid and didn't have a clue on the details, so

> **George W. Bush is the most accomplished, bold-faced hypocrite ever to have come down Pennsylvania Avenue.**

nobody called him on the way he mangled the facts as well as the language. Now we know better.

At the time of Bush's inaugural in 2001, *The Onion,* the satirical magazine out of Madison, Wisconsin, published a mock version of a speech for the new president in which he reassured the nation: "Our long national nightmare of peace and prosperity is over."

I remember having the same premonition. But George W. Bush

was such an empty suit—such a lifelong nothing—that, at the beginning, it was hard to know what his presidency was going to be about.

Republicans have always said they were about fiscal responsibility and balancing the budget, so I thought maybe his administration was going to be about solid economics and financial stewardship.

But during the first three years that George W. Bush was in office, he managed to turn a surplus of $236 billion, a nest egg left over from the Clinton administration, into a deficit of $374 billion.

In the same State of the Union address in which he misled the American people about the situation in Iraq, he also said, "Our first goal is . . . an economy that grows fast enough to employ every man and woman who seeks a job."

In reality, during Bush's first three years, the American economy lost nearly three million jobs. In November of 2003, even after the economy had rebounded and the Dow Jones Industrial Average had returned to 10,000, the economy lost another 17,000 manufacturing jobs. No American president has screwed up that badly for working men and women since Herbert Hoover and the Great Depression.

Still, Bush, the cowpoke from Midland, said, "The tax relief is for everyone who pays income taxes. . . . Americans will keep, this year, an average of almost a thousand dollars more of their own money."

The truth is, speaking in terms of averages is nonsense. *Averaging* out what Donald Trump saves from the Bush package with what a schoolteacher saves is just a way to lie with statistics. Nearly half of all taxpayers got less than $100, and 31 percent of all taxpayers got nothing at all.

Summing up our leader's way with dollars and cents, George Akerlof, who won the 2001 Nobel Prize in economics, described Bush's as "the worst economy in two hundred years." Lawrence Kutikoff, chairman of economics at Boston University, says that in terms of present value (meaning all resources set against all bills currently on line) this country is now effectively bankrupt. Which is the punch line to the Bush administration's Big Hustle: a flat-broke government is just the way some radical, anti-government conservatives want it. As we'll see in Chapter 3, they've been talking about cutting off the oxygen supply to government for thirty years or more.

Clearly, solid economic numbers is not what George W. Bush is about.

Well, George W. Bush also said he was going to be a "uniter, not a divider," yet he has had the most divisive presidency since Richard Nixon came out with his enemies list. His cabinet appointments, his judicial appointments, his environmental and social policies, and his foreign policy have all been a big wet kiss to his rich friends and a poke in the eye to everybody else. The Bush II crowd has the ignorance and zealotry of the Reagan bunch, combined with the ruthlessness and craving for raw power of the Nixon group. In fact, a fair number of Bush's inner circle *are* the Nixon group, brought back after thirty years of cold storage like Austin Powers and Dr. Evil.

> A fair number of Bush's inner circle *are* the Nixon group, brought back after thirty years of cold storage like Austin Powers and Dr. Evil.

Bush told us he was a "compassionate conservative," but his administration has tried to offset the cost of tax cuts for fat cats by cutting back on health care for children. Then the "just folks" guy from Andover and Yale told us, "We achieved historic education reform, which must now be carried out in every school and in every classroom." The truth is that, after stealing the phrase "No Child Left Behind" from an advocacy organization and using it as part of his platform, "the education president" cut $8 billion from the funds that had been promised to pay for it. As it turns out, education reform back in Texas—the one accomplishment on Bush's resume that seemed worth something—turned out to be mostly smoke and mirrors. Later audits showed that Texas test scores were wildly exaggerated, and Houston's "too good to be true" drop-out rate was . . . too good to be true.

So maybe Bush was going to offer us what his father called "the vision thing." Maybe he was going to deliver on our claim to moral leadership in the community of nations. But, unfortunately, once George W. Bush gets beyond his chuckle-head, "good ol' boy" act, he is shamelessly arrogant.

After 9/11 we had the whole world's sympathy and support, but Bush changed that to anger and resentment, much of it focused on his go-it-alone, shoot-first-ask-questions-later style. Bush completely blew off world opinion when he invaded Iraq. Then, six months later he was looking for somebody else to share the cost. "To some degree," wrote *New York Times* reporter Richard Bernstein, "the resentment is centered on the person of President Bush, who is seen by many of those interviewed, at best, as an ineffective spokesman for American interests and, at worst, as a gun-slinging cowboy knocking over international treaties and bent on controlling the world's oil, if not the entire world." Bernstein sees this mood of resentment in changes ranging from Canadian hockey fans booing the American national anthem to high school students in Switzerland who no longer want to come to the United States as exchange students.

Incurious George

As for Bush's leadership style, one thing people who have dealt with W seem to agree on is that he is the least intellectually curious person they've ever met. This is a president who says he ignores the media entirely and gets all his news from his staff. Columnist Paul Krugman says to that: "Two words. Emperor. Clothes."

George W. Bush is always in a rush to arrive at a "cast in stone" opinion, then go jogging or take a nap. Which means that he doesn't spend much time looking at all the angles, much less all the details. Especially not when he believes that some of his ideas come directly from God. He doesn't want to go through a real debate with smart people in the room. He hated his fancy schools, not because the other kids were snootier than he was, but because they were smarter and harder working than he was. Now, forty years later, he dresses down an NBC reporter for asking a question in French . . . to the president of France . . . as if that were the height of snootiness.

It worked to Bush's advantage in the 2000 campaign to play the class clown to Al Gore's nerdy brown-nose, but for Bush as president, his inability to go toe to toe with really smart people means that he gets stuck with the judgment of the loudest partisan zealot in the room, whether that's political hack Karl Rove, Defense Secretary Donald Rumsfeld, or national security guru Paul Wolfowitz. It means that he makes decisions by boiling down complex issues into bumper sticker–sized nuggets.

> **Didn't anybody in charge give any serious thought to what would happen *after* they flattened the Iraqi army?**

Which is exactly how we got into the mess in Iraq—an invasion that had a half dozen different justifications as it unfolded, and ended up as a military victory followed by a quagmire. Didn't anybody in charge give any serious thought to what would happen *after* they flattened the Iraqi army?

In the fall of 2003, we got a glimpse of our fearless leader's limitations when the commander in chief and leader of the free world came back from a meeting with moderate Islamic leaders in Asia all confused. According to David Sanger of the *New York Times,* "Mr. Bush has only begun to discover the gap between the picture of a benign superpower that he sees, and the far more calculating, self-interested, anti-Muslim America the world perceives as he speeds by behind dark windows."

I guess being puzzled by Islamic attitudes comes naturally to a man who first described his new effort to combat terror using the word "crusade." Given the behavior of certain sword-carrying European invaders about nine hundred years ago, "crusade" is not exactly a crowd pleaser in Islamic countries. Or for a man who, to help keep the peace in Iraq, wanted to bring in Turks, the country's former colonial masters who are blood enemies of Iraqi Kurds.

Now, let me tell you what even a smut peddler knows about foreign relations. I publish porn in eighteen foreign countries, so I know that you can get arrested for carrying a Victoria's Secret catalog into some Muslim countries. In Japan, you can spend five years in jail for showing pubic hair. A smile in one country means something different from a smile in another. There's a whole etiquette to receiving a business card in some countries. You have to know these things if you're going to do business overseas.

Our president, on the other hand, just invades first and asks questions later.

He tries to make things simple and clear-cut, even when they're not, which makes him ignorant by choice. Fact is, he simply doesn't do his homework, and he never has.

Bush's platitudes may be written by speech-writers—"They hate freedom" is how he explains Iraqi resistance to the U.S. occupation of their country—but all the evidence suggests that our president actually thinks in these kinds of "easy listening" formulations. The guy never reads. He's never challenged himself, except maybe while working out in the gym. With all the money and privilege in his background, he never really traveled anywhere to see what the rest of the world was like. This is a man who always felt safest—and for whatever reason *needed* to feel safe—in the cocoon of an isolated, small-town, Midland, Texas, perspective on the world. Seven years at Andover and Yale and a daddy in the White House didn't enlarge his perspective one bit. He's clung to that country club/Cadillac dealership/First Methodist Church/ "our crowd is the right crowd," Midland, Texas, pin-hole view of the world his whole life. He went to fancy schools but never studied, he spent his early years drinking and carousing, his father bought him out of scrapes all his life, and, even with all his father's back-up, he never could succeed at anything until, around the time he hit forty, his dad's cronies literally dropped a million-dollar deal in his lap for a baseball team. And even there, with the Texas Rangers, he was the mascot, rolled out for meet-and-greet sessions. It was just like when he was back at school—the cheerleader for the team.

But with a world this complicated, we don't need a feel-good mascot. We need somebody in charge who knows his stuff. Bush thought he could "spin" our conflict with the Arab world by hiring Charlotte Beers from Madison Avenue to sex up an ad campaign, sort of like "I'd like to buy the world a Coke," with weapons.

But there are 90 million Arabs in the world today between the ages of fifteen and twenty-four, and 14 million of them are unemployed. If they hate us, it's not because they hate freedom. That's the stupidest crap I've ever heard. And no PR campaign is going to make it better.

> If they hate us, it's not because they hate freedom. That's the stupidest crap I've ever heard.

If they hate us, it's because we have everything and they have nothing, and we're always pushing them around. They hate us because they feel humiliated, and because we always seem to be on the side that's making it worse for them.

Neither piety, platitudes, or PR is going to fix this problem. Even with all our money and military might, we can't fight a never-ending guerilla war against 90 million people who have nothing to live for and don't mind dying.

Asleep at the Wheel

As for George W. Bush not being up to the task, you don't have to take my word for it. I'm just a smut peddler with opinions. But I read the papers and watch the news, and I have a lot of respect for the reporters and commentators who are gutsy enough to tell the truth about what's going on. Take John Dilulio, for instance. Dr. Dilulio is a professor of government at the University of Pennsylvania, who was actually right there inside the Bush administration. During the first year of Bush II, Dilulio was head of the White House "faith-based initiatives" programs, and what he reports back about the Bushies gets down to fundamentals that are truly frightening.

Dilulio gave an interview to Ron Suskind of *Esquire*, then sent a follow-up letter to Suskind that was a bombshell. You can Google "*Esquire* Dilulio" and read the entire letter, if you like, but the gist of it is that Dilulio couldn't believe how much the Bush administration was all about image over substance, how it was all politics all the time, and policy was sort of like a stage prop to be moved around for the sake of effect.

Dilulio is a Bush supporter, and the first half of his letter is full of mushy praise about what fine fellows Bush and all his buckaroos really are. But then he begins to describe his time in the White House, and he tells us how during eight months of staff discussions, he heard real policy talked about maybe three times. The main topic was how to hammer the other side—meaning the Democrats. In the West Wing, he said, you could count on the fingers of one hand the people who even cared about policy, much less *knew* anything about it.

He described their ignorance, and their complacency about their ignorance, as "breathtaking." When they tried to talk substance, he said, they couldn't keep Medicaid straight from Medicare, and the senior people made it very clear to the gofers that really knowing what you're talking about didn't matter—it was all about the spin. Dilulio came up with the description "Mayberry Machiavellis" for these White House staffers who thought it was perfectly okay to pontificate in simplistic, black-and-white terms when they didn't know what the hell they were talking about.

If you don't believe Dilulio, of course, you can always turn to Paul O'Neill. He's the very successful, very Republican former CEO of Alcoa. But when he was secretary of the Treasury for Bush, he was just as appalled as Dilulio. O'Neill got himself crossed off the White House Christmas list by opening up to Ron Suskind in Suskind's book *The Price of Loyalty.*

O'Neill described George Bush as a "blind man in a room full of deaf people." O'Neill admitted that he and Colin Powell and Christie Whitman were all just window dressing, brought in to try to dilute the (accurate) image of the Bush administration as being stuffed with die-hard, radical conservatives. He complained about always having to kowtow to Karl Rove and Karen Hughes, the Texas spin doctors and political hacks, and always having a chief executive who never was quite focused on the problem.

He tried various ways to bring some moderation to the conservative huddle, but he got nowhere. He said he pleaded with Vice-President Cheney to have a better, more open debate on all the issues, especially the deficits. He begged them to make the tax cuts contingent on continuing surpluses. But when O'Neill questioned the wisdom of this payoff for the rich, Cheney shut him up with, "Reagan proved that deficits don't matter. We won the midterms. This is our due." O'Neill says that even W wondered out loud if they hadn't delivered enough presents for the fat cats already. Rove told Bush that he should stick to the cuts on principle. Send the economy into the crapper for generations—some principle. But O'Neill's strongest criticism was his claim that the war on Iraq was being planned from the moment Bush took office, *nine months before 9/ll.* He said that, after one of these early discussions, Bush said, "Fine. Go find me a way to do this."

Ignorance and arrogance are always pathetic and obnoxious, just like it is when you hear on the radio from Laura Ingraham, Rush Limbaugh, and Bill O'Reilly. But when the people *actually in power* operate this way, when "don't know nothing and proud of it" moves into action, it's a lot more dangerous. Considering the number of lives that have been lost and the amount of debt racked up carrying out Bush's half-baked policies, it's tragic.

> **The Bush presidency is about the character of the man in the Oval Office.**

So the Bush presidency is not about economic initiatives. It's not about unity, or education, or world leadership, or compassion, or anything else Bush says it is. I think we have to recognize that, in fact, the Bush presidency is about the character of the man in the Oval Office.

A History of Hypocrisy

Has this president restored "honor and integrity to the White House," as he said he would, or is that kind of claim just a cover for lies and manipulation?

One thing I will show is that Mr. Bush has his own way with facts and figures, and he is also very inventive with his self-image. Near as I can tell, he appears to live in his own moral universe, one in which you're either for him or against him, where every issue is either black or white. He thinks he and his friends are always on the side of righteousness, restoring honor and integrity even when they're advocating unfair and irresponsible tax cuts, cutting sleazy deals with their cronies, and getting us into a deadly and unnecessary war by lying about the threat as well as their own motivations.

But this kind of behavior didn't just pop up once W was in power.

During his campaign in 2000, Bush took credit for a Patients' Bill of Rights in Texas, even though it passed despite his attempt to *veto* it. He lied to the *Dallas Morning News* by saying he had never been arrested after 1968—it later came to light that he was arrested for drunk driving in Maine in 1976. He at first refused to answer a reporter's questions about using cocaine, then came up with a dodge that anyone with half a brain can see meant that, yes, he had used coke sometime before 1974. In his campaign autobiography, *A Charge to Keep,* he claimed to have flown with his Texas Air National Guard unit until 1973, when the record shows not only that he skipped out on his last year of service (the base commander Brigadier General William Turnipseed was "dead certain" that Bush never showed up), but that he avoided taking mandatory physicals—the most logical explanation for which is not wanting the drug use exposed.

You could see his true character back in 1988, when W was the enforcer in Bush Senior's first presidential campaign and he worked with Lee Atwater, who was in my opinion one of the most underhanded political operatives on the planet. Atwater was the mastermind behind the famously racist attack ads featuring Willie Horton, the black murderer who had been furloughed from a Massachusetts prison while the Democratic candidate, Michael Dukakis, was governor. And you sure as hell saw his true character the moment W first began to hit some serious opposition on his own campaign trail in 2000.

Shortly after W appeared in South Carolina, sucking up to the God-fearing racists at Bob Jones University, the buckle on the Bible Belt, Republican contender John McCain started coming on strong. The Bush campaign showed not only its hypocrisy but also its shamelessness. McCain is a true military hero, a genuine patriot who spent years enduring a Vietnamese POW camp. He is also a politician with the integrity to try to put a lid on the soft money from corporations that fueled the Bush campaign. So what did the Bushies do? Push polling, where they

> So what did the Bushies do? Push polling, where they pretend to be taking a survey, and instead, call people up to plant ideas in their heads.

pretend to be taking a survey, and instead, call people up to plant ideas in their heads. The script for the call went something like: "If you were to discover that John McCain had fathered a black, illegitimate child, would you still be inclined to vote for him?" I am not exaggerating—this actually happened.

But the most shameless moment of all was "Top Gun," May 1, 2003, when Bush got to strut in a borrowed flight suit on the deck of the *U.S.S. Abraham Lincoln.* Let's review the White House honesty during Top Gun. Remember when White House spokesman Ari Fleischer was asked about the cost of having the president joyriding in a S-3B Viking? Fleischer said that Bush couldn't arrive by helicopter because the *Lincoln* would "be hundreds of miles from shore." It turned out that the *Lincoln* was, in fact, so close to port that it had to go back out to sea so that the cameras wouldn't catch the San Diego skyline just behind Bush as he made his speech.

Later, on October 28, 2003, in a Rose Garden press conference, Bush began to distance himself from the idea for backdrop for the stunt. He told the world that the "Mission Accomplished" banner, which the passage of time has made increasingly absurd, was "suggested by those on the ship. They asked us to do the production of the banner, and we did. They're the ones who put it up." Right. And those presidential heads on Mt. Rushmore just happened to pop up behind Mr. Bush when he gave a speech out in South Dakota. And Scott Sforza, the former ABC producer on the White House payroll whose job it was to create such backdrops was off getting his teeth cleaned while Bush pulled off the biggest photo op of his life. General Wesley Clark told reporters that Bush's "blaming the sailors for something his advance team staged was outrageous."

No matter which way you slice it, George W. Bush is simply not a man of character. I know it's ironic for a porn king to say that about a president, but at least I'm not pretending to be something I'm not.

So what *is* the Bush administration about?

Hypocrisy.

It's about pretending to have homespun virtues in order to cover up the abuse of political power, which serves to increase the wealth and privileges of the Bush family and their friends.

In George Orwell's classic book *1984*, Big Brother was the man in charge, and if he said black was white and white was black, then it was so. Thanks to corporate fat cats, the NRA, the Christian Coalition, and a gutless media that won't expose a lie when they hear it, we have another man in charge who can say anything at all and have a huge portion of the populace accept it as fact. Only he's not a grim Big Brother. I think the Republicans did focus groups and Big Brother didn't test well with soccer moms. What we have instead is goof-ball "Little Brother." He's not intimidating. He's a likeable nitwit in a cowboy suit, sort of like Howdy Doody, with Wyoming-bred Dick Cheney as Buffalo Bob, holding the puppet on his lap. Howdy's so darn nice that everybody cuts him slack. He mouths platitudes about compassion and integrity while Cheney and the rest of the boys in the back room clean out the safe.

When Bush wants to increase the amount of air pollution allowed, he calls his program the Clear Skies Initiative. When he wants to open up old growth timber to logging, he calls it The Healthy Forest Initiative. *1984* was supposed to be a warning, not a guidebook for how to run an administration!

> *1984* **was supposed to be a warning, not a guidebook for how to run an administration!**

These carefully orchestrated deceptions are killing us economically, killing us in Iraq, killing us in the neglected war on terror, and killing us in the war Bush has declared on our civil liberties at home.

The Mother of All Bait and Switch Operations

When W first started the war talk about Iraq, it supposedly had something to do with 9/11, the war on terrorism, and Iraqi ties with al Qaeda. A short time afterward, though, Bush's own CIA director told us there was no evidence that Iraq had any ties with 9/11 or al Qaeda. After all, Iraq was run by fiercely anti-religious members of Saddam Hussein's Baath Party, and al Qaeda is run by nut-case Islamic fundamentalists—so Bush needed a change in talking points. That's when the justification became weapons of mass destruction.

We invaded, gave the Iraqis a little taste of "shock and awe," and expected their citizens were going to greet our troops with sweets and flowers. Iraq, a foreign power that was supposedly such a threat to us, collapsed in about three weeks. We rolled into Baghdad, no problem. The only glitch was that, with each passing day, it became more and more obvious that there were no weapons of mass destruction to be found. The people didn't greet us with sweets and flowers—they greeted us with suicide bombs and rocket launchers on donkey carts.

So the Bush administration rolled out more of their weapons of mass deception. The talk shifted to regime change. Now the line was that we had invaded Iraq—without actual provocation, mind you—to "liberate" the Iraqi people from Saddam Hussein. With every passing day, as the country descended further into chaos, it became more obvious that nine-year-olds attacking a tree fort would have given more thought to what happens next. There was widespread looting, but we had already disbanded the Iraqi army, and there was no police force in place to enforce the law. There was also no electrical power, no water—no order of any kind. All along, the U.S. Army War College had said we'd need 400,000 troops on the ground to maintain order "the day after" the fall of Iraq, but nobody in the administration would listen.

Unfortunately, as David Ignatius reported in the *Washington Post,* Bush had sent our military on such an ass-backward, ill-conceived mission, that the Pentagon's special operations chiefs have been reduced to screening a 1965 movie, *The Battle of Algiers,* trying to learn why the French suffered a colonial disaster in a guerrilla war against Muslims in Algiers.

Obviously, I'm not the only one troubled by this state of affairs. Long before his "I have a scream" speech in Iowa, Howard Dean, who reminds me of a rabbit on speed, rode to prominence on little more than boiling anger at Bush's policies. After almost four years of this "compassionate conservative," even objective journalists and academics are hardly able to restrain their contempt.

Maureen Dowd says that what Bush and his cronies have done is "cynically attack a villainous country because they knew it was easier than finding the real 9/11 villain, who had no country. . . ." She adds that, "by pretending Iraq was crawling with al Qaeda, they've created an Iraq crawling with al Qaeda."

In her column, she offers a little insight into just how sincere the Bushies were when they trumpeted those big guns Saddam supposedly had pointed at our heads. "Mr. Rumsfeld, who was so alarmed about Saddam's WMD [weapons of mass destruction] before the war, is now so nonchalant that he said he did not even bother to ask David Kay, who runs the CIA's search for WMD, what progress he'd made when meeting with him in Iraq last week. 'I have so many things to do at the Department of Defense,' Rummy told *The Washington Post.* Asked at the press club why our intelligence analysts did not predict the extent of Iraq's decayed infrastructure, Rummy said dismissively, 'They were worrying about more important things.' "

"The leading Bushies almost never admit serious mistakes," *New York Times* columnist David Brooks tells us. "They never acknowledge that they are listening to their critics. They never even admit they are shifting course. They don these facial expressions suggesting calm omniscience while down below their legs are doing the fox trot in six different directions."

Paul Krugman, the Princeton professor of economics who also writes a column for the *Times,* focused on Bush's use of the words "unity" and "sacrifice." But, Krugman said, "What he means by unity is that he should receive a blank check, and it turns out that what he means by sacrifice is sacrifice by other people." Krugman added, "If Mr. Bush had admitted from the start that the postwar occupation might cost this much, he would never have gotten that last tax cut. . . . He squandered American credibility by selling a war of choice as a war of necessity."

As I write, there are roughly 180,000 American troops in Iraq and Kuwait, some 20,000 of them from Army Reserve and National Guard units. Sixteen of the army's thirty-three combat brigades are now there and five more are on other foreign assignments. The remaining twelve are needed for rotation in Iraq or standby duty related to North Korea. The army is considering back-to-back combat tours for the first time since Vietnam.

In September, 2003, after two years of doing everything he could to suggest otherwise, the president finally admitted that he had seen no evidence that Saddam Hussein was involved in the September 11 terrorist attacks. Vice-President Cheney was forced to admit that he had "misspoken" during a television interview last spring when he said Iraq had "reconstituted nuclear weapons."

And it appears that Americans were waking up and smelling something other than the coffee. A *Newsweek* poll in September 2003 showed Bush's approval ratings in the toilet on domestic issues: 32 percent on the budget, 38 percent on health care, 41 percent on the economy, 42 percent on energy policy.

> **Americans were waking up and smelling something other than the coffee.**

There was Republican Senator Chuck Hagel, admitting that the White House "did a miserable job of planning for a post-Saddam Iraq," and Democratic Senator Robert Byrd of West Virginia, chiding Bush about his request for $87 billion—no questions answered—by saying "Congress is not an ATM."

President Top Gun, the one who could go it alone, thumbing his nose at world opinion, agreed to begin negotiations in the United Nations Security Council to authorize a multi-national force for Iraq. When the president called for financial contributions, other countries did not exactly fight to be at the head of the line. Of course, Bush was still insisting that all operations remain under American command, while France wanted authority to be transferred to the U.N. itself. Bush's request for help was what the *New York Times* called "a tacit admission that the current American-dominated force is stretched too thin." Some reserve units have been mobilized since shortly after the September 11 attacks. In September 2003, tens of thousands of reservists learned that their tours would be extended into 2004. They were essentially being drafted as full-time soldiers.

By October 2003, Bush was beginning to sound punchy with double-speak, suggesting that the out of control violence in Iraq was actually a sign of progress. The *Times* had him explaining this strange bit of reasoning by saying "the more successful we are on the ground, the more these killers will react." The *Times* added that this goof-ball pronouncement "left even some Republicans wincing."

Ditto every time he talked about his "coalition of the willing." Poland, Denmark, Bulgaria, El Salvador, Norway—who is he kidding?

The president's truth-impaired antics led Maureen Dowd to write a column in which she compared Blind-sided Bush with "Baghdad Bob." Remember him? He was Muhammad Said al-Sahhaf, the Iraqi commentator who kept broadcasting "There are no American infidels in Baghdad. Never!" with the sound of our tanks and rockets in the background. "We are winning this war, and we will win the war. . . . This is for sure!" Baghdad Bob assured the world. The trouble with Bush is he can't seem to keep his delusions straight. Even after admitting that Saddam had no connection to 9/11—after six months of relentlessly using that supposed connection as justification for an invasion—Bush thumped his lectern and said that we would stay the course in Iraq, adding, "We must never forget the lessons of September 11."

October 28, 2003, was the same day that the White House announced that they were shifting intelligence officers in Iraq away from the search for "weapons of mass destruction," reassigning them to help keep American soldiers from getting their asses blown off by Iraqis—those surprising little devils who were supposed to have been "shocked and awed" by our weapons, then groveling at our feet with thanks for delivering them from Saddam. Good decision about the spies, though. Those guys might as well have been searching for the "real killer" of O.J. Simpson's wife. Backing off the Easter egg hunt for WMDs seemed like an especially good idea, given that the former British foreign secretary, Robin Cook, had come clean. Cook told us that Prime Minister Blair admitted to him privately that there were no threatening weapons of mass destruction in Iraq in the first place. This came out in extracts from Cook's memoir, *Point of Departure,* published in the Sunday *Times* of London. Cook appears to be that rare bird in public life—a man of integrity. On hearing Blair's confession, Cook resigned his job in protest over Britain's being "Bush's poodle" and following W into an unnecessary war.

October 2003 was also when it came to light that the White House knew all along that Iraq oil would never be able to pay for reconstructing that country—which is *not* what Incurious George was telling us as he revved up his engines for war. Six months before the invasion, the Pentagon had produced a book-length report saying that Iraqi oil production was so screwed after a decade of trade embargoes that it was just limping along. But Deputy Secretary of Defense Paul Wolfowitz told Congress that Iraq oil could carry the cost anyway. We got stuck with the check for $87 billion after the fact. Are you beginning to see a pattern with these guys?

This was also the month when the Senate Select Committee on Intelligence gave a deadline—October 31—for information about pre-war assessments they had requested from the CIA in July. But the CIA had already been burned with Republicans on the Committee—stand-ins for the president—blaming the Agency for bad information about nonexistent weapons in Iraq. Four senior spooks held a briefing at CIA headquarters to say that a top-secret internal review showed that the spy guys had done their job properly. "What [the internal review] has shown us is that the judgments were not only sound, they were very sound, and backed up by more than one source," one of these senior officers said. But what they knew was the Republicans, by diverting blame, were trying to provide cover for the president's blatant misuse of that intelligence.

While campaigning in New Hampshire, Wesley Clark said, "You can't blame something like this on lower-level intelligence officers, however badly they communicated in memos with each other." He cited that non–Yale educated Democrat from Missouri, Harry Truman, who knocked on his White House desk and said, "The buck stops here."

Clark also lamented the fact that Donald Rumsfeld "had to leak his own memo," also in October, to fess up to a bleaker assessment of progress in Iraq "because no one would have believed him that we've been two years in the war on terror and we don't have a strategy and we don't know how to measure success."

At the same time, the chairman of the commission investigating 9/11, former Republican governor of New Jersey Thomas Kean, threatened to subpoena the White House in order to obtain documents the Bushies have been hiding ever since the attacks took place. They stonewall, they blame the sailors, blame the CIA, they blame Clinton.

> They stonewall, they blame the sailors, blame the CIA, they blame Clinton.

Let's face it—October 2003 was a lousy month for Bush. But it was even worse for the troops in Iraq. With the number of attacks up to thirty-three a day from twelve a day in July, October marked the turning point at which the death toll after "mission accomplished" exceeded the 116 combat casualties that occurred during the actual "war" itself.

A Big Fake Turkey

November was the time for Bush's second and, actually, most appropriate photo of the war. He showed up unannounced in Baghdad, and was pictured on front pages all over the world holding up a platter with a big fake turkey.

Things were looking better for Bush's war by December, at least in terms of images for public consumption. U.S. forces pulled Saddam Hussein out of a hole in the ground, bearded and haggard, looking like one of the millions of homeless men left wandering the streets of American cities since the Reagan administration began de-institutionalizing the mentally ill. Trouble is, the suicide bombings and the attacks on our troops did not end just because the "butcher of Baghdad" was captured. And the administration just kept bungling along.

Just as Bush began trying to sweet-talk France and Germany and Russia into forgiving some of the $9 billion debt that Iraq owes them, a memo by Deputy Secretary of Defense Paul Wolfowitz hit the Pentagon Web site. The memo declared that countries that did not send troops to fight in Iraq would not be allowed to share in the war profiteering—countries like France, Germany, and Russia. Of course, Iraq previously bought most of its heavy equipment from these three countries, which is how the Iraqis wound up owing them $9 billion. So in terms of spare parts and detailed knowledge of the Iraqi infrastructure, it doesn't make a lot of sense to exclude the people who built the infrastructure in the first place. *Time* magazine called the Wolfowitz memo "sophomoric," and said that "In its tact, timing, and logic, it was a disaster." Not too surprising considering what Professor Dilulio and former Secretary of the Treasury Paul O'Neill had to say about the

Bush policy-making apparatus. But the scariest thing was Wolfo-witz's reference to how these same countries would be excluded from "future operations" as well. What exactly were these "future operations" he was talking about?

With Friends Like These . . .

Which leads us to how we got into this mess in the first place—a man named Ahmad Chalabi, the man with a plan for the Middle East. Because W and the rest of his circle of "all politics, all the time" chuckle-heads are such lightweights, they can be manipu-lated by the few "experts" they have on the payroll. But experts can be manipulated too, especially if they are zealots and ideo-logues. And the guy who took them all for a ride is an aristo-cratic Iraqi expatriate who had not been in Baghdad since the 1950s.

After the first Gulf War, Chalabi started cultivating the right people, namely Richard Perle and Paul Wolfowitz, and the other neoconservative wing nuts over at the American Enterprise Insti-tute and the Heritage Foundation. Chalabi set up the Iraqi Na-tional Congress, which, at least in the eyes of all these Republicans in Washington, was sort of a shadow government for Iraq, just waiting in the wings. Only trouble was, the Iraqi people were not in on the joke. They didn't know Ahmed Chalabi from Adam.

Back in Washington, however, he was talking up not just regime change, but how Iraq could become a kind of Kiwanis Club in the Middle East, a model of democracy and Republican virtue. It was Chalabi's gang who were talking up Saddam's weapons, as well as how the Iraqi people would greet us with open arms. The CIA and the State Department knew he was full of crap, but that made him even more beloved to the hardcore true believers over at the Pentagon.

They landed Chalabi and 500 of his followers in Iraq shortly after the fall of Baghdad, and he went over like a lead balloon. It seems all the Iraqis saw is the colonialists sending in their hand-picked guy once again, just like they always do. It was the same arrogance and stupidity that had us heavily guarding the oil ministry while the National Museum, the National Library, the Ministry of Health, and just about every other institution in Iraq was looted. It was the same blind, arrogant stupidity that led us to disband the Iraqi army, creating 450,000 sworn enemies in one day—all those guys no longer getting a paycheck.

What does the Bush war strategy come down to? Fundamental mistakes that any common sense, common man can see. There are no real policy people in the White House, the political hacks who are there don't do their homework, and they try to dumb everything down to a clear black and white level that just doesn't match the complex, murky reality.

By the time of Bush's 2004 State of the Union, which Ahmad Chalabi watched while sitting in an honored place with Mrs. Bush, the rationale for this war had dissolved into thin air, replaced by repeated statements that "the world was a better place" because of it. All the 2003 talk about weapons of mass destruction held like a knife at our throats was replaced by a reference to "dozens of weapons of mass destruction–related program activities and significant amounts of equipment that Iraq concealed from the United Nations."

I guess the finale to that rousing rhetoric came a few days later when David Kay, who had just resigned as the head of the inspection program, said once and for all that there were no weapons of mass destruction. The *Washington Post* reported having documents suggesting that any biological weapons had been disposed of as early as 1991.

> The radical conservatives are all for democracy, but only if they can guarantee the outcome through dirty tricks.

Meanwhile, Bush has backed off on his plans to establish democracy in Iraq within six months. It's not too surprising. The radical conservatives are all for democracy, but only if they can guarantee the outcome through dirty tricks. When it really is up for grabs, and they see themselves losing, they simply change the rules.

Bill Clinton said that unless we plan to occupy every country on the planet, we have to develop some allies. We can't go it alone with Bush's tough guy swagger and shoot-first, make-up-a-reason-later policies. Especially when even the Army War College describes the trip to Baghdad as a "detour" that contributed nothing to the war on terror.

Bush's whole policy shows both ineptitude and childishness. The story behind the invasion sounds like something dreamed up by a Boy Scout troop. His adolescent fantasies of instant gratification left him blindsided when he realized he'd taken on such a grown-up responsibility. When it didn't turn out as planned, he hedged on the price tag until it was too late, and Congress had no choice but to support an ongoing operation to the tune of $4 billion a month.

Huntin' Down Them Evil-Doers

What about the war we were supposed to be fighting—the war against the people who actually attacked us, who were not the secular Baathists from Iraq, but Islamic fundamentalists, most of whom were from our dear ally Saudia Arabia?

I don't think we are ever going to know the real story about 9/11, or, for that matter, the whole truth about our invasion of Iraq. I think it's going to be like the Kennedy assassination—one of those events that people will be debating forty years from now.

What we do know is that there is far more connecting the House of Bush, the House of Saud, and the House of bin Laden, than the president's handlers are comfortable talking about.

It's been reported in *The New Yorker* and elsewhere that on September 11, 2001, a day when every other civilian airplane in the country was grounded, a private jet flew from Los Angeles, to

Orlando, to Washington, to Boston, picking up twenty-four members of Osama bin Laden's family and taking them back to Saudia Arabia. It seems that the FBI was easily persuaded that these people had nothing to offer our investigation of the "evil-doers." Does that make sense to you? It doesn't make a bit of sense to me.

A year later, Dick Cheney was still trying to derail an investigation into 9/11. *Newsweek* quoted a GOP staffer as saying that there was "a general philosophy that the less the world knows, the better." When Bush could no longer avoid creating such a commission, he nominated Henry Kissinger to lead it. Kissinger, Richard Nixon's secretary of state who launched the secret war in Cambodia, has about zero credibility in terms of being honest, open, and non-partisan. To me that looked like just a *fine* choice to assure everyone that there would be an exhaustive search for the truth and full disclosure of all findings, however damaging to those in power.

As 2004 began, Bush was still withholding documents from the federal commission. These include the intelligence reports that reached Bush in August, 2001, only a few weeks before the attacks, while George was on vacation. (During his first eight months in office, our nap-prone president spent over 40 percent of his time either on vacation, at Camp David, or in Crawford.) The fact that these reports clearly stated the possibility that al Qaeda could very well attack using commercial airliners was confirmed by the White House in 2002.

> As 2004 began, Bush was still withholding documents from the federal commission.

Max Cleland, the former senator who left two legs and an arm in Vietnam, and who is now a member of the National Commission on Terrorist Attacks Upon the United States, told the *New York Times,* "It's obvious that the White House wants to run out the clock here. . . . As each day goes by, we learn that this government knew a whole lot more about these terrorists before September 11 than it has ever admitted."

Senator John McCain was more direct. He called what the White House was doing "obfuscation," which is a nine-dollar word for filling the air with horseshit.

Let me ask a question. Does this administration's peculiar behavior have anything to do with the Bush family's long connection to the Saudi royal family, and, for that matter, with the bin Laden family itself?

For all the billions we spend on defense and intelligence, how did we get caught napping through the build-up to 9/11? The answer might just be that, to the extent that those in charge of investigating such things didn't see it coming, it was because certain areas of investigation were put off-limits. But even more damaging is the fact that plenty of people outside the Bush circle did see it coming, did warn against it, and were ignored by an arrogant, smug, and self-satisfied administration.

Greg Palast is an investigative reporter and a friend of mine. He's an American who works for the BBC (and does maybe five stories a year for *Hustler)*, because most American outlets can't handle news that cuts close to the bone. In his book, *The Best Democracy Money Can Buy,* he quotes a top-level CIA operative as saying that, as soon as Bush took over the White House, "there was a major policy shift" at the National Security Agency. Investigators were ordered to "back off" from any inquiries into Saudi Arabian financing of Islamic terror, especially insomuch as it touched on Saudi royals and their friends. Given that the Saudi royals and Osama's family are joined at the hip, this took the billionaire bin Ladens off the investigators' radar. It was okay to keep tracking bad boy Osama; it was not okay to "follow the money" from other Saudi billionaires to the door of his cave. According to Palast, Osama had a nice racket going, extorting money from his cousins to keep him from acting up inside Saudi Arabia.

It seems that the Saudi royals, the Bush family, and the bin Laden family are all kissing cousins as well. They go way back. You may even recall that it was the Saudis who put up the $30 million to buy arms for Iran in the Iran-Contra affair while George senior was "out of the loop" as vice-president.

As for George W, Palast makes the point that "while some people have guardian angels, our president seems to have guardian sheiks." According to Palast, back in the seventies and eighties, every time W was about to disappear down one of the dry holes he drilled in West Texas, Saudi money in one shape or another seemed to swoop in and catch him. In 1977, W set up his exploration company, called Arbusto (Spanish for "shrub"). His principal backer was James R. Bath, who used money that came, in part, from Sheik Salim bin Laden—Osama's cousin. Bush nearly went under in 1981, until he was bought out—and at a price that made no market sense—by Philip Uzielli, a crony of James Baker III, the lawyer who would later mastermind Bush's theft of Florida's electoral votes. Bush became part of Uzielli's Spectrum Oil, which in 1986, needed salvation itself. In swept Harken Oil—again, paying a surprisingly high price—and within the year, Harken received a healthy investment from Saudi Sheik Abdullah Bakhsh. In 1990, Harken itself was all set to fold when the government of Bahrain selected them to drill in the Persian Gulf. The fact that Harken had no experience drilling offshore was no problem, it seemed, so long as one of their principals was the son of a sitting president.

But the "Bush of Arabia" connection got even thicker. In 1987, a number of former government employees stumbled upon the idea that they could make considerably more money being a sort of "state department" in the private sector, and they founded a company called the Carlyle Group to grease wheels and broker deals. Frank Carlucci, formerly Reagan's secretary of defense, as well as deputy director of the CIA, joined in 1989 and became CEO, bringing with him a slew of former civil ser-

Until 9/11, their happy little investment club also included the loving family of Osama bin Laden.

vice types from the CIA and the Pentagon, as well as the Bush family. And until 9/11, their happy little investment club also included the loving family of Osama bin Laden.

The first President Bush does speeches for Carlyle and was paid in equity shares worth $80,000 a pop. In 1999, he traveled to Saudi Arabia for Carlyle and stayed at the Bin Laden palace. James Baker was in on the Carlyle action, too. (Baker's firm later represented the Saudi royals in lawsuits filed by the families of 9/11 victims.) In 1990, George W. was appointed to the board of one of Carlyle's first purchases, an airline food business called Caterair, which—you guessed it—they eventually sold at a loss.

What's so bad about being in bed with the Saudis, or even the bin Ladens? That depends on how you look at it. Time was, of course, when young Osama was part of the Reagan administration's "war on Communism." This was in the early eighties, when Osama was often seen at the Afghan training camps in Pakistan, handing out cash to the Muslim groups fighting Soviet troops in Afghanistan. His cousin Sheik Salim funneled the money from the British-run Bank of Credit and Commerce International (BCCI) to help fund the Afghan war. The U.S. supported Osama's efforts until 1988, when the Soviets withdrew. It was then that Osama, with fighters we helped finance and train, could turn his attention to getting the U.S. out of sacred Islamic territory as well.

Meanwhile, the Saudis continued their generosity to the Bush family and its allies. Saudi Prince Al Waleed bin Talal bin Abdul Aziz chose Carlyle for advice in a huge stock transaction, the kind of deal where you'd usually rely on an investment bank. This was about as odd as choosing Harken—a company with no offshore experience—to drill in the Persian Gulf. In both cases, if we didn't know better, we might think that the Saudis were trying to buy themselves into the good graces of the Bush circle. The question is, what did they get for their money?

I would never suggest that it was anything more than a tendency to see them as fine fellows, and to change the subject whenever the talk turned to terrorist activity originating in the Arabian peninsula. It was sort of like the Bushes' "Skull & Bones Society" from Yale. When anybody so much as mentions the name of the organization, members are supposed to walk out of the room. But that little bit of benign neglect just may have contributed to the deaths of nearly 3,000 Americans on September 11, 2001.

Some of the deepest dirt Greg Palast dug up concerns a thirty-page document marked "SECRET," which he was able to obtain from the FBI. It seems that the Bureau had become curious about Abdullah and Omar bin Laden, but the Bush administration sent down the word that these guys were good ole boys, and that Osama had a screw loose and was the only bin Laden worth worrying about. But the Feds already had a file of these two that linked them to the World Assembly of Muslim Youth (WAMY). As Palast tells it, WAMY ran a Florida summer camp in which, instead of learning to make campfires and weave whistle straps, Muslim kids learned "what were presented as the good Islamic practices of hostage-taking and suicide killings."

Blaming Bubba

September 11, 2003, the second anniversary of the terrorists attacks at the World Trade Center and the Pentagon, George Bush got a boost from Showtime Television, which broadcast "DC9/11: Time of Crisis," a two-hour campaign advertisement written by Lionel Chetwynd, one of Hollywood's more outspoken conservatives. In it, the leader of the free world gets to grimace and mouth dialogue like, "I want to inflict pain." That's not a kinky confession about Bush at bedtime. That's the president talking about revenge, over the phone, with Prime Minister Tony Blair.

Oddly enough, though, the film also has President Bush saying that he wants to "bring enough damage so they understand there is a new team here, a fundamental change in our policy."

I wonder what that new policy would be? It sounds to me
like the conservatives are trying
to blame Bill Clinton for whatever goes wrong in the world,
as usual.

> **The conservatives
> are trying to blame
> Bill Clinton for what-
> ever goes wrong in
> the world, as usual.**

During the 2000 campaign,
all the Bush people trash-talked Clinton's supposed weakness on
defense. They said that Clinton had diluted our strength by sending troops to Somalia and Kosovo for what they mockingly called
"nation building." Bush claimed that Clinton had let the military
get soft. In one of his cute little smirking remarks, Bush said that
whole units would have to say, "Not ready for duty, sir."

And yet, in dollars adjusted for inflation, the Clinton defense
budget in 1996 was larger than the outgoing budget of the first
Bush administration, the one developed by Bush's then secretary
of defense, Dick Cheney.

The army Clinton financed was sufficiently "ready for duty" to
overrun Afghanistan in less than a month in 2001, a full year before Bush's first budget went into effect. Donald Rumsfeld has
credited our successful battle plan in Iraq to General Tommy
Franks—a man appointed by Clinton to head the Central Command. Reagan's assistant secretary of defense, Lawrence J. Korb,
went so far as to admit that the army that went to war in Iraq was,
for the most part "recruited, trained, and equipped by the Clinton
administration."

And yet, during the early days of the Bush administration, we
had Orrin Hatch telling any reporter who would listen that Clinton was at fault because he had "de-emphasized" the military. The
surfer congressman from California, Dana Rohrabacher, told us
that, "We had Bill Clinton backing off, letting the Taliban go, over
and over again." All the right wing media piled on. Even Newt
Gingrich came out of his all too brief exile to blame Clinton, at-
tributing the attacks to Clinton's "pathetically weak, ineffective

ability to focus and stay focused." (In the next chapter, I'll discuss how Newt and his friends tried to help Clinton stay focused.)

The fact is, Clinton's being "soft on terrorism" is one more part of the conservatives' Big Hustle. A month before Clinton left office, Robert Oakley, ambassador for counterterrorism under Reagan, told the *Washington Post* that he gave Clinton's administration high marks, except for what he called their obsession with Osama. . . . Paul Bremer, later Bush's administrator in Iraq, was a little closer to the mark when he told the *Post* that the Clinton administration had "correctly focused on bin Laden."

The *Post*'s Barton Gellman wrote that "Clinton left office having given greater priority to terrorism than any president before him."

We lost nearly five hundred American lives to Islamic terrorists during the Reagan administration, and in response Reagan launched one bombing run against Libya in 1986. The Reagan and Bush administrations continued to supply arms to Osama bin Laden in Afghanistan, as well as even deadlier weapons to Saddam Hussein in Iraq.

Al Franken makes the point that, in his four State of the Union speeches, the first President Bush said the word "terror" only once, and that was in reference to "environmental terrorism" that took place when Saddam set fire to the oil fields. Bush the First was busy ignoring the power vacuum left by the Soviet withdrawal from Afghanistan, a vacuum that was filled by the Taliban, who then created a safe haven for al Qaeda. He also pulled a bait and switch on the Kurds who hoped for American help in their uprising against Saddam.

When the World Trade Center was bombed in 1993, Clinton responded by catching and convicting the perpetrators—Ramzi Yousef, Abdul Hakim Murad, and Wali Khan Amin Shah. Clinton also managed to stop separate plots to kill the Pope and blow up twelve U.S. airliners at once, as well as planned attacks on federal buildings, airports, tunnels, and bridges coast to coast. Clinton even put out an official "hit" on Osama bin Laden.

Clinton doubled the funding for counterterrorism, created a new national security position to coordinate counterterrorism activity, and destroyed al Qaeda cells all over the world. He even created a national stockpile of drugs and vaccines.

How did the supremely patriotic Republicans respond? In 1996, when Clinton asked for more antiterrorism funding, the same Orrin Hatch who would later slime Clinton for "deemphasizing the military," said, "The administration would be wise to utilize the resources Congress has already provided before it requests additional funding."

After al Qaeda terrorists attacked the *USS Cole* on October 12, 2000, Clinton put Richard Clarke, our first national antiterrorism coordinator, in charge of finding a way to eliminate al Qaeda. Clarke, a career State Department man with experience in Libya, produced a strategy paper that he presented to Sandy Berger and other top national security people in December of that year. According to a Bush administration official quoted in *Time*, the plan included "just about everything we've done since 9/11"—minus the pointless attack on Iraq, of course.

Unfortunately, the plan was never carried out. A Clinton senior aide told *Time* that they held back to avoid "handing [the Bush administration] a war when they took office." Instead, Clinton's national security advisor, Sandy Berger, arranged ten briefings for Condoleezza Rice, telling her, "I believe that the Bush administration will spend more time on terrorism in general, and on al Qaeda specifically, than any other subject." Richard Clarke laid out the whole "get al Qaeda" plan, then repeated the briefing for Vice President Dick Cheney. But, the Bush people had other priorities.

Here is a play by play of what all the king's horses and all the king's men did to deal with the impending terrorist attacks:

February 15, 2001. The United States Commission on National Security/21st Century, initiated in 1997 by the Congressional leadership, the White House, and the Department of Defense issued its long awaited report on national security. Their conclusion: "This commission believes that the security of the American homeland from the threats of the new century should be the primary national security mission of the U.S. government." Their report warned that "mass-casualty terrorism directed against the U.S. homeland was of serious and growing concern" and said that America was not at all prepared for a "catastrophic" domestic terrorist attack. They urged the creation of a new federal agency: "A National Homeland Security Agency with responsibility for planning, coordinating, and integrating various U.S. government activities involved in homeland security."

The report kicked up some media attention, and a bill was introduced in Congress to establish a National Homeland Security Agency.

> **Bush took the same approach he has taken on global warming—more study.**

But rather than carry out this recommendation, Bush took the same approach he has taken on global warming—more study.

May 8, 2001—Bush set up a task force under Vice President Cheney to see what needed to be done to thwart domestic terrorism. He said that he himself would "periodically chair a meeting of the National Security Council to review these efforts." Bush never chaired any meetings, because the task force never met.

July 10, 2001—FBI agent Kenneth Williams sent a memo to headquarters raising concern about the Arab students at an Arizona flight school. Williams suggested that al Qaeda operatives might be trying to infiltrate U.S. skies, and he urged FBI headquarters to contact the CIA to see if they had information on this kind of plot.

Meanwhile, CIA Director George Tenet, a Clinton appointee, was picking up scattered reports suggesting trouble, and in mid-July he briefed Condoleezza Rice that a major attack was on the way.

July 16, 2001—Administration staffers met to discuss the plans that Richard Clarke had proposed six months earlier and had been pushing for ever since. The ideas cleared this group, and were ready for approval by the president's inner circle. They tried to schedule the meeting for August, but too many of these grown-ups were away. The meeting was postponed.

August 3, 2001—Bush approved a plan to *cut* funding to guard unsecured nuclear weapons in the former Soviet Union. He then left Washington to spend the rest of the month on vacation.

August 6, 2001—The CIA delivered a report to the president with the not-too-hard-to-figure-out title: "Bin Laden Determined to Strike in U.S." The report talked about hijacking airplanes and flying them into buildings.

August 16, 2001—The Immigration and Naturalization Service arrested Zacharias Moussaoui, a Muslim aviation student who was not interested in learning take-offs or landings. The agent who arrested him went so far as to describe him as being "the type of person who could fly something into the World Trade Center." A Minneapolis FBI agent tried to add some urgency to her report to headquarters by describing how a 747 loaded with fuel could be used as a weapon.

September 4, 2001—Cheney, Powell, Rice, and Rumsfeld met to discuss Clarke's plan for dealing with terrorism. They endorsed it, but chose to recommend a phased-in approach, beginning with demands for cooperation from the Taliban.

September 9, 2001—Congress proposed to shift $600 million from Rumsfeld's pet project—a $200 billion missile defense program—and redirect it toward fighting terror. Rumsfeld threatened a presidential veto.

September 10, 2001. John Ashcroft sent his Justice Department budget request to the White House. In it, he itemized his seven top priorities. Terrorism was not on the list. This was the same day that acting FBI director Thomas J. Pickard received official notice

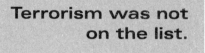
Terrorism was not on the list.

from Ashcroft denying a request for $58 million to hire new field agents, translators, and intelligence analysts to improve the Bureau's capacity to deal with terrorism.

September 11, 2001. Well, we all know what happened on September 11.

The White House fought the idea of a 9/11 inquiry tooth and nail, but then word leaked that Bush had been given a heads-up about the attacks weeks before they happened. When Colleen Rowley, the FBI agent from the Minneapolis bureau, made known her efforts to wake up the guys who were supposed to be minding the store, Bush did a 180 and decided to create a cabinet-level Department of Homeland Security. Of course, the Bushies had to slip a poison pill into their adoption of this Democratic idea—they would deprive the new department's employees of civil service protection. When Senate Democrats voted against the measure because of this basic unfairness, Bush slimed them.

"The Senate is more interested in special interests in Washington and not interested in the security of the American people," he said. Now, hypocrisy like that is enough to make Jimmy Swaggart proud.

Exploiting the good faith and desire for unity among Americans in order to launch an "elective" war is criminal.

Shamelessly exploiting a tragedy for political gain is appalling, but exploiting the good faith and desire for unity among Americans in order to launch an "elective" war is criminal.

People are dying because of this, and as one commentator put it, the Americans who will wind up paying the bill are not able to hear Bush's speeches on TV because it's past their bedtime.

That Bill of Rights Is Too Long to Remember, So Why Don't We Just Trim It Down to Size

Truth is always the first casualty of war, but in the Bush administration, civil liberties have been a close second. I don't think you'll find a more passionate defender of our civil liberties than I am (and I put my money where my mouth is—I'm one of the biggest supporters of the American Civil Liberties Union).

Terror alone never accomplishes much. It's the overreaction to terror by the government under attack that achieves the terrorists' objectives. A government under siege tramples on the rights of citizens, which makes people crazy, which leads to infighting and, ultimately, a breakdown of society.

The man in charge of all this trampling is a Christian fundamentalist radical who was named attorney general as a payoff to the most extreme members of the Christian right. John Ashcroft, a career politician, needed a job after losing the race for the governorship of Missouri to a dead man in 2000 (incumbent Mel Carnahan was killed in a plane crash during the campaign). Throughout his public life, Ashcroft has demonstrated again and again that he simply does not accept the rules of the game as the rest of us do. That's why, during six years in the Senate, he introduced or sponsored seven constitutional amendments. He has always wanted to set up a religious state, which—though he might not want to pass laws against kite flying or make women wear burkas—is exactly what the Taliban did.

Ashcroft is also a crackpot whose hobbies include anointing himself with oil to be like the ancient kings of Israel, and writing (and singing!) hymns so awful they could coerce confessions out of all those interned prisoners in Guantanamo. Let's not forget the

January 2002 press conference he gave from the Great Hall of the Department of Justice Headquarters, staged in front of the female statue that represents the Spirit of Justice. The man spent $8,000 of taxpayer money draping her in blue cloth so that her breast would not be exposed.

Through the Patriot Act that he put together and shoved through Congress, Ashcroft has trashed the Fourth Amendment protection from unlawful search and seizure, the Sixth Amendment right to an open jury, and our First Amendment right to free speech. True to form, and true to right-wing hypocrisy, he drew the line at doing anything that might even come close to affecting the Second Amendment right to bear arms. That's why, just a few weeks before 9/11, he halted a search for gun records on potential terrorists. Anyone who criticized him, he told the Senate Judiciary Committee, was "providing ammunition to America's enemies . . . to those who scare peace-loving people with phantoms of 'lost liberty,' my message is this: Your tactics only aid terrorists."

John Ashcroft is no laughing matter.

His grandiosity is laughable, but John Ashcroft is no laughing matter.

Ashcroft's USA PATRIOT Act, an acronym for The Uniting and Strengthening of America by Providing Appropriate Tools Required to Intercept and Obstruct Terrorism, was proposed at the time of the anthrax scare when many members of Congress couldn't even get into their offices to read the bill. This 342-page law was written, passed (by a 98–1 vote in the Senate) and signed within seven weeks of the Sept. 11 attacks, when everyone was still stunned and waiting for the sky to fall.

When the dust settled, people began to realize that this outrage gave the government new powers to wiretap phones, confiscate property of suspected terrorists, spy on its own citizens without judicial review, conduct secret searches, and snoop on the reading habits of library users. As the American Civil Liberties Union tells us, "Ashcroft demanded that his proposal [for this act] be enacted within three days, and, when that deadline was not met, he suggested publicly that members of Congress would be responsible for any terrorist attack that occurred during the bill's pendency. Congress passed the far-reaching law after abbreviated debate, handing Ashcroft virtually all the investigative tools he sought and several he had not even asked for."

In May of 2002, the ACLU released a report in which they described Ashcroft's "insatiable appetite" for new powers that would not make us any safer but substantially less free. Ashcroft has reopened the door for government fishing expeditions into the private lives of citizens. After the illegal wiretaps, unwarranted dossiers, spying on civil rights and anti-war leaders, and other investigative excesses of a generation ago—especially the way the FBI hounded Martin Luther King, Jr.—Congress pressured the Justice Department into adopting far more restrained guidelines for domestic surveillance. Now Ashcroft is sweeping all that away. Time was, you needed some kind of evidence, some basis for an investigation. Not anymore.

Not long after the passage of the USA PATRIOT Act, Justice Department spokeswoman Mindy Tucker announced, "This is just the first step. There will be additional items to come." And come they did. These "items" are buried in secret documents and include the outright removal of the checks and balances that have been the cornerstone of America's democracy. Say good-bye to the American tradition of equality under the law. Just look at how the government continues to question, arrest, and detain people based solely on their race or ethnic background.

In November of 2001, Bush issued an executive order limiting the public's access to presidential records and giving incumbent and former presidents, vice-presidents, and even family members of dead presidents the right to veto the release of presidential records. So the public can no longer obtain documents from earlier Republican administrations with a few unanswered questions outstanding. Convenient, isn't it, now that so many of those good ole boys have been recycled into Bush II?

And consider what Bush and Ashcroft have done with Greenpeace. The Port of Miami refused entry to their ship, *MV Esperanza,* because Ashcroft's Justice Department is prosecuting them for a protest action in 2002. This is the first time in U.S. history that *an entire organization* has been prosecuted for a peaceful protest carried out by its supporters.

In 2002, two Greenpeace activists climbed aboard a ship that was carrying mahogany chopped down in the rainforests of the Amazon. They held up a banner that said "President Bush: Stop Illegal Logging." Greenpeace took this action not only because deforestation helps deplete the ozone layer and adds to global warming, but because logging in the Amazon is a criminal activity involving bribery, extortion, slavery, and murder.

Amazingly, instead of halting the shipment of contraband wood, the government is prosecuting Greenpeace in federal court in Miami. It has charged Greenpeace under an obscure nineteenth-century law never intended for this purpose.

This Justice Department has no charges against Bush's pal "Kenny Boy" Lay, the chairman of Enron who cost investors untold billions (but has been the single largest financial contributor to W's political career). Yet it has time to prosecute tree-huggers. If Ashcroft gets away with this, we can kiss our Bill of Rights good-bye.

> **We wanted to get the Taliban out of Afghanistan— nobody said anything about copying their playbook over here!**

Ashcroft has used 9/11 as an excuse for the government to detain any citizen indefinitely, without access to an attorney, without preferring any charges or producing any evidence, and without justifying its action in a court of law. We wanted to get the Taliban out of Afghanistan—

nobody said anything about copying their playbook over here! But Ayatollah Ashcroft doesn't believe in the Constitution, written, as it was, by mere mortals. He believes that all life should be governed strictly by one book alone, and we all know which one that is.

Ashcroft is running a gestapo without the cool leather coats. He has detained hundreds and perhaps thousands of people without charging them with any crime. He has closed immigration hearings that were once public. He has detained at least two American citizens—Jose Padilla and Yaser Hamdi—without trial and without access to attorneys, on the ground that they are both "enemy combatants." He claims that in wartime—by the way, has Congress made a formal declaration of war?—he has the authority to try American citizens in military courts. He even says that he can hold any American without bail in a detention camp for as long as he sees fit, without a formal charge, and without showing the courts or anyone's lawyer any evidence. Fortunately, in December 2003, federal courts in San Francisco and in New York City rejected the president's claim that they could do whatever the hell they wanted with these people. No thanks to this administration, but the Bill of Rights is still in force.

According to a *Wall Street Journal* report, Ashcroft has even approved plans for detention camps. Instead of reining in this maniac, Chief Justice Rehnquist, the man who put his thumb on the scales of justice to give us this president, appointed a secret "special court" to oversee all this. Do *they* get to wear the cool leather coats? Or maybe they get to wear the black hoods.

Rehnquist hand-selected three veteran judges from the Reagan and Bush administrations for this "star chamber," which has already overruled a circuit court decision that held the government had abused its power to spy on ordinary citizens. As a result, that power was expanded so that the FBI no longer has to meet any meaningful standard of proof before setting up wiretaps or seizing documents or other property.

Even some law and order conservatives—including William Safire, the *New York Times'* resident Republican, and former Republican Congressman from Texas Dick Armey—expressed outrage.

In November 2002, when the Homeland Security Act was about to be passed, Safire wrote, "Every purchase you make with a credit card, every magazine subscription you buy and medical prescription you fill, every web site you visit and e-mail you send or receive, every academic grade you receive, every bank deposit you make, every trip you book and every event you attend go onto what the Defense Department describes as 'a virtual centralized grand database.'" Ashcroft calls it "Total Information Awareness."

On January 10, 2003, he sent around a draft of PATRIOT II, called "The Domestic Security Enhancement Act of 2003." The more than 100 new provisions, Justice Department spokesperson Mark Corallo told the *Village Voice* recently, "will be filling in the holes" of PATRIOT I, "refining things that will enable us to do our job." Among other measures, it calls for the creation of a terrorist DNA database and would allow the government to engage in domestic wiretapping without a court order, to secretly detain citizens, to access a citizen's credit reports without a subpoena, and to ease restrictions on the use of secret evidence.

In the fall of 2003, Attorney General John Ashcroft began a "national victory tour" designed to drum up support for the VICTORY Act, his follow-up performance to the PATRIOT Act. It will include provisions to allow the government to get business records without a court order or search warrant. This will allow the government to track virtually every aspect of your financial life. Your bank records, subscriptions, purchases—you name it, John Ashcroft will own it.

Welcome to the police state.

Welcome to the police state. Liberty-for-security swaps are always put on the table when major conflicts hit. My gut tells me this one is 25 percent about fighting terrorism and 75 percent about our president's—and his whacko attorney general's—personal agenda. I can only hope that the American people have not become so apathetic that they will let this one administration undo more than 200 years of defending personal freedom in this country.

One of the men who helped draft our constitution, Benjamin Franklin, once said, "Those who would trade their civil liberties for security deserve neither." At least for now, the American people still have a say in the matter. The final decision will be theirs when they go to the polls.

New York Times columnist Bob Herbert tells us: "We have a choice. We can fight and win a just war against terrorism, and emerge with the greatness of the United States intact. Or, we can win while running roughshod over the principles of fairness and due process that we claim to cherish, thus shaming ourselves in the eyes of the world and—eventually, when the smoke of fear and anger finally clears—in our own eyes as well."

To me the choice is obvious, and wide open—*anyone but Bush.* Given the outrages I have tried to spell out in this chapter, I can only hope that Americans will get themselves to the polls and not just Flynt this hypocrite, but give him the boot as well.

Which takes us back to the beginning. How did this guy even get in office?

Now, I know this topic has been covered elsewhere, but in case you have been too busy to connect all the dirt, I'm going to do it for you right here. If Al Gore were coming up for re-election in 2004, none of this would matter so much. But with wing nuts currently in the White House, it is vitally important to remember exactly how they got there. We need to be reminded, because it speaks volumes about the man running the country and about the ethics of the people running it with him.

Hail to the Thief

Bush flunkies like James Baker III have been telling us to "move on" ever since the election first got murky down in Florida. It's true that Bush took possession of the White House in January 2001—there's nothing we can do about that. But the history many of us have come to accept is wrong, and that false history is helping to sustain a corrupt regime.

In George Orwell's *1984,* when the political winds would change, and your enemy would suddenly become your friend and your friend your enemy, the official line was never to acknowledge the change. It had always been that way, the leaders would tell you. Just check the record. And in fact, by the time you went to look it up, all the records would have been changed to conform to the new party line.

Near the end of 2003, the *New York Times* did a poll with CBS News in which 38 percent of those polled believed that Bush actually won the 2000 election, and 66 percent of Americans expected him to win the 2004 election. Well, I'll be damned if I'm going to simply "move on" when even 38 percent of Americans still mistakenly believe that this president did, in fact, win the office that he now holds.

> **Well, I'll be damned if I'm going to simply "move on."**

Like many people, I can still remember that strange feeling I had when the networks interviewed W and his parents from Austin on election night back in 2000. There was something weird about the look on his face, this almost serene confidence as W assured everyone that the game wasn't over until the Florida vote was in, and that his brother had "assured" him that it was going his way.

"I'm not . . . conceding anything in Florida," he said. "I know you have all the projections, but people are actually counting the votes. . . . The networks called this thing awfully early and people are actually counting the votes have different perspective so . . ." Given W's way with grammar, it's hard to know what he was trying to say, but, given the way things unfolded, you'd almost think that he knew something at that moment that the rest of us didn't.

With his "compassionate" tactics, Bush won the nomination in

August, but, in a way, his campaign against Al Gore had been going on since 1993. So much right-wing crap had already been thrown up into the air that nobody could see straight, much less get a clear picture of the Democratic nominee.

Yes, serious Al appeared to have a broomstick up his ass, and yes, he did talk like Mr. Rogers when he spoke to the American people, and yes, he couldn't ride too much on Clinton's genuine accomplishments in office without getting too close to Clinton's zipper problem. But Bush's whole thing about "fuzzy math" and "Gore the exaggerator" ("I bet he invented the calculator too") was total bullshit, and fabulously successful, in part, because it was all such a *total* crock. Just ask any totalitarian and he'll tell you straight—when it's time to lie, make it a Big Lie and just keep on talking. Create a whole alternate universe that works by your own rules. They say the same thing in Washington that they say in Hollywood: When you can fake sincerity, you've got it made.

Human beings understand things best by way of stories. Politicians are storytellers, as are journalists. But journalists are often lazy, so they are easy to manipulate. When you're as shameless as the Bushies, you can feed the media story after story that bear no resemblance to the truth. Over time, because nobody calls your bluff, these false stories can form a powerful image in the public mind. Once that image is in place, nobody can shake it.

Bush had a well-deserved image as an intellectual lightweight, which his handlers did nothing to dispel. They were busy creating a false image of him as a nice guy, a regular guy, and even a "compassionate" guy. So when you put it all together, he's not too bright, but he's okay—so cut him some slack. If he blows the facts and can't speak English, much less pronounce the names of foreign leaders, no point busting his balls about it. That's why Bush grins like a fox when he talks about the media "misunderestimating" him. If we set the bar low enough, he can clobber us with it.

At the same time, the Bushies were also busy helping to cement in the public mind the image of Gore as the kind of kid who, just before the weekend, would remind the teacher than she had forgotten to assign homework. Mostly, they did everything they could to boost the impression that it was *Gore* who was wayward with the truth.

So here's the story line for all you reporters: Bush the lightweight—fair enough; and Gore the liar, exaggerating every accomplishment and stretching the truth at every turn.

After the first debate in 2000, Al Gore caught all sorts of hell for having said that he went down to a disaster site in Texas with Federal Emergency Management Agency Director James Lee Witt when he hadn't. In fact, he had gone to that disaster with a *deputy* of James Lee Witt's. Gore, while vice-president, had gone to seventeen other disasters with James Lee Witt, but not that one. So the press ran away with the story of Al the Liar. Even the *New York Times* did a piece in October of that year called "Tall Tales: Is What We've Got Here a Compulsion to Exaggerate?"

Then Gore caught more hell for "claiming to have invented the Internet." The press ran with this one because Gore had said to Wolf Blitzer in a 1999 interview, "During my service in the United States Congress, I took the initiative in creating the Internet." The phrase "invented the Internet" first appeared in a Republican Party press release. Fact is, Gore *was* one of the few members of Congress who saw how the military's emergency computer network, Arpanet, could emerge into something more, and throughout his career as a congressman and senator, he fought for the funding that would turn Arpanet into what is now the Internet. You got a problem with that?

During his second term as vice-president, Gore was in a casual chat with a couple of reporters, including Karen Tumulty of *Time* magazine. The conversation was about movies and old

> **Gore the liar, there he goes again.**

friends, and Gore happened to mention that Erich Segal once told the *Nashville Tennessean* that the lead characters in his book *Love Story* had been based on Gore and his wife, Tipper. When *Time* quoted him, Gore received no end of trashing because of this grandiose nonsense. Gore the liar, there he goes again.

In fact, in 1980 the *Nashville Tennessean* had indeed quoted Segal as saying that Tipper and Al had been the models for the kids in the book, Oliver Barrett and Jenny Cavilleri.

So Bush bases an entire campaign permeated with lies of substance and factual detail on the most important policy and character issues, and he gets "misunderestimated." Gore tells the truth about certain things that strike the media as odd, or that the Republicans distort, and he gets discredited. It's all in the spin, in framing the story of the day and getting the media to run with it. I just wish Al Gore had been as tough on Bush during the campaign as he's been after it. Not long ago, he called Bush a "moral coward" for never saying no to any lie or ploy that might win a vote.

Settling old scores like this might seem like sour grapes if it weren't for the fact that the Bush inventions in question are all part of the same hustle that is sending our soldiers to die in Iraq and sending the federal treasury into the toilet for decades to come. To understand what we are up against now, you have to see it in context. That's what I've tried to do in this chapter—help you understand the degree to which the Bush administration and the folks who brought it to you are totally, fundamentally, and comprehensively corrupt.

We all know that Gore won the popular vote nationwide—meaning that a majority of Americans, despite years of assault from Newt Gingrich and the other Republican hypocrites in Congress, expressed their desire to keep the Democrats in power. That much is a fact . . . a fact that Bush swept aside pretty easily, with typical arrogance, when he came to the White House. Losing the popular vote is not exactly a ringing endorsement, or an overwhelming mandate for radical change. But Bush's first steps in office—trashing the Kyoto agreement on global warming, reversing Clinton's directives to protect federal lands (and protect our water from arsenic), and passing a $1.6 billion tax cut weighted to the rich—were, once again, not exactly designed to "unite, rather than divide."

However, the simple fact is, had he not had Florida stolen from him, Gore also would have won the electoral vote. This fact has been clouded over for many reasons. The biggest one is the right-wing disinformation machine that was blowing smoke from day one of the campaign, right through election night, the aftermath, and all the Monday morning quarterbacking.

In simple English, Bush did not win the presidency, Gore did, and hanging chads was the least of it.

The venerable *New York Times* banded together with CNN and other major news outlets as a consortium to try to clear the air by hiring the National Opinion Research Center (NORC) of the University of Chicago. But once again, the way they couched their findings played into the hustle.

Almost a year into the Bush administration, they released their findings, and the headlines read "Bush would have won." But that was not the actual result. In fact, the NORC research concluded that a majority of Florida voters had actually voted for Gore. By looking at the 180,000 "spoiled" ballots that Katherine Harris had disqualified and never counted, they discovered tens of thousands of ballots with Gore's name circled, but with stray marks on the pages, often caused by the voting machine itself. That's what the newspaper headline writers boiled down into "Bush would have won." They were never allowed to question the legitimacy of Harris's rules, or the enforcement of those rules, in disqualifying those 180,000 ballots.

Okay, there was a war on—remember Afghanistan? The economy had tanked, and for the good of the country, there's something to be said for yielding to the inevitable, at least for a while. No matter how bitter the contest, we have a tradition in this country of closing ranks behind a newly elected president. Even Tricky Dick had the good grace to accept Kennedy's victory in 1960, despite some pretty funky votes coming out of Democratic Mayor Richard Daley's Chicago.

But those 180,000 uncounted ballots were the least of it. What went on in Florida, and then in Washington, at the Supreme Court, was so corrupt on so many different levels, in ways so typical of larger Bush corruption, that we need to be clear about it before going forward.

The story goes way back before the funny business on election night, when the man in charge of the election coverage for Fox News (the "fair and balanced" people) decided that Fox should go on the air and declare that Bush had won. Of course, the man in charge was John Ellis, first cousin of George W and, naturally enough, Jeb Bush, Florida's governor. The Associated Press knew that it was still too close to call. But all the other networks, afraid of being scooped, followed suit.

After the lie was in place, there was no way to correct it. And here's where Bush arrogance (the divine right of sons of kings to be kings) coupled with Bush solemn-faced hypocrisy, proved decisive. Suddenly the percep- **After the lie was in place, there was no way to correct it.** tion was that Gore was being a spoil sport, asking for a "do over." It was as if they'd broken into his house, then called him greedy for not sharing.

Gore was actually ahead at the time, but that was never how the media played it. The count jockeyed back and forth all the way to December 9, 2000. That's when the Supreme Court got word that the recounts in Florida, despite everything the Bushies had pulled off, were going in favor of Gore. By 2:00 p.m. the word was that Gore was down only sixty-six votes and gaining. At 2:45 that afternoon, the Supreme Court stopped the recount.

Funny, but Justice Thomas's wife, Virginia Lamp Thomas, a right-winger from the Heritage Foundation, had just been hired by George W to help line up employees for his administration. Yet Justice Thomas didn't see fit to take himself off the case for an obvious conflict of interest. Neither did Justice Scalia, whose son was a lawyer with Gibson, Dunn & Crutcher—the law firm representing Bush in his claim before the Supreme Court!

To explain their decision, Scalia wrote, "The counting of votes that are of questionable legality does, in my view, threaten irreparable harm to petitioner [Bush], and to the country, by casting a cloud upon what he [Bush] claims to be the legitimacy of this election." In plain English, what the court was saying was that, if we let all the votes be counted and they come out in Gore's favor, and Gore clearly wins the electoral vote as well as the popular vote, then that might impair Prince George's divine right to govern once he's in the White House. (In *1984,* there was an official way of turning the truth inside out known as "doublethink." This strikes me as a fine example.)

With a little nudge, we probably all remember the "butterfly ballot," which made it all too easy to vote for the wrong person because candidates' names and punch holes were crammed unevenly onto opposite pages. The *Palm Beach Post* estimated that more than 3,000 voters, most of them elderly Jews, thought they were voting for Al Gore but punched the wrong hole and ended up voting for wing nut Pat Buchanan. Even Buchanan admitted on TV that there was no way these Jewish voters intended to vote for him.

The joke was that the person who designed this "butterfly" Trojan Horse, Theresa LaPore, was a Democrat, so the Dems had no one to blame but themselves, right? At least that's the story we all heard in the news. But what we didn't hear was that LaPore had actually been a registered Republican until she switched her affiliation to Democrat in 1996. Then, just three months after the Bush coup, she resigned as a Democrat and switched her voter registration to Independent. Nobody in the candy-ass media bothered to question the switch—or the fact that we dismissed the entire issue on the bogus belief that she was a Democrat.

Then there was the whole question of absentee ballots. The *New York Times* showed that there were 2,490 of these from overseas ballots, of which 680 were considered flawed and questionable but were still allowed. Bush won four-fifths of the overseas vote, which would mean that 544 of the votes that went to Bush (four-fifths of 680) should have been thrown out. That would push Bush's triumphant margin of 537 votes down to minus seven.

But the Republicans were already sending out frantic e-mails to navy ships, asking them to scrounge up any ballots that might be lying around. They even tried to pressure Defense Secretary William S. Cohen (a Republican in Clinton's Democratic administration) into forcing the military to send in those cards and letters, but he resisted.

When all was said and done

344 ballots had no evidence that they were cast on or before the deadline of Election Day

183 ballots had domestic postmarks

96 ballots were not properly witnessed

5 ballots were received after the cutoff date of November 17

19 overseas voters voted on two ballots, which wound up being counted twice

Florida law required all ballots to have been "postmarked or signed and dated" by Election Day, but, mysteriously, Katherine Harris, Florida's secretary of state in charge of elections, declined to enforce that regulation. When journalists inquired as to why she had essentially changed the law, the computer records that might have explained her thinking had been erased. This woman now represents Florida in the United States Congress. She's lucky she's not in jail.

The Big Hustle was well in place to make it look as if the Democrats, by complaining about the irregularities, were trying to screw America's men and women in uniform, who were risking their lives for our country. Desert Storm's highly televised hero,

We all know that these liberals are all traitors anyway, right?

General Schwarzkopf, told viewers "it's a very sad day in our country" when Democrats start harassing military voters. We all know that these liberals are all traitors anyway, right?

All this sleaze was a church picnic, however, compared to the way the hustle had gone down long before the voting started.

Black voters tend to vote Democratic, and in 2000, black Floridians flocked to the polls in record numbers. Not surprisingly, Al Gore received the votes of more than 90 percent of the African-Americans who made it to the voting booth. Trouble is, a huge number of them never made it that far, because of a tactic Bob Kutner of the *Boston Globe* called a "lynching by laptop." The NAACP filed a lawsuit claiming that the Florida Republicans had violated the civil rights of thousands of Floridians as guaranteed by the 1965 Voting Rights Act. But the man from Midland (or was it Andover?) is still the man in charge.

You see, owing to a long history of being forced to the bottom of the socio-economic ladder, a greater percentage of blacks than whites not only vote Democratic, but also have had proportionately more experience on the wrong end of the criminal justice system.

The year before the election, Katherine Harris—also co-chair of George W. Bush's Florida campaign—hired a company with strong Republican ties called Database Technologies, a division of ChoicePoint, to go through Florida's voter rolls and remove anyone "suspected" of being a former felon. For this service, Database Technologies' fee was $4 million.

Now, 31 percent of all black men in Florida have at least one felony on their record—considerably higher than the percentage of white men with the same problem. In Florida, at least, this prohibits them from voting. Given the higher numbers of blacks with records of serious crime, it didn't take a Yale graduate to know that purging ex-felons from the voter rolls would knock thousands of black citizens out of the voting booth, citizens with a 90 percent chance of voting for Gore.

Harris instructed Database to err on the side of thoroughness. She told the company to include even people with "similar" names to those of the actual felons. An 80 percent match of relevant information—birth dates the same as known felons, or a similar Social Security number—and bingo, that person (most likely a black person) just lost the right to vote. They would leave it to county election supervisors to sort out any troublesome complaints from those erroneously denied the franchise, *after* those people had been prevented from voting.

All told, 173,000 registered voters in Florida were permanently wiped off the voter rolls. In Miami-Dade, Florida, 66 percent of the voters who were removed were black. In Tampa's county, 54 percent were black, presumably Democratic, voters.

Another 8,000 Floridians were thrown off the voting rolls because Database used an error-ridden list supplied by another state, claiming that all the names on the list were felons who had since moved to Florida. But this list included those who had served their time and had all their voting privileges reinstated. It also included those merely guilty of misdemeanors. As Mr. Rogers might say, "Can you guess what state supplied this list? Would it help if I told you that its name starts with a 'T'?"

Could this possibly be the reason Bush looked like the cat with the canary in the back of its throat on election night? He knew that cousin John was on the case at Fox News, and Jeb and Katherine Harris had whitewashed the voter rolls.

This story, the result of the investigations of Greg Palast, got a lot of play from the British Broadcasting Corporation, but in the States it went nowhere fast. By the time the *Los Angeles Times* and the *Washington Post* picked it up, the Big Hustler was already dining on the White House china. These newspapers had waited until the U.S. Civil Rights Commission Report had verified the de-

> **The lie gets printed in bold headlines on the front page, then the retraction appears beneath an underwear ad on page twelve.**

tails that had been dug up by Palast and his BBC colleagues. But that's the way the hustle works. The lie gets printed in bold headlines on the front page, and then the retraction appears beneath an underwear ad on page twelve. It's the headline that sticks in people's minds. Short term, at least, the headline becomes history.

The official tally in Florida showed George W. Bush receiving 537 more votes than Al Gore. The number of voters kicked off the roles was 66,000, with another 22,000 votes scrubbed by various games.

Palast also makes the interesting point that ChoicePoint's Database Technologies was not the first contractor for the job of whitewashing the Florida voter rolls. In 1998, a company called Professional Service, Inc., was going to do the job for $5,700. A year later, the Florida Department of Elections fired them and hired Database Technologies for a first-year fee of $2,317,800, which, all fuzzy math aside, appears to be several-thousand-percent costlier than the Professional Service bid. And at 27 cents per record, this was easily *ten times* the usual rate within the industry.

In *The Best Democracy Money Can Buy,* Palast tells the story of taking his BBC cameras up to the eighteenth floor of the Florida Capitol Building in Tallahassee to meet with Clayton Roberts, the director of Florida's Division of Elections, to find out why the state was so determined to be fleeced by a private contractor hired to do work that didn't need doing. Especially a company like Database Technologies, which had taken some heat for an alleged association with Bahamian drug dealers, and had run into trouble for improper use of personal data in Pennsylvania.

Roberts, who worked directly under Secretary of State Katherine Harris, had agreed to be interviewed on film. But, as Palast tells it, when the bureaucrat saw that Palast had a confidential memo that dug deep into the dirt, "Roberts sputtered, falling over a few half-started sentences—then ripped off his lapel microphone, jumped up, charged over the camera wires and slammed his office door on me and the camera crew giving chase." Roberts called in the state troopers, but not before letting loose with the more-than-a-little-suspicious parting shot "You know if y'all want to hang this on me that's fine."

The confidential document that caused Roberts to cut and run showed that Database Technology would be paid $2.3 million for their lists and "manual verification using telephone calls and statistical sampling." Yet Roberts and Harris had testified to the U.S. Civil Rights Commission under oath that verification of the voter purge list was left completely up to the county elections supervisors, not to the state or the contractor. However, to quote Palast, "it was the requirement to *verify* the accuracy of the purge list that justified ChoicePoint's selection for the job as well as their astonishingly high fee. *Good evening, Mr. Smith. Are you the same Mr. John Smith that served hard time in New York in 1991?* Expensive though that is to repeat thousands of times, it is necessary when civil rights are at stake. Yet DBT seemed to have found a way to cut the cost of this procedure . . . by not doing it."

So there he was, in the freezing rain on January 20, 2001, George W. Bush, the little rich boy, standing in front of Chief Justice Rehnquist on the Capitol steps to claim the office that James Baker and all daddy's friends on the Supreme Court had set up for him.

> **Twenty thousand protestors had lined the motorcade route, the largest hostile crowd at an inaugural since Richard Nixon.**

Twenty thousand protestors had lined the motorcade route, the largest hostile crowd at an inaugural since Richard Nixon took his second oath of office in 1973.

They held up signs saying "Silenced Majority," and chanted "Hail to the thief!" but Incurious George appeared not to notice. And he certainly didn't have to care—he was now president of the United States.

3

A "Vast Right-Wing Conspiracy"

The preacher caught with his pants down . . . in a motel . . . with a hooker . . . is by now an American cliché. So many moral crusaders have been caught with their hand in the honey pot, or dipping into the cash register, that it doesn't even surprise us anymore. The trouble is, too many Americans are simply numb to this kind of thing. As long as a crooked conservative gives lip service to "American values," then he seems to get a free ride.

In this chapter, I'm going to do some backtracking to show you the ways in which the right has used the holier-than-thou con job for the past thirty years. They've used it to create a movement out of hypocrisy and lies, and as you might have guessed, twisted sexual repression is right at the heart of the issue.

Hypocrisy, self-loathing, and con jobs go hand-in-hand. That's how you got a guy like Roy Cohn, the junkyard-dog persecutor of gays and other "pinkos" back during the Army–McCarthy hearings in the 1950s, who turns out to be gay himself. The same goes for J. Edgar Hoover, the long-running FBI director and obsessive digger into other people's privacy, who in fact was living with his boyfriend Clyde Tolson the whole time. Conservative crusaders for God and country and the flag have a long tradition of saying one thing and doing another, of having a set of values they preach to others and living by a different set themselves.

A perfect example of this right-wing hypocrisy is the late J. Strom Thurmond of South Carolina. Thurmond had the longest run of any man ever in the U.S. Senate—forty-eight years. The cornerstone of his career was laid back in 1948, just about the time I was trying to have sex with a chicken. Senator Thurmond turned his back on Harry Truman's modest plans for integration and ran for president as a "Dixiecrat." Then he led the pack of Southern Democrats who defected from their party, and joined the Republicans, over matters of race. He fought the civil rights movement tooth and nail throughout the fifties and sixties. As his Bible belt followers saw it, segregation "now and forever" was a moral stand not just sanctioned but ordained by God. Way back in 1948, Thurmond made it clear that, "on the question of social intermingling of the races, our people draw the line."

In 1948, Strom's own biracial daughter, Essie Mae Washington, was roughly twenty years old. It seems that the senator had found that "intermingling" was okay when it came to Essie's black mother, Carrie Butler, the Thurmond family housekeeper. Still, the Christian Right loved what Strom Thurmond "stood for," and staunchly supported him up until his retirement, in 2002.

> **What is it about extreme conservatives that makes it so hard for them to walk the walk?**

I think we need to ask ourselves, what is it about extreme conservatives, and extreme conservative positions, that makes it so hard for these people to walk the walk?

Good Old-Fashioned Crackpot Conservatism

In the old days, you had conservatives who may have been one brick shy of a load, but they were straightforward and honest. In fact, many of them had a kind of integrity. Barry Goldwater, the Republican candidate who was crushed by Lyndon Johnson's landslide victory in 1964, was like that. He told you just what he thought and just what he planned to do, even when what he planned to do was drop "tactical" nuclear weapons on Vietnam. Of course, that scared the bejesus out of the American people, which is a large part of why he was a bomb himself as a candidate.

Unfortunately, conservative extremists learned a valuable lesson from Senator Goldwater's failure: When you have nutcase positions, you don't tell the truth. When you have positions that are blatantly unfair, that favor the rich and the special interests while screwing everybody else, lie.

Weave a thick enough fabric of lies and, apparently, you can get a lot of people to hand over their wallets, the car keys, the retirement account—the whole shooting match. Make a big enough noise by lying, become prominent by lying, and nobody but some liberal do-gooder is ever going to call you on it. Certainly the media that matters—television—is never going to say that an American president is flat-out lying, if for no other reason than that it violates a kind of middle-class propriety.

Patti Davis, Ronald Reagan's daughter, wrote in her memoir that "My parents have never gone for simple, state-of-the-art lies. They weave bizarre, incredulous tales and stick by them with fierce determination." I can't say whether this character trait is common to all conservatives, but I know for damn sure that it is the strategy used by the radical conservative movement that now runs the show. And Ronald Reagan was the one who showed them the ropes.

Partly, I think, it has something to do with religious fundamentalism. After all, to "weave bizarre, incredulous tales and stick by them with fierce determination" sounds to me like a pretty good definition of evangelical religion. And God knows there are a lot of God's people in the present Bush administration, with Bibles all over the place and prayer meetings at breakfast.

But when radical conservatives—people who hate government—have to govern, they bring in not just the religious nuts, but a variety of other nuts as well. Bush the First put Clarence Thomas, an avowed opponent of affirmative action, in charge of affirmative action. Bush the Second appointed Gail Norton, who never saw a chain saw or a strip mine she didn't like, to protect our natural resources as head of the Interior Department. Bush II also made gynecologist Dr. David Hager, who opposes prescribing birth control pills for single women, in charge of the Food and Drug Administration's panel on women's health.

> **They bring in not just the religious nuts, but a variety of other nuts as well.**

Loading up an administration with people who directly oppose the mission of their department is a long conservative tradition. James Watt, Ronald Reagan's secretary of the interior, saw no need to worry about preserving our natural resources. For him, saving open space or virgin forests for future generations was not going to be a problem because, as he told Congress, "I don't know how many future generations we can count on before the Lord returns."

The need for appointees to be nuts in order to fit the right-wing agenda is why conservatives have to scrape the bottom of the barrel to find minorities to fill federal judgeships. When they go looking for black or Hispanic conservatives, they wind up with losers like Janice Rogers Brown, the black woman on the California Supreme Court who attacked FDR's New Deal as "the triumph of our socialist revolution," and praised court decisions that struck down health and safety laws for workers. This black judge, selected by Bush the Second, earned fierce opposition from the Congressional Black Caucus and a C- from the American Bar Association, which usually rubber-stamps nominees.

Probably because George W. Bush is a nut himself, his record for judicial appointments is just awful. A *New York Times* editorial drew upon Bush's own words to say that, "President Bush, who promised as a candidate to be a 'uniter, not a divider,' has selected the most divisive judicial nominees in modern times."

Get up on the wrong side of the bed some morning, and you might begin to think that our Republican leaders actually want the government to fail. You might reach the dark conclusion that they don't want an impartial referee moderating the excesses of capitalism, or helping maintain a society that serves both the rich and the poor alike. You might conclude that their policies so blatantly favor the wealthy and the white that any minority who buys what they're selling is into masochism. You might even say that they have been running a hustle for more than a generation in which the most blatant lies and hypocrisies are standard operating procedure.

So who are these people who brought Bush to power, the "lying liars" that Al Franken writes about? They're not just his daddy's friends—this crew is far more conservative than the people who ran the first Bush administration. What makes them tick? What's their problem? And when you Flynt them, what do you come up with?

Feeling Their Pain

City Beat, a Los Angeles weekly, has a feature called "Please Tell Me You Made This Up," and in the summer of 2003, they ran a piece that attempted to explain the conservative mind. It seems a research paper had appeared in *Psychological Bulletin,* in which the psychologists had brought together study results of 22,818 people in twelve countries and concluded that conservatism can be explained by a set of neuroses rooted in "fear and aggression, dogmatism and the intolerance of ambiguity . . . desiring a return to an idealized past and condoned inequality."

I'm not sure what that tells us beyond what we already knew,

> **Right-wingers have set up "liberalism" as the Bogeyman.**

but I do know for sure that there's always been a paranoid style in American politics that is fearful, aggressive, intolerant, and backward thinking, and that explains most forms of inequality as simply God's will. Now that we don't have the "yellow peril" or the "Communist threat" to band together against, right-wingers have set up "liberalism" as the Bogeyman.

In the 1950s, and then even for a while after the Goldwater debacle in 1964, our two political parties were not as far apart as they are today. In other words, there was still such a thing as a conservative Democrat and a liberal Republican. In the sixties and seventies, radical conservatives, the kind with extreme views matching what we have in the Bush administration today, were a laughable bunch of cranks on the political margin. We had the John Birch Society, worrying about commies under the bed and fluoridation in the water, and—no joke—trying to have stories about Robin Hood banned from public libraries. Just about the only hardcore conservative talking politics on TV was William F. Buckley, and he was a sight to see. His show was called "Firing Line," and with his wild, rolling eyes and nervous tics, his voice going up and down and his tongue darting in and out like a lizard, he was a clear demonstration, if you ever needed it, that radical right-wingers are nuts.

Apart from the occasional huckster like Joseph McCarthy during the fifties' Red scare, and even more extreme groups such as the Ku Klux Klan and the American Nazi Party, the right-wing was reasonably decent about the way they played the game. I think most old line conservatives were too uptight to lie, cheat, and steal. They would come right out and accuse the United Nations of being a Communist front organization. They would make it perfectly clear up front they wanted to burn books, and they'd tell you which ones. But they wouldn't lie to you, because lying was dishonorable.

Like Barry Goldwater, these old-time right-wingers had to find their victories in simply slowing down social progress in America. Despite their efforts, Roosevelt's New Deal agenda—things the Democratic Party established such as social security, worker protections, basic regulation for banks and securities on Wall Street— were mostly taken for granted by 1960 or so.

But then Vietnam and the civil rights movement scrambled all the eggs of American politics. Union guys who'd always voted Democratic didn't like kids burning the flag to protest the war. Southerners who'd always voted Democratic didn't like black people agitating for equality. Churchgoers who were scared to death of sex didn't like all this talk about "free love." And so, in 1968, Richard Nixon's Southern Strategy was born.

This strategy was the beginning of playing up "wedge issues," the lifestyle concerns, like religion, that serve to divide people. Nixon and his cronies would present themselves as representing the "silent majority" who were not demonstrating for civil rights or against the war. They would present themselves as the party of family values and unquestioning patriotism. The Republican surge that came from opposing civil rights, war protests, and sex later picked up momentum by opposing the women's movement, environmentalism, and abortion.

Richard Nixon was no conservative ideologue, but he was a cynic and a paranoid through and through, and he knew how to play to the right, including the Christian right. Republicans started praying and putting flag decals everywhere you looked (and hoping no one would notice the duct tape over those door locks at the Watergate office building). But in 1973, the public learned about the Watergate break-in. When the president's henchmen were caught burglarizing Democratic headquarters (as well as running a much larger dirty tricks campaign out of the Oval Office), conservatives feared their ideas had been pushed right back into the ditch where Barry Goldwater had left them in 1964.

Not long after "Tricky Dick" Nixon resigned in disgrace, a Democrat won back the White House, but mostly because of the ineptitude of Nixon's replacement, Gerald Ford. Ford had already replaced Nixon's first vice-president, Spiro T. Agnew, who'd been forced to resign for outright graft. Agnew, the verbal hit man for the "silent majority," pleaded no contest to bribery and tax evasion. However, to save the nation from the embarrassment of a former president behind bars, Ford pardoned Nixon. At worst, Nixon carried the stigma as an "unindicted co-conspirator" in fraud, obstruction of justice, illegal wiretaps, and burglary.

In 1976, the public wanted something very different from Nixon's sleaze, and the Sunday school teaching governor of Georgia, Jimmy Carter, fit the bill. Carter's problem was that he really was as square and morally upright as he let on—so much so that he was even more inept than Ford in trying to exercise power in Washington, D.C.

Carter's sister, Ruth Carter Stapleton, once told me a story about coming into the Oval Office and finding the president down on his knees, but he wasn't praying. She said, "Jimmy . . . what are you doing?" He looked at her and said, "I've called the Department of Agriculture, I've called the Department of the Interior . . . and nobody's been able to get it done. So I finally went out and bought these traps." And there he was, the President of the United States, down on his hands and knees, setting these little traps to catch the White House mice. Needless to say, Jimmy Carter was not the slickest player in Washington.

> The President of the United States, down on his hands and knees, setting these little traps to catch the White House mice.

By the late seventies, the country was in what Carter himself called a "malaise." The economy stunk. We'd had the Arab oil embargo, "stagflation," and the Japanese were kicking our asses in economic competition. All the resentments from the culture clash of the sixties still hung over our heads, compounded by the humiliation of the American evacuation from Vietnam in 1975.

Anti-tax, anti-urban sentiment was hitting the big time. People just wanted to watch "Happy Days" on TV and forget about the problems of black people, sick people, old people, and grimy northeastern cities. Meanwhile, the women's movement and the environmental movement were rubbing even more people the wrong way. The country was already dazed and confused—and then a bunch of religious fundamentalists (Muslims, not Baptists) took over our embassy in Iran.

Carter was even less successful in freeing our hostages than he was in catching mice. He seemed clueless, and the American people saw it. The Democrats had already tilted too far to the left to suit middle-of-the-road Americans. To the big middle, the 1980 Democratic convention looked like a black revival meeting, or a sit-in for welfare rights, and voters decided that they had seen enough "reality TV" for a while.

They'd also had enough of Jimmy Carter. TV viewers had seen him wobble and faint once while jogging. In another photo-op on some river, he seemed to be fending off a swimming "attack rabbit" with a canoe paddle. Public cynicism reached the apex when an editor at the *Boston Globe* sent along the text of a presidential address with "More Mush from the Wimp" scribbled across the top. Only that phrase got printed by mistake. The paper hit the streets with "More Mush from the Wimp" as a banner headline.

As we entered the 1980s, America was ready for a renewed dose of testosterone, mingled with the best of Hollywood myth-making. The nation sent Carter back to his peanut farm and embraced a campaign of flag-waving and platitudes that the Republicans sold to us as "Morning in America."

The Hollywood Version

The Republican party's ability to capture the American mood in 1980 might have been nothing more than smart politics if the re-vamped conservatives, in power at long last, had stuck to the truth. There were certainly things about the Democratic agenda that could have used a course correction—minority groups trying to out-victim each other (my oppression is greater than your oppression) and the liberal b.s. that would turn into all the "politically correct" crap we had to suffer through. This hypocrisy on the left really helped the conservatives capture the political middle. Women and gays, blacks and Indians (sorry, I mean "people of color") had gotten a raw deal, sure. But exclusive attention to their needs is a hard sell to my old neighbors back in Kentucky, white guys trying to raise three kids on $9,000 year.

Americans wanted a man on a horse, a cowboy, and the Republicans had one. Ronald Reagan was a B-movie actor, bankrolled by a bunch of Southern California fat cats, hired to play the part of president of the United States. Oddly enough, the Republican catch-phrase may have been "Morning in America," but the name that stuck for the early Reagan years was the "Teflon presidency." He rode in on such a wave of popularity that nobody in the media would cross him—least of all raise this whole issue about him being just an actor reading lines. After maybe fifteen years of nothing but demoralizing news, nobody wanted to burst America's bubble with such an anticlimactic truth. Besides, Reagan was damn good at appearing Presidential—except when he couldn't remember his lines.

> **Reagan was damn good at appearing Presidential— except when he couldn't remember his lines.**

The Republicans had spent their time out of power learning to play hardball. Several sources suggest there is evidence that in order to influence the outcome of the 1980 presidential election, two Reagan operatives flew to Paris and arranged a deal delaying the release of the American hostages in Iran until after the election. Gary Sick, a member of the Carter administration who was also on the staff of the National Security Council, wrote an article for the April 15, 1991, *New York Times* called "The Election

Story of the Decade." In it he writes, "In the course of hundreds of interviews, in the U.S., Europe, and the Middle East, I have been told repeatedly that individuals associated with the Reagan-Bush campaign of 1980 met secretly with Iranian officials to delay the release of the American hostages until after the presidential election." Kevin Phillips, the Nixon White House strategist who wrote *The Emerging Republican Majority* in 1969, makes a similar case in his recent bestselling book *American Dynasty*. In April 1992, PBS aired a "Frontline" documentary on the topic called "Investigating October Surprise."

Now, if you didn't live through it, it's hard to imagine what a big deal that hostage situation was. This was before cable news, and every night, CBS anchor Walter Cronkite, the most God-like of the three network anchors, railed on it, ending his broadcast with—"And that's the way it is . . . Tuesday [whatever the date was], the one hundredth and [whatever] day of captivity for our hostages in Iran." President Carter's inability to get our guys out of there was like a great big, dead, stinking albatross hung around his neck.

In the context of today's politics, it's interesting to note that the two operatives fingered in this alleged secret mission to Paris were not only William Casey, a former director of U.S. Intelligence in Europe and soon to be director of the CIA, but George H.W. Bush, Reagan's running mate and a former director of the CIA himself. Carter had cleaned house at "the Company," and a great many disgruntled agents had been shown the door. The Reagan administration, by contrast, would bring back the good old days of cloak and dagger operations, creating ample opportunities for the spooks to resume their careers trying to overthrow governments that didn't salute our flag quite smartly enough.

This much we know for certain: Under Reagan, U.S operatives illegally mined Nicaragua's harbors. When Congress cut off support for such activities, they illegally provided arms to terrorists in Iran, in exchange for the release of other hostages held in Lebanon. Then they diverted the cash from the sale to help fund the Contras back in Central America. The whole mess came to be known as the Iran/Contra scandal. For this, and for lying about it, some Reagan officials went to jail. A great many others were pardoned by—guess who—incoming president George H. W. Bush.

As for Reagan, he said he was not fully informed. Later, he said he didn't remember. Then, when forced to admit that he had lied, he said, "A few months ago I told the American people I did not trade arms for hostages. My heart and my best intentions still tell me that's true, but the facts and the evidence tell me it's not."

A hundred years from now, students of political hypocrisy will be studying that bit of double-talk the way history professors study the Gettysburg Address. I guess what his daughter called "state-of-the-art lies" had failed the great communicator, so he moved on to the "bizarre, incredulous tales."

By the time of Reagan's 1984 campaign, he had teamed up with the best Hollywood production team of his entire acting career. His director was a true master of media manipulation named Roger Ailes, a man who had worked for "Tricky Dick" Nixon, but who had begun in television producing a corny, daytime talk show for a washed-up singer name Mike Douglas. Ailes was a pro at packaging images and ideas—at least, ideas "lite." Now this same right-wing media manager is running Fox News. Fox, with more of a sense of humor than conservatives usually display, calls itself the "fair and balanced" network.

Long before Reagan's first election, conservatives had already lost all the most important battles over domestic policy. They had tried to stop workers' rights, civil rights for blacks, women's rights, and environmental protections. So in the eighties, they regrouped, upped the ante, exploited America's exhaustion with social change, and launched an attack on government itself. According to this script, all regulation was bad, and despite the fact that Americans are taxed very lightly compared to every other industrialized nation, all taxation was excessive.

They even devised a name for their agenda that a Hollywood

press agent would love. They called it "trickle down" economics, also known as supply side economics, a bogus theory concocted by one very controversial economist named Arthur Laffer. He was disputed by just about everybody else in the field, but still championed by Reagan political flunkies and Robert Bartley, the famously partisan editorial page writer for the *Wall Street Journal.*

According to the trickle down theory, which even George H.W. Bush called "voodoo economics," if you take care of the rich, sooner or later everyone else will get taken care of too. The theory argues that the tax breaks will spur investment, which will create jobs, which will spur economic growth. The good news for Republicans, of course, was that even if the theory didn't pan out that way in practice, the rich would have gotten their part of the deal already. The middle class would pay for the mistake out of higher interest rates and, ultimately, higher taxes. (As former hotelier and jailbird Leona Helmsley could tell you, the "little people" are all just whiners anyway.)

The Reagan White House sold trickle down and supply side by cooking the books in a way that Enron could appreciate. They made it appear that huge tax cuts for the wealthy really would improve the economy and the financial shape of government, and they did it by lying about the statistics projecting economic growth. The man who perpetrated this lie, Reagan Budget Director David Stockman,

> **The Reagan White House sold trickle down and supply side by cooking the books in a way that Enron could appreciate.**

joked about the code name they had for this plan—a fictional character named "Rosey Scenario."

But something else was brewing at the time that made this little deception look like a high school prank.

Putting the "Con" in Conservative

Back in the dark days just after the Watergate fiasco, a certain number of right-wing Republican millionaires decided to buy themselves a movement. These included the Coors brothers, whom you probably know by virtue of their beer. And then there were the Koch brothers, Charles and David, whom you've probably never heard of, but who own Koch Industries, the second largest private corporation in the country. Their father, Fred Koch, after making his fortune building refineries for the Soviet Union, turned around and helped found the John Birch Society. But the book-burning, Commie-hating Birchers were left-wingers compared to the younger Kochs. These guys supported a movement to deny food stamps to children. They also put up $21 million to found the libertarian Cato Institute, plus another $80 million or so for various other think tanks and political action committees, including, in the 1990s, the money to bankroll Newt Gingrich and his "Contract with America" (or "Contract *on* America," depending on your point of view).

In 1989, a Senate Investigating Committee concluded that the Kochs had been pilfering oil from Indian reservations to the tune of $1.5 billion, but according to charges made by FBI agent Richard Elroy, Bush the First gave them a get out of jail free pass and the investigation ended. The FBI brought attention back to the Kochs during the Clinton administration. Civil lawsuits were filed, grand juries were impaneled, but then this investigation died on the vine too. The implication is that these guys have clout that swings both ways.

Meanwhile, other, even more colorful players emerged on the right-wing nut circuit. One of them was the Reverend Sun Myung Moon of the Unification Church, who, among his other little quirks, claimed to be the second coming of Christ. He founded an ultra-conservative newspaper that is still spewing lies today, *The Washington Times*.

His arranging mass obligatory weddings—Moon hand-picks

brides and grooms who have never met from among his disci-ples—says a lot about his views on freedom of thought. But match-ing him dollar for dollar, and loose screw for loose screw, is America's own homegrown cult leader, the Reverend Pat Robert-son. Robertson, once described by the *Wall Street Journal* as "a paranoid pinhead with a deep distrust of democracy," made his greatest contribution to right-wing politics with his 1988 run for the presidency. Despite his claim of being "endorsed by God," not even the Supreme Court could get him into the White House.

Still, Robertson's candidacy struck gold by generating the million-name mailing list that became The Christian Coalition. These people are the true American Taliban, and the desire to keep them happy is why Bush the Second appointed the equally ex-treme John Ashcroft as our Attorney General. If Mr. Ashcroft has any time left over from writing hymns and destroying our civil lib-erties, he would do well to take a look at Mr. Robertson's business dealings. This "man of God" has been involved in everything from the Ice Capades to diamond mines, in arrangements that are enough to make Nixon blush.

Robertson's fortune, estimated at between $200 million and $1 billion, was built by having his non-profit Christian Broadcasting Network "sell" him, for practically nothing, what became The Family Channel, which the Good Reverend then took public and sold to Rupert Murdoch for between one and two billion dollars. Somehow, this man of God did not see fit to share the proceeds with the little old ladies whose contributions, sent to "spread the word of Jesus," financed the whole thing.

But the wing nut who has had the most direct hand in causing trouble for the rest of us is a pathetic little man named Richard Mellon Scaife. Scaife has more money than either brains or integrity, and what

> **It was Scaife's money, with thirty years' compounded interest, that helped turn radical conservatism into a nasty bloodlust cult.**

poured out of his wallet was like gasoline on a brush fire. It was his money, with thirty years' compounded interest, that helped turn radical conservatism into a nasty bloodlust cult.

Birth of the *Spectator*

Unlike you and me, Richard Mellon Scaife was born filthy rich. That middle name of his comes not from a farm stand but from the Mellon banking family, which also owns large chunks of Gulf Oil and Alcoa. Apparently, young Richard was ignored by his parents and raised by nannies, and he retreated into newspapers to amuse himself. Unfortunately, nothing he read seemed to expand or enlighten his mind.

As a rich boy coming of age in the fifties, Scaife, like our president, was able to get into Yale on family connections, despite the fact that, like our president, he had a numbskull academic transcript. But whereas even a know-nothing, party boy like George W managed to graduate, Scaife was kicked out for being a drunken fool. In 1957, the University of Pittsburgh gave him a bachelor's degree, and he has absolutely no record of genuine accomplishment since that date.

Scaife's business ventures—*The Sacramento Union, Pittsburgher* magazine, and a Pittsburgh all-news radio station—all failed. But in 1972 he found his niche. In that year, he gave money to 107 Republican congressional candidates, as well as $1 million to the master of dirty tricks, Richard Nixon. Such is his lack of talent or charm that even this degree of generosity failed to gain him so much as an ambassadorship to some tiny third world country.

But Scaife's life now had a purpose, and that purpose was to pour money into right-wing causes in order to completely muddy the waters of American politics. He had three foundations dispensing cash for him—The Sarah Scaife Foundation, The Scaife Family Foundation, and the Carthage Foundation. Of course, while funding a "family values" agenda, Scaife, so the *Washington*

Post tells us, openly kept a mistress. He continued to have a problem with alcohol, and he was not on speaking terms with either his daughter or his sister. But hypocrisy was only one of his sins. The one for which he deserves a special place in hell was his bankrolling of *The American Spectator* magazine.

By the time Bill Clinton came to office in 1993, Scaife got it into his head to prove that Clinton was the devil himself, and the *Spectator* was his propaganda machine. At the height of the Clinton scandals with Monica Lewinsky, Hillary Clinton gave an interview to Katie Couric in which she talked about a "vast right-wing conspiracy" that was trying to bring down her husband. At the time, the claim sounded a little desperate, sort of like Al Gore and the Internet. The First Lady seemed to be swinging wildly to cover for her philandering Bill, making excuses and calling names. But the fact is, just as there was truth behind Al Gore's supposed exaggerations, there *was* a vast right-wing conspiracy. It was anchored in the right-wing foundations supported by Scaife and Coors and the other fat cats, and the *Spectator* was at the hot, burning center of the scam.

The really pointy end of the radical conservatives' stick, the mud-slinging hit squad that took the focus off Clinton's accomplishments and onto his supposed crimes and misdemeanors, was called the "Arkansas project." A dirty tricks campaign funded with $2.4 million of Scaife money, this group worked with *The American Spectator* to find anything they could possibly use against Clinton. "Drag a hundred-dollar bill through a trailer park," as James Carville, Bill Clinton's "Ragin' Cajun" political advisor explains, "and no telling what you can find."

The Arkansas Project is the source of all the dirt about Clinton, from Whitewater to Vince Foster to the stories about the White House staff trashing the place on their way out. And it all turned out to be horseshit. "Troopergate" (the Arkansas state troopers who wanted cash for trash on Clinton), even Paula Jones, the state employee he was supposed to have sexually harassed—all of it smoke with no fire.

But several years and several million dollars' worth of mud-slinging had its effect. The distraction stopped the Clinton agenda cold, wasted huge amounts of government time and money, and accidentally led to the one accusation that did stick, and that nearly got the man kicked out of office—a blow job in the White House Map Room.

Queer Eye for the Big Guy

Probably the most notable attack dog in the whole right-wing pack was a young writer for the *Spectator* named David Brock, and if you really want to understand the state of our union today and how we got here, I recommend you read his book *Blinded by the Right*. It gives the whole play by play of how this movement grew, who was attracted to it, their excesses, and most of all, their underhanded tactics that muddied the political waters enough to make a Bush presidency in 2001 possible.

Brock is the guy who wrote *The Real Anita Hill*, trashing the black law professor who accused Supreme Court nominee Clarence Thomas of sexual harassment. Brock was the one who dubbed her "a little bit nutty, and a little bit slutty." Brock also did most of the stories on the Arkansas state troopers and their bogus "trash for cash" on Clinton. And then, after the damage was done, Brock turned around and admitted that it was all lies. After carrying out character assassination on a very courageous woman, helping a twisted Uncle Tom—Clarence Thomas—be elevated to the Supreme Court, helping to poison the political atmosphere in this country, and wasting nearly a decade of our time with bogus accusations, the man said he was sorry.

> After the damage was done, Brock turned around and admitted that it was all lies.

You try to figure out how somebody like that lives with himself, much less shows his face on a book tour. The reason he gives for all his sick behavior, which fits with one of my basic themes, was that he couldn't come to terms with his sexuality. He was a fruit in the wrong basket—a gay man who, he admits, hated himself for who he was and turned all the anger into right-wing, attack journalism.

But the most interesting thing about Brock's story of his twenty years inside the wing nut disinformation machine is not how he characterizes himself, but how he characterizes just about everyone else involved in this movement that torpedoed the return of progressive politics in America.

Brock's own story sounds like an all-too-familiar made-for-TV movie. Gay boy suffers under overbearing, unavailable father, whom he describes as "a conservative Irish Catholic . . . emotionally dead." Boy goes away to college where being a fire-breathing conservative gets him noticed.

Remember that this was in the "politically correct" eighties, when Reagan was in the White House, but the universities were run by people who had been student radicals—or at least students—in the sixties. So to be a right-wing fanatic during this period was to be part of a new counter-counter culture. But as Brock says, it was really all about "anger and confusion about identity . . . a way of standing out." Brock even took it so far as trying to "look like an old fogey in training, donning a bow tie and horn-rimmed glasses and, ludicrously, puffing on a pipe and occasionally even carrying a walking stick." As I've said before, sexually hung-up people sometimes do very strange things.

But then Brock went to Washington where he joined Scaife's *Spectator,* where he could channel his demons into underhanded attacks, and teamed up with a bunch of other oddballs who would become the foot soldiers in a mass temper tantrum known as Gingrich conservatism.

The fact that the movement he had joined made a point of condemning homosexuals was something that Brock was able to compartmentalize, at least for a while.

"Bill Clinton is a bizarre guy," he would write. But then he corrected himself. "It was me, a sexually repressed closeted gay man, detailing Clinton's alleged infidelities to forward the right-wing political agenda, who was the bizarre guy." He attributes this behavior to "a sick sense of my own identity."

It was the same with Clarence Thomas. Uncle Toms like Thomas have been so humiliated and scarred that they have to distance themselves from everything about their past lives, even when it means attacking the less fortunate people they left behind.

Brock was a key player not just in the effort to bring down Anita Hill, but in the much larger effort to trash President Clinton. This makes him a well-placed guide to the conservative culture that is still in power today, a culture he summed up with the words "corrosive partisanship, visceral hatreds, and unfathomable hypocrisy."

"Hate, of course, is an emotional aversion," Brock observed, "not an intellectual one. When I spent enough time talking with a Clinton-hater, I found the problem in the emotional life of the hater."

Throughout his book, he presents a rogue's gallery from the right-wing Washington soap opera that brought us to where we are today. The descriptions he uses do not speak well of the mental and emotional health of these people. He talks of one prominent conservative whose political ideas were all caught up in his "conceptions of manliness"; another who was an "overbearing know-it-all" trying to "overcome a deep well of insecurity." Another was fixated on homosexual pedophilia. Another was obsessed with "white pride" and feared a "war against the white race." Another is simply unhappy and self-loathing, while another is "numbed emotionally"; still another is "emotionally disturbed."

But the hypocrisy and anger and twisted sexuality really took on new dimensions the closer you moved toward the Arkansas Project. Here's what Brock has to say about the key players:

Parker Dozhier, "the project's 'eyes and ears' in Arkansas," was filled with "vein-popping rage . . ."

Cliff Jackson, the Arkansas lawyer who turned on Clinton and who "seethed, shaking with indignation. . . . The more I listened to him, the more I came to believe that Cliff's hatred of Bill Clinton sprang from envy . . . of Clinton's success as a pol, and even of his way with the opposite sex. . . ."

Gil Davis, a Virginia Republican lawyer who took over the Paula Jones case, was head of the Virginia-based Christian Action Network, dedicated to promoting "traditional morality and family values." Davis was reported to be "notorious for his womanizing."

George T. Conway III, was the Wall Street lawyer who advised on the Paula Jones cases, whose "prurience made me wonder why he seemed more excited about my story than I was. I knew Conway was a lonely workaholic whose clumsy attempts at dating right-wing babes like [Ann] Coulter always seemed to fall flat . . . Conway . . . spoke to me about little but Clinton's rumored sexual habits, and the supposed size and shape of his genitalia."

These are the healthy and happy people who were the foot soldiers working for the good of all Americans under the banner of conservatism.

But then we get to the more prominent, and possibly even more deranged.

The Newtonian Universe

Newt Gingrich was the lightning rod, the man who brought the "vast right-wing conspiracy" together, rose to the heights with it, and then exploded right in front of us. Ironically, his most damaging accomplishment was unintended. Gingrich led a partial government shutdown (due to a budgetary stalemate) at the end of 1995, after feeling slighted over which door he got to use while traveling on Air Force One. This gave Bill Clinton the extra time to put his hands on Monica.

David Brock describes Gingrich as "an opportunist, a nihilist even," then admits that even he (Brock, the hypocrite) underestimated "Newt's capacity for hypocrisy."

No kidding. Here was the super patriot who avoided service in Vietnam; the "family values" man who showed up with divorce papers for his first wife, Jackie, while she was in the hospital with cancer. Newt Gingrich was unfaithful to his second wife, Marianne, and all the while he was pontificating about Clinton's immorality, he was having an affair with a female aide to Congressman Steve Gunderson.

One look at Gingrich's childhood and you see the makings of the hateful toad he would become. Gingrich learned not just to endure rejection but to thrive on it. He was an army brat with an adoptive father who seemed to hate little know-it-all Newt. Moving from base to base, forced to make new friends every few years, Gingrich grew up an outsider. Early on, like many frustrated and unhappy people, he decided that if he couldn't find love he'd go for power. And in middle age, he was still the little nine-year-old who would trash somebody else's science project so he could win the prize.

> **One look at Gingrich's childhood and you see the makings of the hateful toad he would become.**

This was the same little toad who, years later, would tell a group of corporate lobbyists that Clinton was "the enemy of normal Americans." In time, conditioned by Newt's barrage of propaganda, one in five Americans would come to say they "hated" Clinton.

"Fights make news," was Gingrich's political philosophy, the birth of tactics that House Speaker Tip O'Neill would denounce as "the lowest thing I've ever seen in my thirty-two years in

Congress." Newt didn't believe in anything. He simply wanted to hurt the other team.

Cutting taxes was one way to do that. He often said that tax cuts were a way to "defund the left" and to "starve the beast" of government. But his greatest weapon was the total smear. He ran his own little training program for right-wing hypocrites, urging Republican candidates and pundits to use "contrast words" to describe anyone who disagreed with them, words like "decay, failure, shallow, traitors, pathetic, corrupt, incompetent, sick . . ."

He knew that conservatism, a pessimistic and negative philosophy, thrives only when it has an enemy, so he declared all-out war on the Democratic Party. It was not enough to oppose them, they had to be destroyed. "There is no 'after the Cold War' for me," he said. "So far from having ended, my Cold War has increased in intensity, as sector after sector has been ruthlessly corrupted by the liberal ethos. . . . We are far less prepared for this Cold War, far more vulnerable to our enemy, than was the case with our victorious war against a global Communist threat."

He made the distinction moral, not political. He called the Democrats "sick," "grotesque," "loony," "stupid," "corrupt," "anti-family," and "traitors." He said that the Democrats were the party of "total hedonism, total exhibitionism, total bizarreness, total weirdness." In a memorable article, one *Esquire* writer concluded, "Gingrich offers up a history of American values in a scheme so hysterically partisan, so transparently dishonest, so willfully stupid, that it's impossible to believe even Newt himself would expect anyone to take it seriously."

Newt could only be so petty and vindictive because he stood for nothing, and his ravings poisoned the political system enough to pave the way for George W. Bush. What brought his hypocrisy to Olympic levels was this: His assault on the Clintons was undertaken partly to distract the House Ethics Committee from what Gingrich had been up to himself. They still found that Newt had violated tax laws and misled the committee in sworn testimony.

They fined him $300,000, and he lost his position as speaker of the House.

> **Other lying hypocrites were more subtle, and that's where my million-dollar ad came in.**

While Gingrich was such a lying hypocrite, and such a fool, that he didn't need any help to spontaneously combust, other lying hypocrites were more subtle, and that's where my million-dollar ad came in.

The larger point is that these are not happy campers we're dealing with here on the right wing of American politics. But they don't lie and cheat just because they have twisted personal lives. As I've said many times, they lie and cheat because they have to in order to have any hope of winning elections. According to John Dilulio, the government professor and former Bush White House staffer who blew the whistle on Bush in that letter to *Esquire,* there aren't ten House districts where, on an honest presentation of policy, Republicans could win a majority vote.

The right-wingers in power today would try to tell you that *Hustler* is obscene, but I find their tax policies obscene. Obscene is not how I would describe a beautiful nineteen-year-old girl running around buck naked, but it is how I would describe a nineteen-year-old soldier getting both his arms blown off in a war we got into on the basis of lies and spin. A president who does not go to any military funerals for fear of calling attention to the ugly reality of war—that's obscene. So is the White House policy that prohibits photographs of all the caskets coming in from Iraq to Dover Air Force Base.

I think it's obscene the way the right-wingers have hidden the truth for more than a generation, the way they shamelessly repeat their lies as if we're all dumb as a post. Obscene is the way I would describe the hypocrisy of right-wing chicken hawks who rattle the saber but never served in the military, men like Pat Buchanan (bad knee), Rush Limbaugh (a cyst on his tail bone), Newt Gingrich (student deferment), Dan Quayle (Indiana National Guard), Dick

Cheney ("other priorities"—what the hell does that mean?), and John Ashcroft (deferment to teach business law). Dick Armey, Tom DeLay, Karl Rove, Phil Gramm, Trent Lott, House Speaker J. Dennis Hastert—none of these guys served in the military.

These guys mock old-line liberals like George McGovern, questioning their patriotism for challenging the waste of American lives in unnecessary wars. They'd have you believe that McGovern was a wimp, and yet he's the combat veteran, the man who won the Distinguished Service Cross as a bomber pilot in World War II. In my view, you first take your chances getting your ass shot off—and then *that* gives you the right to speak about wars.

The same holds for John Kerry. The Republicans try to tar him for being "a liberal from Massachusetts," by which they mean soft on defense, when in fact he's a highly decorated veteran. Kerry saw combat in Vietnam, then came back and led Vietnam Veterans Against the War. The Bush camp wants to turn Kerry's anti-war activism into a liability, but to me, what Kerry did is the height of patriotism—you do your bit, and then you speak your mind, honestly and openly.

We're not little Nazis, you know, unquestioningly following orders. And we don't have to swallow lies for the likes of George W. Bush, who hid out in the Texas Air National Guard, then skipped out to work on a political campaign in Alabama.

Where do these self-righteous, right-wing hypocrites get off calling anyone who disagrees with them unpatriotic? Idiots like Ann Coulter and Laura Ingraham have gone so far as to call all liberals traitors. That's obscene in the biggest way, because it denies the bedrock tradition of open-minded dissent that this country was founded on, by a bunch of liberals, I might add, who stood up to another out-of-touch George—England's King George III. And yet an apathetic public lets these right-wing blowhards get away with it.

Just take a look at what the right-wing allies of our King George W did to Senator Max Cleland of Georgia. Cleland voted against the Homeland Security Bill because the Republicans had put a poison pill inside it, depriving government security workers of civil service protection. Cleland's right-wing opponent for the Senate in 2002, Saxby Chambliss, trashed him relentlessly for this. The Republican ran attack ads featuring pictures of Osama bin Laden, Saddam Hussein, and Max Cleland as partners in trying to destroy America. Chambliss sat out Vietnam with a bad knee. Max Cleland served in that war and came back in a wheelchair. He lost both legs and one arm to a Vietnamese land mine. But the slime attack worked. The draft-deferred chicken hawk attacked disabled war hero Cleland's patriotism—and got away with it!

But not even the outrages of the Bush administration are enough to satisfy the truly rabid right-wingers. After Bush gave his State of the Union address in January 2004, with all its warm and fuzzy talk and hugging Jesse Jackson's granddaughter on TV, he sent Cheney over to give the *real* talk to the Conservative Political Action Conference and the American Conservative Union. These are the hard-core zealots who dumped Bush I for raising taxes. These people call ordinary conservatives "Rinos" for "Republican in Name Only." But at least they're right in one of their complaints— they're ticked off about the deficits, calling Bush the most fiscally irresponsible president ever. At least in that respect, these hard shell types are less hypocritical than Bush. They make no bones about being to the right of Attila the Hun.

We need to Flynt these hypocrites. Their unjustified accusations appear on page one of the newspaper, and then the retraction appears on page twelve two days later, and the false impression lingers. That's the secret of the

> **We need to Flynt these hypocrites.**

right-wing hustle. Lies, jokes, distortions of facts—it doesn't matter. Given the way media works, it's what gets picked up that counts, what sticks in the mind that matters. Images, even blatantly manufactured ones, can become "reality," at least long enough to pull off a scam like the invasion of Iraq or tax breaks for the super rich.

The sticking power of images is why you saw so many black

faces at the Republican convention in 2000. Trust me, 100 percent of black Republican politicians got to speak at that convention, and eight percent of black Americans wound up voting Republican. The pictures on TV said, "Look, see, we're not racists, not just for rich white people—we're for everyone," but most black voters knew better.

The rest of us need to wise up in the same way.

4

Fat Cats and Crony Capitalists

I have plenty of money, but I don't want to have to live behind high walls with razor wire to keep out the rest of the world. I don't want to have to live on a special planet for rich white people. I think America can do better. I think America means more than that. That's why it upsets me to see some picture of George W. Bush smirking on the front page of the newspaper, surrounded by a bunch of Republicans who have just signed into law some new aspect of the Big Hustle. He and his crony capitalist friends need to be exposed for what they are—looters of the public trust.

In the previous two chapters, I showed you the naked truth about the hypocrisies of George W and the right-wing conservatives who put him in power. Now I want to focus on the way W and his backers have rewarded their rich pals at the expense of working-class and middle-class Americans. Let's connect the dots on crony capitalism.

Hustling on Health Care

In December 2003, the Big Hustle was a bill adding a drug benefit to Medicare. The Bush junta held a big to-do at Constitution Hall, with 2000 hand-picked attendees, and a big banner behind the president saying "Keeping Our Promise to Seniors."

Well, they kept their promises, but I don't think it was to seniors. I think they kept some promises that had been made behind closed doors in exchange for some very hefty campaign contributions from drug companies. With the signing of the Bush drug bill, pharmaceutical stocks shot up immediately. This "reform" of Medicare opened up a huge new market for the giant drug companies. It also specifically prohibited the government from negotiating discounts or lower drug prices, and it barred the importation of cheaper drugs from abroad. This was Bush's solution at a time when older people on fixed incomes have to go to Canada to fill their prescriptions or order them over the Internet to avoid the artificially high American prices.

Bush handed the drug companies a windfall. Private insurance companies got to start handling Medicare accounts as contractors to the government. And oh, yes, somewhere along the way, senior citizens will derive some benefit too. Only it won't be nearly as much as they think. That's because the Bush bill is typical Republican bait and switch. The image they present does not match reality in any way, shape, or form. It's the same old conservative hustle.

> **The image they present does not match reality in any way, shape, or form.**

Let's start with the beginning of the idea of government help on health care for the elderly. Harry Truman first proposed it back in the 1940s. It went nowhere because the Republicans opposed it. President Kennedy tried to make it happen, too, but, again, the effort was nipped in the bud by Republican opposition. In 1965, after the Kennedy assassination but before Vietnam dried up all the money and good will, Lyndon Johnson was able to get Medicare through Congress.

Even then, Republicans like Ronald Reagan, the right-wing saint, railed against a health care program for the elderly as socialism, the first wave that would "invade every area of freedom in this country." Always good with a colorful phrase, he said that Medicare would leave old people to spend their "sunset years telling our children and our children's children what it was like in America when men were free." Republican Speaker of the House Newt Gingrich was still railing against Medicare thirty years later during the Clinton years, comparing it to "centralized command bureaucracies" in Moscow.

Republicans simply hate the idea of government assistance on health care—or most anything else—and they always have. More important, they have always done everything they could to block it. The Democrats succeeded in establishing Medicare in spite of them, and it became one of the most popular government programs ever, helping 40 million older citizens. Republicans don't dare try to kill it now, at least not in broad daylight. Even so, Bush's first choice for his prescription drug program was one that would have required patients to leave Medicare entirely in order to qualify, only it wouldn't fly in Congress. Bush couldn't gut the program outright, so he proposed to "reform" it.

By 2010, this bill the Republicans passed for the prescription drug program will force Medicare to compete against private, profit-making health plans in selected areas. Only it's going to be a rigged competition. The private healthcare plans are going to be subsidized by Medicare money, and they'll be able to cherry-pick the healthiest patients, and leave the hopeless to the government. When the new program starts, it has a complicated formula for what you get when.

Bottom line: If your drug cost is $5,000 a year, you're still going to have to pay $3,500 out of pocket. Drugs worth $500 will still cost you $313, and $4,000 worth will cost you $2,500. In other words, it sounds a lot better than it delivers. It's going to be like phone service—a million different plans from a million different providers. Good luck to the ten percent of Medicare seniors who have Alzheimer's or some other form of diminished capacity in figuring out which plan to choose.

The benefits could have been much more generous, because the whole thing would be much cheaper and more efficient if delivered the same way other Medicare benefits are delivered now. But the Republican reverse Robin

> **Their whole idea is to scam the people's money and hand it over to the special interests.**

Hoods wouldn't stand for that, because their whole idea is to scam the people's money and hand it over to the special interests, while eating away at the government program one bite at a time. On second thought, the benefits *were* pretty generous—to the pharmaceutical industry.

Hustling at Halliburton

Ironically, this Medicare bill signing happened in the same news cycle as another story that cried out to be Flynted. Fortunately, this time the media had the guts to investigate. The vice-president's old company, Halliburton, had overcharged the government $1.09 a gallon for 57 million gallons of gasoline trucked into Iraq. That thumb on the scale cost the taxpayer an extra $57 million, on a contract that was awarded to Dick Cheney's friends without competitive bidding. In 2002, as it turns out, Halliburton had to pay a $2 million settlement for overcharging the government for work at Fort Ord, California. And in 1997, it came to light that Halliburton's subsidiary was charging $85 for $14 plywood, and billing the government to clean offices four times a day.

Is it any wonder Republican fat cats are always crying about waste and fraud in government and how we should turn everything over to private companies? They want to make sure that all the waste and fraud goes into their own pockets.

In the 1980s, Reagan Republicans deregulated the Savings and Loan industry, supposedly to help all Americans make more money. What you got instead was the savings and loan scandal that may have cost American taxpayers as much as $1.4 trillion. The Bush I Republicans deregulated the energy industry and you got Enron and blackouts (and near bankruptcy) in California. The Bush II Republicans now want to "reform" Medicare out of existence, and you get . . . Well, we don't know yet. But one thing we do know is that everywhere you look, we get the foxes—big money Republican campaign contributors—taking charge of the henhouse.

Crony Capitalism Casino

One of the foxes put in charge of the deregulated savings and loans was my old friend Charles Keating. This particular episode of "No Millionaire Left Behind" holds an especially warm place in my heart because it put ol' Charles in the slammer. If you saw *The People vs. Larry Flynt,* you may remember Keating as the blue nose moral crusader who tried to have me locked up for obscenity back in the seventies in Ohio.

Before 1982, when Reagan signed deregulation into law, S & Ls had been a stable and "conservative" place for generations of middle class people to save money. Jimmy Stewart ran a savings and loan in *It's a Wonderful Life*—you can't get any more small-town American values than that. But the right-wingers were convinced that, once again, the idea of government refereeing a vital asset—mom and pop's nest egg—was an outrage. The free market could turn all this under-utilized capital into an engine of economic growth, they said. Instead, it turned people's life savings into a casino, where sleazeballs like "holier than me" Keating ripped off the folks on Main Street and caused the biggest financial disaster in history.

Which is not to say anything bad about casinos per se. I own one myself in Los Angeles, and we treat our customers very well. But you don't have to take my word for it, because we are closely regulated by the California Gaming Commission. My question is—if gaming tables, where you might risk $100, are regulated, how can institutions that risk your entire life savings *not* be regulated?

The Bush family knows the deregulated S & L territory pretty well. Jeb Bush, now governor of Florida, once took out a $4.56

My question is—if gaming tables, where you might risk $100, are regulated, how can institutions that risk your entire life savings *not* be regulated?

million loan from Broward County Savings in Sunrise, Florida, in order to construct an office building. After the federal government closed down the Broward S & L, Jeb's building was reassessed for only half a million. He and his partners paid back that amount and defaulted on the rest, leaving you and me—the American taxpayers—to cover the remaining $4 million.

W's other brother, Neil, was made a director of the Silverado Savings and Loan in 1985, and three years later it went belly up, costing the American taxpayer $1.6 billion. Two Bush cronies, Ken Good and Bill Walters, had set up Neil in his own oil exploration company, called JNB. (They put up $160,000; Neil put up $100.) Then Neil approved $138 million in loans for his buddies from Silverado, another $3 million of which found its way back into Neil's company, JNB. Walters and Good then defaulted on the whole thing. Because of sleazy dealing like this, the head of Silverado was sent to jail for three and a half years. After the Reagan administration dragged its heels for as long as it could on the investigation, Neil was slapped on the wrist with a $50,000 fine.

I had never even heard of brother Marvin Bush until I started looking into what political commentator Kevin Phillips called the "never-ending hustle" of the Bush family business dealings. Marvin, it seems, was a principal in a company called Securacom (now Stratesec, Inc.) that provided security not only for the World

Trade Center, but also for United Airlines (two of their planes were hijacked on 9/11), as well as Dulles International Airport, where one of the 9/11 planes took off. Some security, right? The company also provided security for Los Alamos National Laboratory, where, if you follow the news, you know they've had more security breaches of late than Carter had mice. One of the backers of the company was a Kuwaiti-American firm with long ties to the Bush family. The Bush White House, of course, has succeeded in promoting legislation that limits both their liability and their exposure to investigation. The same is true for HCC Insurance Holdings, which held some of the insurance on the World Trade Center, and another company on whose board Marvin Bush holds a seat.

Where it stops, nobody knows.

It's a Family Affair

The Bushes are big on family loyalty. But then again, so are the Gambinos and the Bonannos. In all of these families, being a loyal retainer has its advantages.

Joe M. Allbaugh, who stands 6-foot-4 and weighs close to 300 pounds, was George W. Bush's chief of staff during the governorship in Austin. He was also Bush's campaign manager in the 2000 presidential election. He is now chairman of New Bridge Strategies, a broker for contracts to rebuild Iraq. Here's how the New Bridge web site sums up their business plan:

> The opportunities evolving in Iraq today are of such an unprecedented nature and scope that no other existing firm has the necessary skills and experience to be effective both in the United Sates and on the ground in Iraq.

In other words, "We've got the contacts. We can get you inside the door. Bring your carpet bag and come on down!"

Republicans like the Bush family and friends never stop saying how much they hate government. But it seems to me they only hate government when it's trying to keep them from pouring acid into rivers, or doing insider trades, or running sweatshops. When government is handing over those big checks, it appears they can't get enough of their dear old Uncle Sam.

> **They only hate government when it's trying to keep them from pouring acid into rivers, or doing insider trades, or running sweatshops.**

New Bridge is a prime example of the crony capitalism that has been a guiding principle for our president his whole life. You can work and study hard if that's your thing, but what counts is knowing the right people. Other directors of New Bridge include M. Rogers, Jr., and Lanny Griffith, lobbyists who worked in the White House for W's father.

The way New Bridge is drooling over postwar Iraq used to be called "war profiteering," and in earlier years you could get shot for it, or at least put in jail.

In his day, W's grandfather, Prescott Bush, went well beyond simply making a buck off death and destruction. He was a managing director of Union Banking Corporation, financial operatives for Fritz Thyssen, the steel and coal baron who bankrolled Hitler. After World War II, the assets of eighteen Union Banking Corporation clients were seized under the U.S. Trading with the Enemy Act, yet Bush and his colleagues continued to move money into Switzerland, Panama, Argentina, and Brazil, on behalf of their Nazi clients. They had done the same sort of things for the Nazis who wanted to move assets out of Germany during the days leading up to Hitler's invasion of Poland.

These days the Bushes simply hand out hundreds of millions of dollars' worth of contracts, sometimes in no-bid deals like the Halliburton fiasco. In November of 2003, the army asked for permission to do the work itself and save the $1.09 a gallon Cheney's friends were bilking the government out of. About the same time, NBC News reported that conditions at Halliburton-run mess halls for our soldiers were worse than the monkey house at the zoo.

U.S. News & World Report says the Bush administration has dropped "a shroud of secrecy" over what's going on—as if corruption in business and government is some sort of family squabble that should not be made public. It's no longer possible to tell where government ends and business begins. Under Bush, the greatest nation on earth is being run like some small-town zoning board packed with realtors and land developers.

Revolving Doors in D.C.

> **Under Bush, the right-wingers have closed ranks around the bad guys. They *are* the bad guys.**

There was a time when bad guys had to pull off a coup if they wanted to gain control of a government and raid the nation's assets. Under Bush, though, the right-wingers have closed ranks around the bad guys. They *are* the bad guys.

The Defense Department has become one big "Petroleum Club," a place where millionaires can put their feet up for a while, sip some scotch, and work their next deals. It's a luxury hiring hall for plutocrats as they go through the revolving doors of government agencies, corporate jobs, and high-level consulting. Defense contractors go into government, and retired spooks and military guys go into defense industries and corporate security firms.

Of course, it's not just happening in the defense industry. Jim Hightower, the former Texas agriculture commissioner, used to complain about Monsanto's lobbying the secretary of agriculture. In the Bush administration, as Greg Palast points out, "Monsanto executive Ann Venamin *is* the secretary of agriculture." Hightower told Palast, "They've eliminated the middleman. The corporations don't have to lobby the government anymore. They *are* the government."

Then you get Republican stalwarts like Richard Perle, who does both government and private enterprise at the same time, stuffing his pockets with both hands. Perle, who was one of the cheerleaders for the Ahmad Chalabi invasion strategy in Iraq, had so many fingers in so many government pies that he was forced to resign as chairman of the Defense Policy Board. But oddly enough, his financial conflicts of interest did not induce him to resign from the Board itself. The *L.A. Times* pointed out just where this kind of thing leads. While chairman of that board, Perle received a classified briefing on Iraq and North Korea. He promptly turned around and sold that information to the investment company Goldman Sachs.

Since 9/11, the media has been too busy waving the flag and filming Bush photo ops—strutting in a flight suit, holding up a fake turkey—to report on where that bad smell is coming from. Could it be all the rotting food they've uncovered in those Halliburton-run army mess halls?

Another Halliburton subsidiary, Dresser Industries, couldn't even wait for the invasion to start ringing their cash registers. From 1997 through mid-2000, they sold $30 million worth of oil field equipment to Saddam's Iraq. Federal law prohibits U.S. companies from doing business with state sponsors of terrorism, but those rules must be, to use Leona Helmsley's famous phrase, "just for the little people." Halliburton dodged the restrictions the same way U.S. corporations dodge taxes—by setting up subsidiaries in places like the Cayman Islands.

Now that Halliburton has received more than $1 billion in federal contracts for rebuilding Iraq, Cheney has tried to make it "clear" that he no longer has any ties to the company. Of course, the vice-president holds 433,333 Halliburton stock options, and continues to receive deferred compensation—about $150,000 a year through 2005—but I guess, for the veep, that's just walking-around money not worth mentioning.

Just after the invasion of Iraq, the initial feeding frenzy of Bush cronies at the trough of public expenditure was so appalling that the Senate has since demanded that all contracts be awarded on the basis of competitive bidding.

> **Those desert sands are green pastures if you know the right people and have made the right political contributions.**

But the good times—at least for well-connected corporate contractors—still continue, at a cost to the taxpayer of $4 billion a month. Those desert sands are green pastures if you know the right people and have made the right political contributions.

Bush's cronies at New Bridge Strategies are also minority partners of a company called Diligence Iraq. Now that we've got "mission accomplished" and the Iraqis are greeting us with sweets and flowers, you can go over and investigate your share of the spoils of war. Diligence will set you up in a three-car convoy of armed S.U.V.s driving 90 miles an hour across the desert to avoid bandits and shoulder-fired missiles. Looks like the Bushies thought of everything, except how to explain what we're doing in Iraq, establish order, and keep our soldiers from getting killed.

Quid Pro Quo

As for managing the political contributions that lie at the heart of crony capitalism, there is nothing subtle about the way the game is played.

The New York Times ran a piece on political fund-raising that shows why presidential politics has become more of an auction than a horse race, and why certain legislation never makes it out of committee, while other legislation can't be stopped. The *Times* ran excerpts from a series of letters that appear in the record in *McConnell v. Federal Election Commission,* the challenge to the

McCain-Feingold campaign finance law now before the Supreme Court. A letter from the Republican party to Bristol-Myers Squibb makes it quite clear that they're looking for a $250,000 contribution. In return, Jim Nicholson, then the Republican National Committee chairman, had enclosed a copy of the Republican health care package and asked for suggested changes. In closing, he refers to how "we must keep the lines of communications open."

At other times the letters sound like ladies after a garden club luncheon, with their "see you in the Hamptons," and "thanks so much for introducing me to the governor." Except that these favors come at a price. In one particularly revealing letter, the finance chairman notes that approval for a merger has gone through, and so, he writes, "I am taking the liberty of enclosing an invoice for an additional upgrade" to this person's contribution. In other words, we delivered the goods—now you pay the price.

People in California have seen, up close and personal, what happens when the Bushes take care of their own at the expense of everybody else.

Throughout their political careers, both George Bushes have fought to remove any form of control over corporate sleaze. As a governor, W fought environmental regulations and consumer protections. Then, working with a group called Texans for Lawsuit Reform, founded by none other than Ken Lay, George managed to change the law in Texas so that even after you've been royally screwed by a corporation, the executives walk away scott free. I think Ken knew that, sooner or later, the scam he was running at Enron was going to blow, and he didn't want to be left holding the bag.

Bush would later claim that he hardly knew Ken Lay, which seems odd, given that the former Enron chairman holds the record for lifetime donations to George W. Bush's political career. In 2000, Lay was a "pioneer." That's Republican for a fat cat who pledges to raise $100,000. He also was a personal adviser to Bush during the pre-inaugural "transition," as well as an adviser to Dick Cheney on energy policy.

As I write this in early 2004, the vice-president is still trying to keep the public from knowing exactly how he and other disinterested advisers like Ken Lay devised their famous energy plan. The Sierra Club sued and won the right to find out. The Bush administration appealed and lost. Then Cheney invoked executive privilege.

Still, we have a pretty good idea of what went on. In a November 8, 2003, editorial, the *New York Times* said, "The results . . . have been plain as day: policies that broadly favor industry—including big campaign contributors—at the expense of the environment and public health."

> **Are we supposed to believe for even one minute that kind of money doesn't call the shots?**

In 2003, Bush took in $130.8 million in political contributions. Are we supposed to believe for even one minute that kind of money doesn't call the shots?

Power to *Which* People?

On December 14, 2000, just after the Supreme Court's conservative majority shamelessly handed the election to the Republicans, President Clinton issued an order to prohibit the kind of uncontrolled speculation then going on in the California electricity market. That same month, as Clinton was packing his bags, Dick Cheney began a series of secret meetings with power company executives. On their advice, within three days of Bush's inaugural, the Energy Department overturned Clinton's new constraints.

Did that decision have anything to do with $18.9 million in campaign contributions from the utilities industry? Or the $4.1 million in campaign contributions that Enron and four of its partners in price gouging and profiteering had laid at Bush's cowboy boots? All we know is that, as a result of W's reversal of government policy, Enron profits shot up $87 million in the first quarter of 2001. Then again, what goes up, when it's crooked, can quickly come back down.

This sort of "you fill my pocket, I'll scratch your back," behavior was not unusual. The petrochemical industry was worth $48 million to W's campaign, and W's first budget contained absolutely nothing for the Environmental Protection Agency civil enforcement team. A couple of years later, in November 2003, Bush's EPA decided to drop investigations into more than 140 power plants and refineries busily fouling the air in violation of the Clean Air Act. This pattern of caving in to special interests was so outrageous that several states filed suit against the federal government for not enforcing the law. The blatant violation of what we used to call the public trust had reached the point at which Congress began calling for an investigation.

Presumably, this is the kind of behavior you can learn from your dad, when your dad is the King of Cronyism, George H. W. Bush. After all, legalized gambling with our power supply had been made possible by the elder Bush. In 1992, he overturned the regulations that, since the days of FDR, had given us the lowest priced, most reliable electricity service in the world. But Bush the Elder owed favors to his big money backers. Also under Bush pressure, the FCC gave up many of its controls on the size and power of media empires, and accounting rules were softened into the mush we would later see in the clean bill of health Arthur Andersen gave Enron.

In 1998, Bush the First wrote to the oil minister of Kuwait on behalf of Chevron Oil Corporation. According to Greg Palast, Bush maintained that he "had no stake in the Chevron operation," which may be true, but which doesn't quite account for the $657,000 the company contributed to young Bush's 2000 campaign for the White House. The senior Bush lobbied President Carlos Menem of Argentina to grant a gambling license to Mirage Casino Corporation—a Bush Junior contributor to the tune of $449,000. Father Bush gave a single talk to the board of Global Crossing, the telecom start-up, in exchange for stock worth $13 million after the IPO. Perhaps as a tip, Global Crossing's employees also kicked in another million for Son of Bush.

> **The corporations buy the politicians, who then rewrite the rules the way the corporations want them.**

Government is supposed to be the referee so that we get prosperity without huge numbers of people getting screwed. Crony capitalists, however, have learned how to rig the game. The corporations buy the politicians, who then rewrite the rules the way the corporations want them.

With a free hand from newly neutered federal regulators, Enron and its ilk set their sights on two states where voters seem to have forgotten how the West was really won. They ignore all the barn raisings and wagon trains and other forms of cooperation, as well as federal troops in those Fort Apache blue uniforms, that made modern life in the West possible. The only part of frontier mythology that conservatives remember is the bit about the lone cowboy riding across the plains, which means that, like Ronald Reagan, they got their all their ideas from watching movies. That "rugged individualism" from the nineteenth century got turned into blatant hucksterism in the twentieth. The "cowboy" was replaced by the developer who, of course, relied on federal dams and irrigation systems to make his land worth anything, but the myth of "government had nothing to do with it" lived on.

In 1996, thanks to a *$53 million* campaign led by Southern California Edison, Pacific Gas and Electric, and their allies, California led the way in opening up its power grid to the hucksters' extortion racket. All the utilities had to do was hold back power from a single generator and they could turn the law of supply and demand into a license to print money. False shortages drove prices up 1000 percent. According to Greg Palast, in North Carolina, one of twenty-three other states conned into this game, Duke Power simply threw away the replacement parts they needed to keep the plants operating.

When the game got out of control, California again led the way with rolling blackouts. Then, in May 2001, W was "shocked, shocked" to find that this wild speculation was going on. Actually, the suckers were simply raising too much of a fuss and he had to tell his boys to cool it. Of course, Bush's solution was as comical as his surprise and crocodile tears. He put Dick Cheney in charge of the committee to save California consumers, which is, once again, putting the fox in charge of the henhouse.

Cheney's creative, forward-thinking ideas? Build nuclear power plants. Who you gonna call? Well, it so happens that Halliburton's Brown and Root does a fine job building power plants. His second idea: Open up oil exploration in Alaska's Arctic Wildlife Refuge. California does not burn oil in its power plants, but no matter. Commerce Secretary Don Evans, former CEO of a billion-dollar oil and gas corporation, thought it was a great idea. Drilling in one of the last wild places on earth flipped the bird to all those tree huggers. It was red meat symbolism for W's wing nut core constituency.

As Greg Palast put it, "California didn't run out of *energy*, it ran out of *government.*" What's really pathetic, though, is that, even after Enron managed to drive Pacific Gas & Electric into bankruptcy, Jeb Bush, true to family tradition, was talking to Ken Lay about deregulation in Florida. Meanwhile, the International Monetary Fund and the World Bank, under pressure from Bush, had made "privatization" of public utilities—including water systems—a condition of loans to developing nations. This put $4 *trillion* in public assets in the hands of American, French, and British corporate colonialists. (I assume they're working on finding ways to turn the air into a marketable commodity as well. After all, we've got oxygen bars in L.A.) Former World Bank chief economist Joseph Stiglitz summed up this program by saying that it wasn't privatization, it was "briberization."

On the international scene, thanks to the Bush family, Enron was given a sweetheart deal, not just on an Argentine gas pipeline, but on the entire water system of Buenos Aires province. Enron fired so many workers, and left the water so contaminated, that in October 2001, the provincial government finally came to its senses and rode Kenny Boy's team out of town on a rail.

Back in the 2000 campaign, Joe Lieberman made a joke about Cheney's $20 million farewell gift from Halliburton. He said, "And I see, Dick, from the newspapers, that you're better off than you were eight years ago."

Cheney shot back with, "And I can tell you, Joe, that the government had absolutely nothing to do with it."

But it looks to me like Halliburton was on the government sugar tit to the tune of $3.8 billion in government contracts and taxpayer-insured loans while Cheney was running that company.

When the government bailed out Chrysler Corporation back in the eighties, a lot of anti-government conservatives had to shut up at least for a day or two. But now, twenty years later, corporations don't just get bailed out—they run the show.

Corporations don't just get bailed out— they run the show.

I can see federal agencies going the way of the big civic auditoriums like the Staples Center in L.A. or the Fleet Center in Boston and offering naming rights. Someday soon we'll have The "Cisco Systems Department of Justice," the "Boeing Department of Defense," and the "Pfizer Department of Health and Human Services."

For decades we've had direct government subsidies for tobacco and sugar and any other commodity that has friends in high places. But a woman who's evicted with her three kids and needs a little help for a few months becomes a "welfare queen" and an abomination to these "self-reliant" Republicans. Poor people are supposed to pull themselves up by their own bootstraps; corporations get subsidies and bailouts—not to mention billions in cozy government contracts.

And If You're Not a Millionaire?

Middle class and working class people get screwed in this country mostly because politicians like Bush are complete hypocrites. People in the big middle believe the Republican con job, in part, because the outright lies are hidden behind the smokescreen of religious and moralistic crap.

In part, good-hearted Americans believe the lies because they are so blatant and outrageous. Decent people simply can't believe that this "nice man" they see on TV could possibly lie to them outright, and that's mostly because they don't *want* to believe it.

Why do so many people who are not rich go along with policies that favor the rich? I think it's because so many people in this country want to be millionaires, or think they can be, so they identify with the higher rungs on the economic ladder. The idea of being a blue-collar guy and proud of it, of taking care of your family and being part of your community and letting it go at that— that is way out of style. Partly, that's because good blue-collar jobs and friendly blue-collar neighborhoods hardly exist anymore. The same guy a generation ago who would carry a lunch bucket to a factory somewhere now wears a tie to fix your office copy machine. He drives a Honda instead of a pick-up truck, and he lives in a three-bedroom ranch in a suburb with all the community of a strip mall. His kids go to crap schools because there's no money for education. Local school districts can't even finance sports these days, much less things like music and art. You see teachers down at K Mart spending their own money for classroom supplies.

This is what a knee-jerk reaction against taxation leads to. Starving the beast of government means that budgets have to be cut. When you put radical conservatives in charge of making those decisions, you can count on having to make sacrifices in your community, not theirs.

There's nothing wrong with aspiring to having a few bucks. But you can't let your aspirations delude you into thinking that what's good for the Bush family and the Cheney family is good for you.

In *Lies and the Lying Liars Who Tell Them*, Al Franken points out that during the first seven years that the two Bushes were in power, not one new job was created, net. Franken speculates that with a little fuzzy math, an economist could prove that had Bushes been running the country from the Revolution until now, not a single American would have ever worked.

During W's first three years, the U.S. economy shed over two million private-sector jobs. But in a speech in Indianapolis, September 5, 2003, just hours after the government announced the loss of 93,000 American jobs the month before, Bush remained upbeat. He said that if Congress wanted to help, it should make the recent tax cuts permanent and enact other parts of his agenda, from limiting malpractice judgments against doctors and suits against companies, to allowing more domestic oil and gas drilling and further easing regulations on business. But what did he say about job creation?

Considering that over 80,000 jobs were shed each month during the first two and a half years of his presidency, Bush's mid-2003 announcement that he was creating a new undersecretary of commerce post devoted to job creation sounded like very little, very late. Echoing that great Republican role model Herbert Hoover, Bush told union workers on Labor Day 2003, "There are better days ahead."

As further good news, the Federal Reserve Bank of New York recently issued a study that describes this recession's job losses as far more structural and permanent than in the past. That might explain why there are nine million people still looking for work, and uncounted others who have simply given up.

> **There are nine million people still looking for work, and uncounted others who have simply given up.**

Meanwhile, Bush's buddies are busily exporting American jobs. The Labor Department estimates that at least 15 percent of the two million plus jobs lost since Bush took office have reappeared in Mexico or China, or somewhere else where workers don't have rights and work for cheap. White-collar workers who voted Republican never seemed to care much before, but now the "offshoring" of work has worked its way up the skill ladder. Thoroughly middle class, college educated people like engineers, software designers, and stock analysts are finding that their white-collar job can be done by someone in Russia, or in Ireland, or in India. Boeing is hiring design engineers in Moscow. Morgan Stanley, the investment house, is hiring number crunchers in Bombay. Business consultants are telling the corporate class to junk their high-priced American workers and get in on the overseas action, where you can save fifty cents on the dollar for every job. Which is why companies like IBM and Microsoft are telling their people to "think China."

A Census Bureau report shows that the number of Americans living below the poverty line increased by more than 1.3 million in 2002, even though, technically, we were supposed to be edging out of the recession. That's a total of 34.8 million Americans—12.4 percent of our people desperately poor, including 6.6 million families and 12.2 million kids growing up without basic things the rest of us take for granted. Meanwhile, the trade imbalance is way out of whack, and the federal budget deficits have grown so huge that even the International Monetary Fund has begun expressing concern about our credit-worthiness. In terms of debt, we're already a banana republic. And don't count on faith-based solutions. According to the Chronicle of Philanthropy, donations to charity in 2002 dropped for the first time in twenty years. It seems that hard times have dried up contributions everywhere, except the kind corporations make to politicians, and vice versa.

Bush could become the first president since Herbert Hoover to manage an absolute decline in employment over the course of his term in office. Even at the end of 2003, when the economy had supposedly rebounded and we were having the biggest growth spurt in twenty years, we still were creating only 80,000 jobs a month—which isn't enough just to keep up with the number of kids coming out of school and hoping to earn a living.

Nine million unemployed, and the new jobs pay three bucks an hour less, on average, than the jobs that have been lost. Nine million unemployed, and in December of 2003, Bush refused to extend benefits, while persisting in his plan to try to kill overtime protection for millions of workers. And that growth spurt? Economists refer to an "increase in productivity." What that really means is that companies are squeezing more work out of fewer people. We're "rebounding" by keeping nine million people off the payroll, while turning those who are employed into wage slaves.

> We're "rebounding" by keeping nine million people off the payroll, while turning those who are employed into wage slaves.

The median household income has fallen each year of Bush II. Fewer family members are working, and the people who are working are having their hours cut back, often to part-time status. To make matters worse, 2004 will be the fourth straight year of double-digit increases in health insurance premiums. People in employer-sponsored health plans are paying 48 percent more out of their own pockets for care than they did at the beginning of Bush's term. Almost two-thirds of large employers raised the amounts that employees have to contribute. Even if a family got a check for a federal tax break, it was all eaten up by higher local taxes to compensate for the loss of federal money, and the higher cost of health insurance.

Can't We Blame Clinton Again?

When Clinton came to Washington, he discovered that his "fiscally conservative" predecessors Reagan and Bush had left the country in what Joe Conason calls "deep voodoo." The '93 deficit would be $300 billion. With the national debt "supply sided" up to $3 trillion during the Reagan years, Clinton saw no choice but to raise taxes. The conservatives trashed him for the "largest tax increase in history." Which wasn't even true. Even the *Wall Street Journal* admitted that the largest tax increase in history was Reagan's 1982 deficit reduction package. The Gipper cut taxes one year, then pushed them back up the next.

What drove conservatives crazy about the Clinton tax package was that he raised taxes on the wealthiest 1.2 percent of Americans. Gingrich screamed that "the tax increase will kill jobs and lead to a recession, and the recession will force people off of work and onto unemployment and will actually increase the deficit." Then Texas Senator Phil Gramm, since retired, intoned, "We are buying a one-way ticket to a recession."

But, defying their predictions, Clinton presided over the longest period of uninterrupted growth in American history—115 straight months of economic expansion at an average rate of 4 percent annually. His eight years at the controls saw the creation of 22 million new jobs, more than any other president in history, and more than Reagan and Bush combined.

The top tax rate was increased in 1993, and the economy boomed. The unemployment rate dropped to 4 percent—the lowest unemployment figure since 1970—without inflation. Clinton increased the minimum wage twice during his administration, and contrary to all that right-wingers consider holy, the economy still produced a record number of jobs. More jobs meant the smallest welfare rolls since the sixties, and the poverty rate dropped to the lowest percentage of the population since 1980.

In the last two years of his administration, Clinton's treasury paid off more than $360 billion of the national debt, saving taxpayers billions annually in interest payments. The deficits left by the Reagan and Bush eighties had been converted into surpluses. And by the time Clinton left office, federal income taxes as a percentage of income for the typical American family were lower than they had been at any time since 1966.

There were 281 billion extra dollars in the budget Bush inherited from Clinton, and the Bush administration, looking a decade ahead, predicted that the cumulative budget surplus would be $5.6 trillion by 2011. Bush vowed to pay off the national debt, and said that he would strengthen retirement and health plans by setting aside trillions in savings.

But then the surplus disappeared in a puff of smoke and mirrors, replaced the next year with a budget deficit that has since grown to record size. In comparing the Clinton years to the Bush regime, Robert D. Reischauer, a former director of the Congressional Budget Office, compared the financial free fall to Adam and Eve getting booted out of Eden in *Paradise Lost*. The $5.6 trillion surplus once predicted for 2011 is now a $2.3 trillion cumulative deficit under the Congressional Budget Office's best-case scenario. The *New York Times* pointed out that the decline in the long-term budget forecast in just two years under Bush matches the total revenue collected by the United States government from 1789 to 1983.

By the summer of 2002, the White House Office of Management and Budget admitted that its sunny fiscal projections of a few months earlier were completely wrong. Bush's repeated pledges not to fund the tax cuts by tapping into Social Security revenues were history. So were his campaign promises to pay down the federal debt. But not the three tax cuts he pushed through Congress in three years.

> **The White House Office of Management and Budget admitted that its sunny fiscal projections of a few months earlier were completely wrong.**

The times kept changing, and his story kept changing too.

In 2000, the idea was that the surplus was excess that should go back to the people.

By 2001, the surplus was evaporating, and the reason for tax cuts shifted to economic stimulus. By 2003, we needed tax cuts on dividends for long-term growth. But the 2001 budget projections were false; the 2001 cuts would do very little to stimulate the economic short term, and the supply side rationale for 2003 was nonsense. Bush was simply paying off Kenny Boy and all his other wealthy backers. Even if it hammers our long-term financial health, and it does nothing for the average American but increase interest rates down the road, Bush's tax cuts put millions more dollars into the pockets of the already rich. Mission accomplished.

Pedal to the Metal and Into the Ditch

Robert Greenstein, executive director of the Center of Budget and Policy Priorities, told the *Times,* "Once it was clear that the confident predictions had blown up and the picture was frightening, they still refused to step on the brakes. Instead, the administration pushed the accelerator down closer to the floor. It's flabbergasting."

The terrorist attacks of September 11, 2001, not only made the economic downturn worse, they also brought heavy increases in domestic security spending. The budget office estimated that we would need another $300 billion in military spending long before Iraq entered the picture. When it did, Bush's toady, Tom Delay, the Republican House majority leader, told us sagely that "Nothing is more important in the face of war than cutting taxes."

On June 11, 2002, for the first time in five years, the White House was forced to ask Congress to raise the ceiling on the national debt. Undaunted by fiscal reality, former senator Phil Gramm chose this same day to propose permanent repeal of the federal estate tax. He spoke of it in terms of saving family farms, but it was actually just a windfall for America's richest heirs and heiresses, sold as if it were part of Willie Nelson's "Farm Aid."

With $1.5 trillion in tax cuts and at least $100 billion in new defense spending, something had to give. Not surprisingly, the Environmental Protection Agency saw itself with 5.5 percent less to spend. Even construction of housing for military families is being cut by 6 percent. Bush has demonstrated the meaning of "compassionate conservatism" by cutting after-school programs, schools on military bases, child vaccinations in Third World countries, prosecution of polluters, and health care for veterans. "No child left behind" has not received the funding Bush promised, and its focus on test scores is having the perverse effect of pushing school administrators to kick out troubled kids to boost testing averages. At the same time, the conservatives are killing off programs for job training.

If Congressional Republicans and the administration get their wish and extend all the tax cuts, with no increase in spending the deficit will have built up to $6.2 trillion by 2013. Deficits will push up interest rates and impose huge costs on Social Security and Medicare at precisely the moment that the baby boom generation will begin expecting its retirement benefits.

In the last thirty years, the top 1 percent of families, those with incomes starting at $230,000, have seen their after-tax incomes rise 157 percent. Their share of the national income has doubled, and is now as large as the combined income of the bottom 40 percent. The thirteen thousand families at the very top have almost as much income as the poorest twenty million households in America.

The White House "economic stimulus" proposal of 2002 included rebating more than $7 billion to corporations—with as much as $250 million in the package for Bush's friends at Enron. The central feature of the second tax package was the elimination of taxes on dividends. This means that money you work for gets taxed, but money you make because you already had enough money to put some of it in the stock market does not get taxed. This, of course, is where the money in really big estates comes from, so Buffy and Brad get a free ride again. Likewise, George, Jeb, Neil, Marvin, and Dorothy. The kind of estates we're talking about make your 401K look like sixteen cents found under the sofa cushion. Do *not* think what's good for them is good for you—it isn't.

In late October 2003, the House pushed the biggest overhaul of corporate taxes in twenty years—relief to the tune of $128 billion over the next decade—removing taxes on everything from the excise on tackle boxes to foreign royalties on movies. The public interest journal *Tom Paine* calls Bush "the gift that keeps on giving," at least to contributors like Bank of America and Pfizer and H-P. Corporate taxes have been slashed by 40 percent in the Bush years. This gift for corporations is called the American Jobs Creation Act. It'll create plenty of jobs for Americans—if they move to Guatemala.

> **It'll create plenty of jobs for Americans— if they move to Guatemala.**

The Houdini Hustle

When you look at the numbers on the 2001 tax cut, you find a transparent trick. They rely on "phasing in" the cuts over time, as well as "sunsets," which means they have an expiration date of 2011, in order to make the numbers look much better than they are. But what do you think is going to happen in 2011? Conservatives are going to pressure Congress to extend the cuts, even though the expiration date is what made the model work in the first place. And if Congress refuses to do it? They'll be accused of raising taxes! Can you believe it? Pure hustle. And to present these cuts as helping the middle class is pure lies.

The 2001 cuts will deliver 42 percent of their benefits to the top 1 percent—families making over $330,000 a year. The 2003 cut delivers 29.1 percent to the top 1 percent, but it really delivers for those making over a million a year. This 0.13 percent of the American people will receive 17 percent of the benefit, which is more than the benefit for the bottom 70 percent.

Half of Americans received no tax cut at all in 2003. Out of those who did receive a cut, half saw their taxes go down by $100 or less. Meanwhile, the Congressional budget office says that half of the 2003 deficit of $400 billion is due to these Bush cuts.

Once the bill comes due for the retirement of the baby boomers, the whole system is going to collapse, which is just the way all the right-wing anti-tax crusaders want it. They've got their gate-guarded communities, and their armor-plated limos. Reagan already pushed the mentally ill out into the streets, and the number of homeless sleeping in cardboard boxes makes American cities now look like the Third World. Republicans don't care if older Americans have to eat dog food or if young people grow up to be illiterate criminals.

And these are the people who claim to be such super patriots? How can you say you love your country when you want to see its social structure go down the toilet, or when you feather your own nest by profiteering from war, all the while providing shoddy goods and services to the people doing the fighting?

What Happened to Restoring Honor and Integrity to the White House?

Once again, it comes down to the issue of character I raised earlier. W seems incapable of choosing a genuinely tough path, of risking his political popularity with the same aggression with which he risks the country's economic stability and international credibility. In challenging times, a president needs to play it straight by asking the American people to make sacrifices

> **W has never played it straight in his life, and the only kind of sacrifice he knows anything about is a throw to first base.**

that are fairly distributed. But W has never played it straight in his life, and the only kind of sacrifice he knows anything about is a throw to first base.

He launched a purely elective war that costs billions while

telling civilians they deserved big tax cuts. He wants to remake the Middle East, but he does nothing to reduce our dependence on Middle East oil. His energy policy is a grab bag of giveaways to his cronies.

W talked about compassionate conservatism, but there just isn't a compassionate bone in George Bush's body. He made a big deal out of his No Child Left Behind education package, which he then refused to fund. Similarly, in his African AIDS initiative and his faith-based initiative for social services, he tries to take credit without paying the political dues necessary to get things done. In December 2003, he let benefits expire for 80,000 unemployed. The unemployment figures had dropped a bit, but only because people stopped looking for jobs. Still, Bush touted those numbers as "a positive sign that the economy is getting better." Sure it is, if you're CEO of a Fortune 500 company with a nice big golden parachute to protect you.

The economic recovery that George Bush is so excited about is a party not everybody has been invited to. In the third quarter of 2003, the gross domestic product rose 8.2 percent. During the same time, corporate profits rose 40 percent. Congressional pork is up 40 percent. Wages and salaries, however, rose at an annual rate of only 0.8 percent.

Americans are killing themselves working longer hours, which yields productivity and profits like never before, but the worker gains nothing. The fat cats tell him he's lucky to have a job. Which is true, since they have plans to ship that job off to India next week.

A hundred years ago, Henry Ford figured out that in order for companies to make money, the workers needed to be consumers too. That's why he built a cheap car, paid a decent wage, and gave people time off for newfangled ideas like the "weekend." He wanted them to be able to buy things—starting with his cars. But the new fat cats think they can get by selling luxury cars to pluto-crats. Times are great if you're a fat cat. Everyone else is just out of luck.

The Assault on Government

Right-wing propaganda has been trashing government ever since Franklin Roosevelt saw the country through the Great Depression. The reason is that government was reinforcing its role as referee in the blood sport of capitalism. Don't get me wrong—capitalism ain't always pretty, but it's the only system that works. It works because it's human nature. Some people's human nature, though, is to ride roughshod over everybody else. Some people are just plain greedy and mean, and they need adult supervision, and government happens to be the only "adult" we have.

In the 1990s, the anti-government tantrum got so extreme that we had militias arming themselves up in the woods of Idaho, and nutcases blowing up federal buildings. Our friends on the wing nut radio programs were trash talking about "jackboot thugs in black helicopters" descending to rub out good, God-fearing Americans. Part of that was ignorant, anti-social paranoia, and part of it was cynical jerks on the radio stirring up trouble to make a buck.

Today's computer programmer and copier repair guy are from a generation that has no first- or even secondhand knowledge of a time just before World War II when millions of perfectly average, mainstream Americans went hungry. Woody Guthrie's union songs and *The Grapes of Wrath* don't register with these young, upwardly mobile people. They've never seen those photographs of haunted and hungry American faces that Walker Evans took for Franklin Roosevelt's Works Progress Administration. That's why I'm paying so much attention to what's gone on in the past thirty years.

The Democratic party, the party that dug us out of the Great Depression, that gave us radical ideas like five-day work weeks punctuated by weekends; electric lights in rural areas; social security for old age; voting rights; and medical care for the elderly no longer appealed to these new folks moving to the suburbs, and especially not those who moved to the suburbs of the rapidly growing Sunbelt.

The real and more lasting damage is when people of modest means are hustled into thinking that government is their enemy. Sure, a lot of things our government has done over the years have been stupid, and it's safe to say that bureaucracy needs to be minimized. But government is all that stands between **Government is all that stands between average people and complete domination by the rich and powerful.** average people and complete domination by the rich and powerful. And bureaucratic bungling and waste can be fixed.

Don't Starve Government, Reinvent It

There's nothing wrong with government that a little competition and efficiency can't cure, as soon as the right-wingers stop wasting our time trashing the very *idea* of government.

The question is, What do we want government to do? We sure as hell want government to clean up the mess when firestorms wipe out hundreds of homes in California, or hurricanes wipe out whole towns in Florida or the Carolinas. We want government to keep airplanes from crashing into each other (and we wish that government did a better job of keeping psychos off the passenger lists). You don't see a movement urging faith-based air traffic control. And you don't have to have kids, and you don't even have to care about having a decent society, to want government giving the best education money can buy to every child in America.

All you have to know is a little economics to see that you can't retire unless there's a good, educated work force coming along behind you, generating profits to support the value of your 401K and paying your Social Security benefits. That's how it works, you know. It's not *your* money you get back. *Your* money was used to pay for your grandparents' and parents' retirement. *You* retire on what young people pay in after you get the gold watch. Social Security works like a chain letter, and whether you like the idea or not, we're all in it together.

Short-sighted corporations don't want government policing their excesses—keeping poisons out of our air and water, or poisons out of our food or medicines—because regulation creates overhead. They don't want government keeping mutual funds traders or the New York Stock Exchange honest, because, as recent headlines attest, corporations and stock traders sometimes want to be *dishonest.*

Republican farmers want government crop subsidies, and Republican corporate leaders want government contracts and a government international police force—the military and the state department—to make international trade possible. They hate Social Security, Medicare, Medicaid, the Securities and Exchange Commission, the Interstate Commerce Commission, the Federal Trade Commission, the Federal Communications Commission, the Nuclear Regulatory Commission—all the agencies that try to prevent public health epidemics like food poisoning, social problems like millions of homeless, and financial disasters like the S&L scandals. Before Republicans changed the rules, these agencies might have prevented both mad cow disease and Enron.

Hating government while profiting from government in all sorts of ways is two-faced hypocrisy of the worst kind, and the banana Republicans have perfected it. And the baby that gets thrown out with the bathwater in this whole "anti-tax, we hate government" hustle, is the fact that government does things that we need doing, things that nobody else can do.

In 2001 Bush actually called the disappearing federal surplus "incredibly positive news" because it would put Congress in a "fiscal straitjacket." He was echoing Grover Norquist, president of Americans for Tax Reform, the anti-government wing nut who has been pushing for thirty years to reduce the size of government by "draining its lifeblood." They can't win by arguing that we don't need or want Social Security or Medicare, because by a huge majority of Americans do want this safety net. The hustle is to sneak in the back door through tax cuts that will make these programs impossible.

Right-wingers have tried to incite ordinary voters to also hate government by arguing that we're being gouged by taxation. *The Wall Street Journal* editorial page has said that the idea is to shift taxation onto the neediest to get their "blood boiling with tax rage." These are the same guys who referred to those so poor that they don't pay income tax as "lucky duckies." Are they insane?

In *The Great Unraveling,* Paul Krugman, the Princeton economics professor who has a column in the *New York Times,* sets the record straight about this part of the Republican hustle. According to Krugman, each citizen of the United States now pays in state, local, and federal taxes combined roughly 26 percent of his share of the gross domestic product. When you isolate those at the very top of the income ladder, they're paying 35 percent.

By contrast, in Canada, the *average* tax bite for everyone—rich and poor alike—is 38 percent. In France, they pay on average 45 percent. In Sweden, its 52 percent. In short:

We Pay Less in Taxes as a Percentage of Our Wealth Than Any Other Industrialized Nation on Earth.

So, once again, the American voter needs to stop complaining about taxes and start asking what we're getting for our money. Good roads? Safe airways? Good education for our kids? Don't we want those things?

Good roads? Safe airways? Good education for our kids? Don't we want those things?

In 2000, at the height of the capital gains bubble (and before the Bush cuts) the average American's tax tab was 29 percent of

GDP. Otherwise, taxation for middle class Americans has been more or less stable at 26 percent since Sonny & Cher were on top.

However, those raking in big bucks have seen their tax rate cut in half. (In the seventies they were paying 70 percent!) Taxes on corporations also have been cut in half. And by the time all the Bush cuts are in place, the rich will be taxed at the lowest rate since the Hoover administration.

So the other message in all of this is:

Anti-tax Crusaders—You Won. Now Shut Up. What say we move on now to making life better for everyone?

Ever since the California tax revolt of 1978, the Republican anti-government hustle has been right there alongside the morality and family values hustle. David Stockman, the same guy who created "Rosey Scenario" to sugar coat his "supply side economics," coined another cute phrase for attacking government programs that make big business play by the rules. He called it "starving the beast," and supply side was just one of the weapons.

Anyone who says that Reagan's "supply side" tax cuts did wonders for the economy is pissing on your leg. Economies always rebound after recessions—that's called the business cycle. The question is, where do they rebound to? To a much bigger pie, or not? The late eighties saw growth of about 3 percent a year, which means that it was pretty much back to where it was before the Reagan recession and the Reagan cuts. Except that we were now hammered with huge deficits, the very same deficits that forced Bush senior to weasel out on his "read my lips" pledge and raise taxes.

Dr. N. Gregory Mankiw, chairman of George W. Bush's own Council of Economic Advisors, once called Reagan's supply siders "charlatans and cranks." Bush senior called supply side "voodoo economics." Paul Krugman, who with his credentials ought to know, tells us that supply side is a creature of the right-wing think tanks and policy wonks, the same "vast right-wing conspiracy" I described in chapter 3. These people aren't economists—they're smash-mouth partisans. Professional economists call supply side crap.

Even Irving Kristol, the godfather of the neo-conservatives, admits that it's crap economics but also says it's brilliant politics. It's a Trojan horse for getting inside the walls to dismantle government. After tax cuts create huge deficits, government won't have the funds to stop the mean and greedy (that would be your conservative Republicans) from doing whatever they want.

To drive the deficit back down, Clinton was forced to push the tax rates on the wealthiest back up to 36 percent, and the economy did exactly the opposite of what supply-side theory predicted. Growth went through the roof—the best since the 1960s. The deficits turned into a surplus, which George W then pissed away. Wing nuts will still try to lay claim to the Clinton boom years by saying that it was the result of tax cuts in 1981! They might as well say it was because of the gold rush of 1849.

> **Wing nuts will still try to lay claim to the Clinton boom years by saying that it was the result of tax cuts in 1981!**

So once again, the conservatives lost the economic argument on its merits, and what did they do? What they always do—they lied. They began to piss and moan again about how we are all being bled to death with taxes. The Bushies renamed the estate tax the "death" tax to make it sound awful. Mostly, they lied to make people think that everyone had to pay it, rather than merely the super rich.

Bush used the death tax issue in practically every stump speech he gave, lamenting the devastation it visited on family farmers and small business owners. The Republicans pushed estate tax repeal as a middle-class tax-relief issue, and once again the Big Lie worked. Seventeen percent of Americans thought the estate tax would apply to them. In fact, the tax affects less than 2 percent of estates. Nearly half of the revenue it produces comes from taxes on 0.16 percent of estates, worth an average of $17 million, belonging to about 3,300 families each year. In 1999, fully a quarter of the estate tax revenue came from just 467 estates. And for the record, family farms have always had a $2.6 million exemption. For family farms worth more than $2.6 million, the heirs have always had a grace period of up to fourteen years to pay the tax bill at low interest rates. Most of all, nobody has ever documented a *single case* of an American farm family having to give up their land because of the estate tax. But now the cost to the rest of us in ditching this tax to keep Buffy and Brad in the manner to which they were born is an estimated $800 billion over ten years.

But the American voter never sees the real price tag on these things. That's because hypocritical politicians can use the government's antique accounting system to hide the long-term implications of the stupid and deceitful things they do today.

Hustler Accounting 101

One of the problems with government is that, like civil service regulations, government accounting was set up to prevent petty crimes. Crimes like stealing a little cash here and there, or putting your cousin on the payroll. That's why there's so much red tape in old-fashioned government. They didn't want anyone (at least not the small fry) to do anything wrong, even if it meant they couldn't do anything at all.

One result of this is that governments by and large use "cash accounting." Set up to keep some clerk from pocketing a few bucks, cash accounting focuses almost exclusively on current transactions. The bad news for us is that cash accounting ignores the big picture. It zeros in on the short term to the neglect of long-term financial obligations.

Businesses use "accrual accounting." This means that any future obligation is carried on the books as an expense now. In cash accounting, nothing shows up on the books except the checks and the bills coming in today. That's how cash accounting allows governments to rack up enormous future obligations without any trace showing up as a cloud hanging over this year's election. This means that governments can—at least for a while—get away with ignoring things like pension obligations that are going to come home to roost say, ten years from now.

In accrual accounting, businesses have to face up to their debts, and to admit that things like equipment decline in value with age. This "using up" of an asset's value has to be accounted for as a form of spending, which they call "depreciation." However, the government can act like there's no tomorrow. When government builds a bridge or a dam or an airport, it creates a valuable asset. But as that structure ages, its value declines, because without costly maintenance and repair, that asset eventually will go to hell. But cost accounting takes no notice of this. Government agencies don't have to depreciate the value of their physical assets, because cost accounting only tracks money that's coming in and going out today.

That explains why politicians can focus on building the new airport, for which they get credit, while neglecting the roadways that are falling apart. The books aren't being charged for that decline in value, and the neglect doesn't show up anywhere. In the same way, neglecting to prepare for the financial tidal wave of massive retirements of baby boomers doesn't show up anywhere. The Bushies can claim that things are okay, right up until the bridge (or the social security system) collapses.

That's the nasty little secret of Bush's tax cuts for his friends. The $400 billion deficit for 2003, and the $4 trillion national debt, doesn't tell you the whole story.

Social Security tallies up its money using the rules of cash accounting. For 2003, there was a surplus of $160 million that got shaved off the total federal deficit for the year. Without that little accounting fiction, the deficit would be $560 million.

But that's nothing compared to the long-term problem. The

Social Security System has future obligations to retirees totaling $14 trillion dollars. That's trillion with a "T." But the system has only $3.5 trillion in assets. That number includes reserves of $1.4 trillion, plus the present value of all the taxes today's workers will pay in until they retire—$2.1 trillion. See the problem?

If the government used the same method of accounting that Flynt Publications has to use, their books would be flashing red ink to the tune of $10.5 trillion in the hole! And Bush would be selling tax cuts! If our accounting system told the truth, I doubt even Bush's Big Hustle could pull the wool over our eyes.

> **If the government used the same method of accounting that Flynt Publications has to use, their books would be flashing red ink.**

When people talk about the "social security" crisis, this is what they mean. Cash flow accounting allows politicians to leave tomorrow's problem for another day. It doesn't appear on the books yet, so it doesn't really exist. And all W's rosy scenarios are so just much horse manure—until he takes the real numbers into account and faces up to the dry hole he's drilling for your "golden years."

> **When you're trying to pull off a really big hustle, you have to keep saying the exact opposite of the truth with a straight face until people start believing that black is white.**

There's a reason that this administration, more than any in history, has made such claims about this president's honor and integrity. It's the same reason that radio wing nut Laura Ingraham makes such a point about railing against "the elites." When you're trying to pull off a really big hustle, you have to keep saying the exact opposite of the truth with a straight face until people start believing that black is white. For example, that Laura, who graduated from Dartmouth and the University of Virgina Law School, speaks for the "little guy." Or that Bush, who shamelessly uses every trick in the book to make his rich cronies even richer—at the expense of the American people—has restored honor and integrity to the White House.

5

Media Piranhas and Poodles in the Press

Shelf space in any retail outlet is highly valued real estate, and as everyone knows, the first three rules of real estate are location, location, and location. So when I recently dropped in at a bookstore in L.A., I thought it was significant that a whole slew of political books were right up front and face out, and by far the majority of them were written by people who called themselves conservatives. Clearly, these were the books the store managers expected their customers to pick up. In no particular order, here are the titles I came upon:

Treason: Liberal Treachery from the Cold War to the War on Terrorism by Ann Coulter

The Savage Nation: Saving America from the Liberal Assault on our Borders, Language, and Culture by Michael Savage

Useful Idiots: How Liberals Got it Wrong in the Cold War and Still Blame America First by Mona Charen

Tales From the Left Coast, True Tales of Hollywood Stars and their Outrageous Politics by James Hirsen

Why the Left Hates America: Exposing the Lies That Have Obscured Our Nation's Greatness by Daniel J. Flynn

What's So Great About America by Dinesh D'Souza

Hillary's Scheme: Inside the Next Clinton's Ruthless Agenda to Take the White House by Carl Limbacher

Bias: A CBS Insider Exposes How the Media Distorts the News by Bernard Goldberg

Dereliction of Duty: The Eyewitness Account of How Bill Clinton Endangered America's Long-term National Security by Colonel Robert "Buzz" Patterson

The New Thought Police: Inside the Left's Assault on Free Speech and Free Minds by Tammy Bruce

Looking at this small sample, I could identify several big ideas in the conservative world view.

The first idea is that conservatives see the U.S. as pathetically insecure, like some aging movie star who needs to be reassured she's still beautiful, or some senile businessman who surrounds himself with yes-people to tell him only what he wants to hear. I'm a pretty successful businessman myself, and I can tell you that sealing yourself off from the truth is a sure way to go broke.

The second idea is that we have been seriously wronged, and even at this late date continue to be threatened by, a pair of evil-doers named Bill and Hillary Clinton, the Bonny and Clyde of "liberalism."

The third and most general impression is that liberals, who are all elitest America-haters, are the most sinister threat this nation has ever faced. To the conservatives, liberals are the source of all our problems.

> **To the conservatives, liberals are the source of all our problems.**

Fortunately, I stay pretty well informed, so I know that these books are nothing more than a way for radio personalities and other entertainers to make a buck. If they didn't sway voters, I wouldn't care about them at all. I know that this country has no reason to be insecure. America is the strongest cultural, economic, and military power on earth, and I believe that our core values of tolerance and openness to dissent are the foundation of that strength. We don't have to gild the lily to make ourselves feel good.

As to the second point, last time I checked, Bill Clinton had been out of office for several years now. I also know that the Clintons' image was systematically distorted from the moment they first showed up on the national radar coming in from Arkansas.

As to the third point, by last count there are just about enough old-fashioned, tax-and-spend liberals left in Washington to fit inside Teddy Kennedy's car. Based on his driving record, however, I do not recommend the ride.

Still, the word "liberal" is like the "Applause" sign that lights up in a television studio, only it says "Jeer" or "Hiss and Boo." The term no longer describes a point of view that a reasonable person could argue for or against. Instead, it's red meat to dangle in front of a bunch of right-wing piranhas ready to strip it to the bone.

Where did these ideas come from, and why are they so popular? The answers lie in our newspapers, magazines, radio, and television, and in the people who run them. On the right, you have media piranhas who lie, distort, and "work the ref" until our heads spin. On the left, you have press poodles who either just do what they're told, or are too reasonable and polite to compete with ranting, conservative lunatics.

The So-Called Liberal Bias

Most reporters for quality news outlets are reasonably well educated and well informed. As a result, their opinions are what I would call "enlightened." They actually understand a little history and economics and psychology and the other background issues feeding into what's going on. So they don't just buy in to simple-minded crap like "they hate freedom." It's also a reporter's job to question those in power, to keep the politicians honest. Knowing what you're talking about and being critical of the people in power is what right-wingers call adding a "liberal bias" to the news.

With Bush in the Oval Office, right-wingers don't understand the concept of "loyal opposition." They rant and rave that even the mildest criticism is somehow treason. They hate enlightened opinions that run counter to their Big Hustle.

When you're in the magazine business like I am, or even just trying to put together a Web site, you become very aware that it's difficult to get beyond an eighth-grade reading level and still hold the attention of the American people. Democrats try to play it straight on the issues and their ideas sail right over the heads of casual observers, who are like kids shooting spitballs in the back of the room. The Republicans figured out long ago that politics is like a popularity contest, so they're the teachers who decide to cut back the assignments, show the video, and keep the kids happy.

> **A few well chosen —and misleading— pictures with easy-to-read labels like "patriotic" and "regular guy" and "family morals" carry the day, even when those images are *totally manufactured crap.***

A few well chosen—and misleading—pictures with easy-to-read labels like "patriotic" and "regular guy" and "family morals" carry the day, even when those images are *totally manufactured crap.*

Some people pay attention to politics, but many are really just getting their thumb sucked by some entertainer. If they weren't watching "The McLaughlin Group" or listening to Rush or O'Reilly, they'd be watching roller derby or mud wrestling. It's all the same kind of smash-mouth smackdown. Those shows have nothing to do with a serious look at the issues.

Fleecing the Faithful

What Ann Coulter, Laura Ingraham, Sean Hannity, Rush Limbaugh, and Bill O'Reilly are doing stands in the long tradition of American radio preachers putting on a show to fleece the faithful. That's fine, as long as you don't take these blowhards seriously. Go ahead and lay your hands on the radio, if that's what entertains you. But please do not confuse the crap that they spew with the truth. The next time you hear a right-wing talk show bashing Clinton, remember this.

The last Democratic president, the one the right-wingers still love to hate, balanced the budget, decreased the size of the federal government, promoted free trade, and eliminated welfare as we knew it. He also was on the case with Osama bin Laden and on the alert to al Qaeda. Contrary to all the conservative pissing by Sean Hannity and others, there's no way the Democrats were asleep at the wheel in terms of the terrorist threat. As I said in chapter 2, the question Hannity and his pals should be asking is: How much did the long business association between the House of Bush and the House of bin Laden have to do with Bush's "don't ask, don't tell" policy about al Qaeda during the first year of his administration?

But the biggest fact to offset the "evil liberals" fantasy is this: Bill Clinton was not even particularly liberal. He was a centrist Democrat, elected as a "third way" candidate, fighting what he called the "brain dead" politics of left and right." The main criticism of his Demo-

> **The most robust economy this nation ever experienced was on Clinton's watch.**

cratic Leadership Council was that it was too pro-business. As it turned out, Clinton was incredibly good for business. Another obvious fact: The most robust economy this nation ever experienced was on Clinton's watch. Because he'd found a way to blow past the conservative propaganda machine to create a solid, middle-of-the-road majority for the Democrats, the right-wingers decided to assassinate his character before he ever showed up for work.

Bill Clinton is on the History Channel. Since 2001, it's been a Republican making the mistakes. It's time to stop piling on Bill and Hill and kicking the crap out of their imaginary band of traitors, and to spend that time looking at the government that actually *is* in power. It would sure be a fresher and more legitimate source of outrage.

Blowhards on the Right

I'm not usually one to gloat over someone else's troubles (unless he's a total bastard). And certainly I'm not going to moralize over someone else's addiction to pain pills. I've been there myself. But I have to say, I was not entirely unhappy to see Rush Limbaugh's fat face (with a $12 cigar in his mouth) plastered all over the tabloids as his drug problem made front-page news.

We already know what a ridiculous snob—and hypocrite—Limbaugh is with his fine wines and fancy hotels and cigars. Rush was interviewed in *Cigar Aficionado,* where the supposed voice of the little guy goes on about how he likes to spend part of his $200 million salary package on Chateau Haut-Brion '61 (that's wine to you and me) at $2000 a bottle. Thank God we have Rush to protect us from "the elites." We already know that Mr. Family Values has been divorced twice, has no children (which, in his case, is a plus for the gene pool), and does not go to church.

But in case you missed it, in the fall of 2003, the right-wing motor mouth was busted by his housekeeper, Wilma Cline. She'd been his drug connection for years, and, according to the *New*

York Daily News, he had slipped her an extra $120,000 to keep quiet about it. Instead, she wore a wire and gave the tape to the cops in Palm Beach County. It appears that she thought her employer was a major asshole. I guess Rush doesn't speak for the "little guy" when that guy is the woman who cleans his toilets.

Cline said she'd supplied Rush with 4,350 pills in one forty-seven-day period, and that he took "enough to kill an elephant." OxyContin—known as "little blues" or "hillbilly heroin"—was his favorite. It's a narcotic similar to morphine. Rush is also a big fan of Lorcet and hydrocodone. Maybe Rush will be able to broadcast from jail. I know from personal experience that the acoustics are great.

Of course, the drug bust came shortly after Rush was fired from ESPN for a racist attack on a black quarterback, but that you'd expect. He said that Donovan McNabb of the Philadelphia Eagles was overrated, and that McNabb got all the credit just because he was black, when nothing could be further from the truth. Rush blamed the flap on the liberal media. At least he didn't blame it on Clinton.

So the mighty wind has been brought down a little. But so far, no one has laid a glove on the twin harpies of the right, Ann Coulter and Laura Ingraham. Every circus needs its dancing girls, and that's where Ann and Laura come in. The right-wing babes are making out like bandits, exploiting anger (and lust) in the hearts of conservative men.

> **Every circus needs its dancing girls, and that's where Ann and Laura come in.**

Laura Ingraham has a Web site that markets her like a pin-up, photographed in a tight T-shirt with a slinky look in her eye. The biggest joke is that tag line of hers, "Keep the elites on the run." What are we supposed to do with her then? She's a graduate of Ivy League Dartmouth College and the University of Virginia Law School, and she got a clerkship on the Supreme Court. What does it take to be an "elite" in her eyes? Has Laura been working the counter at Walgreen's? I don't think so. And since when did trying to stand up for the average American become an "elite" idea? I think what they mean by "elite" is anyone who knows what he's talking about and therefore disagrees with Laura Ingraham and Rush Limbaugh.

Eric Alterman did a great piece on Ingraham for *Salon*, in which he described her "amazing audacity and embarrassing ignorance." Apparently, he and Ingraham were both on the set of MSNBC just after TWA flight 800 blew up over Long Island, and former Israeli Prime Minister Shimon Peres was there for an interview. She asked him if he didn't think it was a good idea for the U.S. to bomb Syria or Libya in response. As Alterman describes it, "Peres clearly thought she was nuts and did his best to explain that no one even knew if foul play had been involved yet."

From this and other encounters, Alterman came to the conclusion that "this woman was more full of shit than just about anyone I had ever met." But then again, "She is young, sexy, and ambitious. She argues politics the way lawyers argue cases, as if there can be no possible interpretation other than her own, and what can possibly be the matter with her pathetically out-to-lunch opponent?"

By being that opponent, Alterman learned a thing or two about how the media game is played in the age of images. Back in 1996, in a debate on the tube, Alterman tried to argue that the real issue between Clinton and Dole was the effect of global capitalism on people's daily lives and on their local communities. "She just laughed," he said. "We were, after all, on television. Just how did I expect to explain to soccer moms that their problems lay not with taxes or family values but with highly mobile capital markets? Laura looked and sounded great and responded with some snappy Republican campaign slogan. I was toast."

The Big Hustle distorts logic, facts and figures, even the historical record, and replaces them with great visuals. The words come and go; the pictures stay in your mind.

Ann Coulter, like Ingraham and Limbaugh, is an entertainer.

She earned her chops on "Politically Incorrect," which, you may remember, airs on Comedy Central. She grew up in ritzy New Canaan, Connecticut, where her father was a lawyer for Phelps Dodge mining, and her mother was a Daughter of the American Revolution. She went to Ivy League Cornell, then worked for Senator Spencer Abraham, founder of the Federalist Society. Can you say . . . *elites?* She joined the Paula Jones defense team, but could not keep Paula from being sentenced to Fox's "Celebrity Boxing," where she had the crap kicked out of her by disgraced ice skating champ Tonya Harding.

David Brock described Coulter's "virulent anti-Semitism," and said that she often talked about wanting to leave her New York law firm "to get away from all these Jews." He described her as venting her anger and cruelty by hurling insults at liberals and poor people. And, according to the *New York Observer,* she did most of her moralizing against Clinton while she carried on a relationship with my fellow pornographer Bob Guccione, Jr.

Ann is like a sick comic who just happens not to be funny. She gets paid to say stupid, outrageous things, like "liberals instinctively root for anarchy and against civilization." Given conservative attitudes toward the arts and arts organizations, their refusal to pay for educational reform, and their lack of interest in promoting a civil society, I'd say that Ann has it exactly backward.

Some of her more insane remarks got her booted as a columnist for *National Review.* I think it was the bit about how our policy toward all Arab nations should be to "invade their countries, kill their leaders, and convert them to Christianity." I think she just sits around trying to come up with the craziest thing she can think up, then practices saying it with a straight face.

Bill O'Reilly is the best reason for censorship I've ever seen.

As much as I believe in free speech, Bill O'Reilly is the best reason for censorship I've ever seen. The only thing O'Reilly and I have ever agreed on is that we both oppose the death penalty. Other than that, I think he's an arrogant SOB who, if he were a journalist, would give journalists a bad name. He only invites two kinds of people to his show. He either brings on someone who agrees with his position and sucks up to him, or he brings on some pathetic slob who's unable to defend himself, then beats up on him.

O'Reilly's greatest moment was during the summer of 2003, when he pushed Fox to sue Al Franken over the use of Lord O'Reilly's graven image on the cover of *Lies and the Lying Liars Who Tell Them*. The suit also claimed that, because Fox had a trademark on the words "fair and balanced," Franken couldn't use them to describe his book. I'm convinced that O'Reilly put Fox up to suing, because anyone with half a brain and a lot less ego inflation could see that the claim was laughable. Filing that suit was a vanity project, a loss leader Fox had to take on to salve their star's wounded pride. And the judge did laugh them out of court, making O'Reilly look like the idiot he is. Paul Newman wrote a piece in the *Times* saying that he was going to sue the Department of Housing and Urban Development for using an acronym that stole the name of his first big starring role, *HUD*. Franken came back by saying that he had trademarked the word "funny."

The unbelievable arrogance that O'Reilly demonstrated seems to have become a conservative trademark. They truly worship their icons, which are often themselves.

Remember the Reagan biopic that was scheduled to be on CBS in the fall of 2003? This was a $9 million investment, scheduled for the November ratings sweeps—a pretty big deal. But then word got out that the script did not depict the Gipper as Jesus on a flaming bun, and all hell broke loose. Apparently, the biggest infraction against the Republicans' myth-making was a slight paraphrase of something Reagan actually said, a line quoted in the *Dutch* biography by Edmund Morris, to the effect that AIDS might be the judgment of God in retribution on these sodomite sinners. The radio call-in people got hold of this, the screamers on

"The McLaughlin Group" screamed, and the chairman of the Republican National Committee grabbed the phone. Next thing you know, the President of CBS, Leslie Moonves, personally sends the show back to the minor leagues to air on Showtime, a pay cable channel.

When the Reagan movie actually aired, it had all the bite and controversy of the Weather Channel. But free and open debate clearly is not a part of the American tradition that conservatives seem interested in conserving. And sadly, they have the power to either buy or bully into oblivion anyone who disagrees with them. They even have their own cable news network to help them.

When Fox News Guards the Henhouse

On November 1, 2003, the *L.A. Times* offered a little insight into how the images come to be made at that "fair and balanced" network—one of whose commentators, by the way, was recently overheard referring to Michael Moore as a "pinko" and a "commie." What is this, 1950?

Charlie Reina, a veteran of ABC, CBS, and the AP, left Fox after working there for six years. In October 2003, he posted a letter on the Web site of the Poynter Institute, an organization that promotes journalistic ethics. As I've mentioned, Fox is run by Roger Ailes, the Nixon and Reagan image-maker. Lee Atwater once described Ailes as having two speeds, "attack, and destroy." Reina's letter referred to Fox as "Roger's revenge" against the mainstream media who always thought Ailes was a creep. Reina also makes the point that Rupert Murdoch, who owns Fox, is willing to lose $40 million a year on the *New York Post* in order to do his part for the Big

> **Lee Atwater once described Ailes as having two speeds, "attack, and destroy."**

Hustle in the Big Apple. Fox allows him to keep the disinformation flowing and make a profit.

Reina's letter described how, unlike legitimate news organizations, the Fox newsroom "is under the constant control and vigilance of management . . . a news network run by one of the most high-profile political operatives of recent times." Reina told the *Times,* "I'd never worked in a newsroom like that. Never. At ABC . . . I never knew what management or my bosses' political views were, much less felt pressure to make things come out a certain way. . . . At CBS or the AP, if a word got in that suggested bias—liberal or conservative—it was taken out." But the roots of Fox's "day-to-day on-air bias come in the form of an executive memo" from John Mood, the network's vice-president for news, and these memos are "distributed electronically each morning, addressing what stories will be covered and, often, suggesting how they should be covered."

In his interview with the *Times,* Reina offers examples of how the story of the day gets hammered and hammered, just as if it came from the White House press office and Karl Rove. Which, ultimately, it does. Av Westin, executive director of the National Television Academy, told the *Times,* "Nothing about this surprises me. The uniform smirks and body language that are apparent in Fox's reports throughout the day reflect an operation that is quite tightly controlled. The fact that young and inexperienced producers acquiesce to that control by pulling stories is further evidence that nonjournalistic forces are at work in that newsroom. Roger runs that place with an iron hand and he was put there by Murdoch who selected him for his politics." Describing the young anchors, Reina said, "As they near the time to get their own show, the hair gets blonder and the bias gets clearer."

CNN's Christiane Amanpour expressed some regret about the way her network went along with Bush's march to war, admitting that "Perhaps, to a certain extent, my station was intimidated by the administration and its foot soldiers at Fox News." A spokesman for Fox came back with: "It's better to be viewed as a foot soldier for Bush than as a spokeswoman for al Qaeda." Is admitting you were "had" by a deceitful administration the same as being a supporter of the terrorists? Does that Fox spokesman *really* think that Christine Amanpour is a spokeswoman for al Qaeda? Or is he just an asshole who will say any stupid thing to toe the party line and hurt the other team? And how "fair and balanced" is that?

Intimidating reporters by constantly haranguing about "liberal bias in the news" as well as spinning false images that linger as false impressions—these techniques work. Is it any wonder, then, that the White House has been trying to weaken the Federal Communications Commission so that fat cats like Fox owner Murdoch can buy up more and more media outlets anywhere they please?

> **The White House has been trying to weaken the Federal Communications Commission so that fat cats like Fox owner Murdoch can buy up more and more media outlets.**

In the past, we maintained the very American idea that no one person should gain too much control over the news. But Bush's FCC chairman, Michael K. Powell, never saw a right-wing special interest that he didn't like. The good news is that even Republicans in the Senate have more sense—sometimes—than the radical Republicans in the Bush inner circle, and in September 2003, they voted down Bush's rule changes. Even conservative columnist and former Nixon speech writer William Safire came down in opposition to the Bush camp on this one, calling their efforts "the ruination of free TV."

As for the intimidation factor in today's media, reporter Joe Conason got to the heart of it in an interview with Rich Bond, former chairman of the Republican National Committee. "There is some strategy to it," Bond told Conason. "I'm a coach of kids' basketball and Little League teams. If you watch any great coach, what they try to do is work the refs." "Working the ref" means yelling and screaming about the unfairness of every call against you so the referee will think twice before blowing the whistle. You see this every night in pro basketball—guys acting outraged, pretending that the other guy fouled them. As Bond put it, the point is that "maybe the ref will cut you a little slack on the next one."

For ten years or more, the mainstream media has cut the right-wingers far too much slack. Thoroughly intimidated, they tiptoe around Bush's deceptions, just like they did when Gingrich was trying to steal the government back during the Clinton years. The right-wingers have learned to work the ref so well that their supposedly "biased" treatment from the mainstream media is all you hear about, endlessly, from all the right-wingers who have their own huge pulpits in the mainstream media! This is nonsense. Rush Limbaugh can broadcast this absurd complaint each day to 20 million listeners. As Conason says, "It is a subject that essentially has its own cable outlet . . . in the form of Fox News Channel."

Press Poodles

Just after Labor Day 2003, nine candidates for the Democratic Party nomination for president met for their first nationally televised debate. The event was upstaged the same evening by NFL Kick-off Night in Times Square, a big blowout featuring Bon Jovi and Enrique Iglesias. But what really made headlines, as well as magazine covers, all over the world, and was by far the most reported and analyzed event of that week, was Madonna slipping her tongue down Britney Spears's throat at the MTV awards a few nights before.

There are two things political observers can learn from this:

Point #1: The nation as a whole is made up of a great many not exactly deep thinkers.

If we don't pay attention, the lying hypocrites will rob us blind.

When we're waiting in line at the checkout counter, we're flipping through *People*, not *Foreign Policy Review*. Trouble is, though, democracy is not just a spectator sport. If we don't pay attention, the lying hypocrites will rob us blind.

Point #2: While there was once a profession called journalism, which used to serve as a sort of bullshit detector in opposition to power, it has been replaced in all but a few places with what is known as "the media." The media doesn't dig to find the truth and confront politicians with it. The media simply goes along with whatever is put in front of its cameras. Everyone in the "entertainment-news" business knew that Madonna's tongue-wrestling episode was a stunt meant to give a boost to two flagging careers, but that didn't matter. Networks and newspapers can be—and are—routinely manipulated by anyone savvy enough to do so, and Madonna is the greatest manipulator since P. T. Barnum.

Whether they're wise to the game or being duped, mainstream news organizations continue to play along. Instead of serving as the watchdogs they're supposed to be, they've been turned into cute little poodles—and neutered, to boot.

We're all lazy to some extent, and we want to get our information as quickly and painlessly as we can. So we don't always read other information that would expand on what we hear on the tube, or help clarify what's really true, or even just give us another point of view. We tend to believe the first thing we hear, or the image the spin-doctors hand us, and stop there. American voters need to understand more about how we're being spun around and what the rules of engagement really are. And then we need to become engaged. We need to demand more from the media than commentary about John Kerry's hair.

How Dumbed Down Is Dumb Enough?

If you want to blame the media poodles for something, forget the phony "liberal bias" accusations the conservatives love to throw around. Instead, blame the media for dumbing down the level of political discussion. Blame them for setting up their cameras just where Karl Rove wants them to as they play along with a photo-op presidency. They allow themselves to be manipulated, they trivialize the real issues, and they play up horse race issues that are easy to grasp. As a result, they've turned politics into a sideshow and paved the way for politicians who are pure media creations.

In Hollywood, there's an old joke that politics is show business for ugly people. Who would have guessed that the joke would become literally true, that politics would *actually* become show business? Frank Rich, the *Times'* op-ed writer, didn't mince words in a September 14, 2003, piece he wrote: "Only in America could a guy who struts in an action hero's Hollywood costume and barks macho lines from a script pass for a plausible political leader." Comparing our new governor in California, Arnold Schwar-zenegger, to W, Rich added, "At least Schwarzenegger is a show-biz pro. He never would have signed on for a remake of *Top Gun* without first ensuring that it would have the same happy ending as the original."

Arnold's showbiz savvy paid off in his bid to be governor of California, just like many of us predicted. But just because we saw his victory coming didn't mean we knew how to make sense of it. When he was elected, the *Onion* reacted by publishing its first factually correct headline:

MUSCLEMAN PUT IN CHARGE OF WORLD'S FIFTH LARGEST ECONOMY

They didn't know how to make a joke about this, because it was already a joke—on us, the citizens of the golden state. Arnold is all image all the time, which is why he's the perfect politician for today. Forget ideas. It's all about seeing yourself on TV, and checking out how you look in the mirror. Arnold has spent the last forty years staring at himself in the mirror, trying to perfect every muscle in his butt. As Bob Herbert wrote in the *Times,* "He doesn't

Arnold has spent the last forty years staring at himself in the mirror, trying to perfect every muscle in his butt.

want to govern. He just wants to be adored." Herbert offered up some prize quotes from a book proposal Arnold circulated back in the seventies: "The feeling like Kennedy had, you know, to speak to maybe 50,000 people at one time and having them cheer, or like Hitler in the Nuremberg stadium. And have all those people scream at you and just being in total agreement with whatever you say."

Kennedy, Hitler . . . what's the difference? To someone like Schwarzenegger, it's not about policies or ideas. It's all about screaming crowds. So it was perfect that he announced his candidacy on "The Tonight Show."

The Pew Research Center has done studies showing that about a third of Americans under thirty now consider Jay Leno and David Letterman to be "news sources." Leno went on to participate in Arnold's victory party, breaking a long tradition in which the late night hosts stayed out of politics. Now that they get taken seriously as news sources, they're becoming political.

I don't think Americans should get their news or political views spoon fed to them by talk show hosts. And I don't think "all image, all the time" is a valid way to make our national decisions. There are still some of us who care about real issues and who want hard news. I'm one of them, which is why I sued Donald Rumsfeld and the Department of Defense in 2002.

Suing Rummy

Anyone watching the news on American television during the winter of 2002 would have seen the map of Afghanistan with nifty, full color graphics, and journalists standing by who appeared to be covering the war. The fact is, we had no media with the troops

in Afghanistan. Hardly anyone realized that most western reporters were being kept far from the front lines. The war news
was being censored. We were being spoon fed commentary and
military press releases masquerading as hard news. That was not
only an insult to the American people, it was a huge disservice to
news coverage in general.

I remember Geraldo Rivera "reporting from Kandahar." He
walked the hallowed ground where Americans had died, said the
Lord's Prayer, and got choked up. Later, we found out that he was
in Tora Bora, hundreds of miles away from the incident he was reporting on!

The lack of real coverage of these significant events was a serious violation of our First Amendment rights and a significant
warning to us that, in the Bush administration's war on terrorism,
our rights as a free people were fading fast. To deny the press access is to deny the American people knowledge of what their government is doing in their name. I felt very strongly that citizens
had a right to know what our leaders were getting us into, especially with all the potential for a wider conflict, including reprisals
in the form of further terrorism back in the States.

On November 16, 2001, I filed a lawsuit against Donald Rumsfeld and the Department of Defense seeking press access to the
military action in Afghanistan.
This was the first time in the
history of our country that anyone ever sued the government
to get press access to the battlefield. I simply thought that
Rumsfeld and Bush should do
whatever they were going to do
in full view of the American
people.

This was the first time in the history of our country that anyone ever sued the government to get press access to the battlefield.

There were two hearings before Judge Paul L. Friedman in the
District of Columbia. Just like in my battle to defend parody as a
form of social commentary, I was once again doing the heavy lift-

ing for the networks and all the mainstream newspapers. I had even sought out Floyd Abrams, the best First Amendment attorney in the country, to represent me. But his clients included most of the major television networks, as well as the *New York Times,* and the *Times* would not give him permission to act on my behalf.

The major media never even acknowledged my legal action by covering it as news. A few local radio shows picked up the story, and a couple of local television newscasts mentioned it, but the national debate I hoped to stimulate never happened.

In the 1980s, when Reagan invaded Granada, the press didn't have a clue what was going on then either. I filed a similar suit demanding press access, but the judge simply sat on it, and the war ended before he was forced to render a judgment. I didn't want that to happen again.

The press had not been included when the first President Bush invaded Panama. During the Gulf War, only a small press pool was allowed access. The American people didn't realize this, but the only person giving us real, first-hand coverage was Peter Arnett, standing on the rooftop of his hotel in Baghdad, giving a blow-by-blow report on the war. No one was on the ground with the troops.

Our initial hearing was on January 4, 2002. The few reporters who were paying attention asked if this was a publicity stunt. I can get irritated when reporters refer to what I'm doing as "publicity," and I like to remind them of the following: When my investigation during the impeachment hearings was released, resulting in Speaker-Elect Bob Livingston's resignation, nobody could say that was a publicity stunt. When I defended the First Amendment in Cincinnati in 1977, and was sentenced to twenty-five years in prison, nobody could think that was a publicity

> **When I stick to my beliefs and act on them—often for the benefit of all Americans, often at great personal cost —I may attract publicity. But please don't call it a "stunt."**

stunt. I won that case on appeal. In 1978, when I was shot while fighting a legal battle for the First Amendment in Georgia, and the bullet confined me to a wheelchair for the rest of my life, nobody could think that was a publicity stunt. During the DeLorean cocaine trafficking case in Los Angeles, when I refused to give up my source and was sentenced to fifteen months in prison, nobody could say that was a publicity stunt. When I stick to my beliefs and act on them—often for the benefit of all Americans, often at great personal cost—I may attract publicity. But please don't call it a "stunt."

In May 2002, the United States District Court of the District of Columbia recognized that there was "a substantial likelihood under the First Amendment that the press is guaranteed a right to gather and report news involving United States military operations on foreign soil, subject to reasonable regulations to protect the safety and security of both the journalists and those involved in those operations, as well as the secrecy and confidentiality of information whose dissemination could endanger United States soldiers or our allies, or compromise military operations."

I was very encouraged that the Court recognized a "substantial likelihood" of a First Amendment right of access, and the restrictions outlined by the Court appeared reasonable. But still I was concerned that the president would invoke executive privilege to cloak the Defense Department. We were looking forward to making everyone directly involved—Donald Rumsfeld, Victoria Clarke, Tommy Franks, the joint chiefs of staff, the field commander in Afghanistan—appear and give a deposition. That way, we could ask them directly why the press was not being allowed near front lines. What were they trying to hide?

Why should the executive branch, including the Defense Department, be exempt from the kind of scrutiny the other two branches are subject to? The legislative branch—the House and the Senate—has to conduct its business in the open, with full access for the media. The judicial branch, likewise, conducts trials that are open to the public as well as reporters.

The military could always say that the press might interfere with their operations by revealing tactical information. That's why I made concessions in my suit that the field commander could screen reportage and footage that is gained by independent reporters.

A television crew might shoot fifteen minutes of film, and the military might authorize only two minutes of it for broadcast. That's fine, but what you have left is thirteen minutes, and when the conflict is over, those valuable minutes are preserved for posterity. An accurate record should be made and preserved to inform the public how the war was conducted and to learn from it.

One argument against access might be that "reporters will lose their lives," but reporters were *volunteering* to go. If journalists want to risk their lives to cover the war, how can the government say they don't have a right to do it? I think the only reason the Defense Department wanted to deny reporters access was the fear that if the ground troops made a mistake, it would be broadcast all over the world.

It's the obligation of the press to report on how our nation conducts itself in armed conflict. We have a tradition of press access to the battlefield dating back to the Civil War, when Lincoln himself changed strategies based on news of what was happening supplied by reporters. World War I, World War II, the Korean conflict, and Vietnam were all aggressively covered by the media. But after Vietnam, the president and top advisors started treating the press either as adversaries, or as children to be spoon fed selected images.

How could the press be so passive in accepting this kind of censorship? After 9/11, why didn't they care that that they weren't being allowed to do the jobs they'd been trained for? Why was I the only person fighting the Department of Defense? Were the mainstream reporters too worried about retribution? Were they afraid of being shut out of the next interview or photo op with George or Laura?

Who was on the scene to report whether the people in Afghanistan were really being treated fairly? Who was on the inside to let us know what was really going on? Why were most reporters perfectly okay with hearing only what those in power wanted us to know?

Mainstream passivity over the issue of access was the same as when I went to trial against Jerry Falwell in the eighties. When I lost that case in its preliminary stages, I couldn't get a single member of the mainstream media to file a "friend of the court" brief to show their support for the First Amendment issue at stake. But when the Supreme Court stunned them all by agreeing to take my case, suddenly the mainstream media was all on the bandwagon.

> **When the Supreme Court stunned them all by agreeing to take my case, suddenly the mainstream media was all on the bandwagon.**

Human Rights Watch Is Watching Us

After the action in Afghanistan, I was also concerned about the prisoners being taken away for detention in Cuba. Roughly 660 people from forty different countries, including some teenagers, have been held without being charged and without access to attorneys. Because the Guantanamo Naval Base land is leased from Cuba (a "perpetual" arrangement established a century ago) the legal status of these people is murky, to say the least. Because they are non-U.S. citizens held in a non-U.S. territory, the president and his circle have maintained that the U.S. courts have no jurisdiction.

Donald Rumsfeld has said, "As I understand it, technically unlawful combatants do not have any rights under the Geneva Conventions." Rumsfeld's interpretation means that these people could be held forever. That's why Human Rights Watch is now watching *us*. Are we all comfortable with that as Americans? Eight governments have filed formal complaints. A spokesman for Amnesty International told Reuters News Service that America's "treatment of the detainees is in our view a human rights scandal that violates international law and damages U.S. claims to be a country upholding the rule of law." They also described the camp at Guantanamo as a "black hole."

Terry Waite, the former special envoy to the Archbishop of Canterbury who was held prisoner for five years in Beirut, said that the U.S. "seems to be making up rules as it goes along." He was "appalled" by what we were doing and asked "is this justice or revenge?" Fortunately, the U.S. Supreme Court agreed in November of 2003 to review the notion that these people fall outside the jurisdiction of U.S. courts.

Initial reports said how dangerous and violent these prisoners were, and that they needed to be medicated, but those claims where not backed up by any reporters who were actually there to see it firsthand. This information was fed to reporters by the Defense Department. Without unbiased observers on the ground, all we know is what the Defense Department wants us to hear.

The BBC carried the story of a Kabul taxi driver who said he simply went to work one day and, next thing you know, he's swept up by U.S. forces and carted away to Cuba. He was detained for nine months before being released. He was never charged. No explanation was ever given, nor, presumably, will it ever be, because no one is on the scene to document what is going on or to hold the U.S. government accountable.

On the morning of January 23, 2003, Court TV called to inquire about the status of my lawsuit against the Defense Department. They were airing a show the following day on the lack of satisfaction we were getting from the court system. They asked me if I was angry because my suit was basically being ignored. I told them of course I was, and the American people should be angry too.

On February 19, 2003, U.S. District Judge Paul Friedman threw out our suit. He claimed that the Pentagon had placed my

Hustler reporter on a list of journalists who would be allowed to travel with ground troops under special conditions. The judge said because Defense Department officials did not formally deny access to the reporter, he had no jurisdiction to address the issue of whether journalists have a constitutional right to accompany U.S. troops engaged in ground combat.

As hostilities relocated and the war in Iraq got under way, the Pentagon agreed to allow the press to accompany the troops. I believe my initial lawsuit helped propel the Pentagon to make the decision to allow the press in. The Pentagon's decision also gave the judge a convenient way to dismiss my suit. In that brief, I was asking for press access to *all* wars, be they wars of "terror" or otherwise, and I am still seeking a decision, whether it be from the Appellate Court or the Supreme Court, stating that the press has a First Amendment right to cover war—period.

The international press corps has done its job with great bravery in Iraq and far too many have paid with their lives. Unfortunately, we are still not seeing everything they cover because the networks say the images are too graphic. But I think they have it wrong. The people need to see the truth. The government wants to sugar-coat reality in the hope of getting buy-in from an uncritical public. That was the whole point of the DOD's effort to turn Jessica Lynch into some kind of hillbilly Joan of Arc.

> **The government wants to sugar-coat reality in the hope of getting buy-in from an uncritical public.**

Once again, the press is taking its marching orders from the government and not doing what press is supposed to do: report the uncensored truth.

Walter Cronkite, the anchorman who simply would not let Carter off the hook for our hostages being held in Iran, was from the old school. He trained with Edward R. Murrow and the trench-coat guys back when being a foreign correspondent was serious business and had nothing to do with info-tainment. When Cronkite went to Vietnam, he interviewed General Westmoreland, the man in charge, and he asked him about deceptive body counts and who was really winning the war. You'll never see reporters today asking Tommy Franks, our battlefield commander in Iraq, such blunt questions.

Our journalists are too constrained by buttoned-down corporate behavior, as well as don't-buck-the-system corporate financial concerns. They—or their bosses—have stockholders to answer to, and apparently, that trumps their sense of responsibility to the public.

A Different Kind of Gag Rule

For a few months after I placed the million-dollar ad in *The Washington Post* in October 1998, I held press conferences about sexual hypocrisy in Washington. The events were standing room only, with rooms overflowing with media from every news organization on the planet, news cameras banging into one another, reporters yelling their questions out of turn.

I had established myself as a reliable investigative source. I had shown that I was able to uncover and confirm information that others were drooling to get. I was interviewed and written about by every major newspaper and magazine in the country. But when I was ready to reveal an unpleasant truth about the most powerful family in America, I went back to being a pariah that no one would touch.

What I had to say might have saved us all a great deal of grief, if the media had not refused to do their jobs. That's because character counts. Character counts everywhere, but especially in the White House, where the most difficult decisions on the planet need to be made. I've already discussed the hypocrisy, as well as the moral and intellectual vacuum at the top there now. Lack of leadership has allowed the most disastrous foreign policy in American

SEX, LIES & POLITICS   171

history to unfold on top of the most disastrous economic policy in American history. And I could see it coming, because I had received a tip.

Back in 2000, I got a phone call from an attorney from Houston. He represented a woman we'll call "Susan," who supposedly could prove that, back in the early seventies, George W. Bush had arranged an abortion for his girlfriend.

This woman, Susan, told us that in 1971, she was dating a guy who was a Bush family friend. She said that she had been in the room when this boyfriend of hers—we'll call him "Clyde"—took the call from a very agitated W. The way she told the story, Young Bush was in a panic because he'd gotten his girl knocked up. According to Susan, Clyde told Bush to relax, that he'd take care of everything. She gave us the name of the hospital where the procedure supposedly took place; she even gave us the name of the doctor who supposedly performed it.

Now if this story was true, I thought it was something the American people ought to know about. After all, here was this ultraconservative, anti-abortion governor of Texas running for President as a "family values" candidate. Was he playing by the hypocritical double standard of the conservative rulebook, namely, that certain indulgences are okay for the rich, but not for ordinary Americans? This abortion, if it occurred, was carried out before *Roe v. Wade* made the procedure legal. Bush was successfully slipping past allegations of cocaine use, drunk driving, and being a useless rich boy, but arranging for an abortion was a more serious matter. Bush's own supporters said that abortion is murder.

I sent a couple of reporters down to Texas to check out Susan's claims. My investigators were able to substantiate the following: In 1971, Bush, Clyde, and the supposedly pregnant girl in question—let's call her "Rayette"—all lived at the same singles apartment complex in Houston, one that was known for its party scene. They confirmed that Clyde was loosely assigned to keep the family black sheep, young W, out of trouble. They also found the doctor in question. He said he remembered Rayette—described her as the best-looking woman at the apartment complex—and he confirmed that he had done procedures at the hospital Susan had named. But of course, he denied ever having performed an illegal abortion.

My reporters were unable to gain any evidence from the hospital: the institution had been sold several times over the years and their records were spotty. They found Rayette living elsewhere in Texas. Through her husband, she denied having had the illegal procedure—which is not surprising.

Susan, in an effort to jump-start the investigation, contacted Clyde, told him that some reporters were bugging her about the incident, and asked for his help. She told us that he first casually denied any knowledge of what she was talking about, then in a later conversation, threatened her and told her to keep her mouth shut.

Now if this Susan was a liar, she was a liar who was telling a story that made a lot of sense. Her details checked out but, without solid evidence, this was as far as we could take it. Unless the girl involved would go on record, there was no way we could prove anything. Not according to the standards journalists use in deciding when they can run a story—and certainly not in a court of law, if challenged.

Still, I wanted to make damn sure that the major networks were aware of these allegations. Likewise the *Los Angeles Times* and the *Washington Post. Hustler* isn't a major news organization, and we didn't have reporters on the campaign trail. But I wanted somebody who did have access to the candidate to ask the question, to follow up. The big media had opportunities to confront the man on a daily basis. Surely, with all the legwork we'd done and the circumstantial evidence we'd lined up, there was enough of a basis for asking a freakin' question. After all, they had asked him about his drinking and cocaine use without ever having any proof.

I got a reporter from one of the major network news programs to come to my office to see what we had. I remember him staring down at the files for a long while, then shaking his head. "We just can't do it," he said.

Here was a candidate of the sanctimonious right, running on an anti-abortion platform, and all I wanted was someone from the mainstream press to ask him: "Governor Bush, have you ever paid for or facilitated an abortion?" I pleaded with this guy, but I think he didn't want to take the heat for tip-

> **All I wanted was someone from the mainstream press to ask him: "Governor Bush, have you ever paid for or facilitated an abortion?"**

ping the election with a single story. Little did he know how corrupt that election was going to be.

During the three months before the November election, the late summer and early fall of 2000, I tried to get on network television to pose the question myself.

Howard Stern put me on the air to talk about what we'd found, for which I was grateful, but my interview ran only on his live radio show, and not on his "E!" channel television program.

In L.A., I appeared on KROQ-FM's "Kevin and Bean Morning Show," but it was as if the interview had never happened. Anyone calling the station after my appearance was told that, owing to technical difficulties, my interview was not available as a tape or transcript. That interview with Kevin and Bean aired in August—two months before the election—but no one else would touch the story or have me on to talk about it.

On October 20, 2000, "Crossfire," the debate-style show on CNN, was doing a program about a study that had just come out about blocking explicit material on the Internet. They wanted to have me on as a guest to talk about whether porn sites should screen out certain material from minors. I agreed to come on, in part, because I knew this would give me national exposure to talk about Bush. Once you get on live television, they can't really control what you say. Or so I thought.

The hosts that evening were the conservative Bob Novak and the liberal Bill Press. The show began and we talked for two seg-

> I went into my spiel about Bush and the girl, about what we'd found, and about how the mainstream media wouldn't touch the story.

ments about the restrictions on the Internet—should there be more, should there be less. Then, as we got down to the wire, Novak acknowledged that I had something to say about the election. I went into my spiel about Bush and the girl, about what we'd found, and about how the mainstream media wouldn't touch the story.

Then, as Jerry Politex and his online column, "Bush Watch," reported

> Novak replied at that point, "Mr. Flynt, you said if it's true and you have no proof of that. I gather you are a very strong—" Flynt, whose previous investigation of national-level politicians led to at least one resignation from Congress, loudly interrupted, "The hell we don't have proof!"

> The camera cut from Flynt in L.A. back to Bill Press and Robert Novak, sheepishly grinning in the studio. Novak said, "Larry Flynt, thank you very, very much for joining us."

> Press added, "You never know. Live television."

I had better luck getting the story out in the CNN chat room after the appearance, but still no one would touch it. A few weeks earlier, Gail Sheehy did a profile of Bush in *Vanity Fair* in which she talked about his being dyslexic. Again, the other media outlets wouldn't go near this kind of personal story, except the *New Republic,* which used the article as an excuse to pummel Gail Sheehy.

Unless you were an Internet freak, then, or had seen "Crossfire," chances are you would never have known anything about my interview. There had been a tiny chance for the story to break through to the surface. Maybe some journalist would take the question and put it before Bush. But no such luck.

Syndicated columnist Liz Smith tried to breathe new life into the controversy, but even she was censored. She submitted her story to run the day before the election. Her column appears in over 100 newspapers nationwide. She rarely, if ever, gets edited. Yet the item on Bush was cut from every paper except the *New Jersey Star-Ledger.*

EXCERPT FROM LIZ SMITH'S COLUMN
The New Jersey Star-Ledger, November 6, 2000

TROUBLE FOR GEORGE—Hot on the heels of the George W. Bush DUI revelation (in Maine, it's called OUI—Operating Under the Influence), comes word that porn-king muck-raker Larry Flynt is charging that a girlfriend of W's, back in 1970, had an abortion. But that's not the story, as there's no evidence that Bush even knew about the pregnancy. The real story—according to the Internet's About. com—is that Flynt's remarks were apparently censored from CNN's "Crossfire," and the entire transcript of the show vanished from the CNN web site. The media has been willing to crucify Bill and Hillary Clinton with the worst sort of specious rumor-mongering, so why was this sleazy tidbit too hot for the "responsible" press to ask about?

I contacted Army Archerd, the legendary Hollywood columnist for *Daily Variety,* an industry newspaper. Army has always been a strong advocate of truth in politics, and I should have contacted him months before, but I had been hoping for a major, main-stream paper to pick it up. On November 7, 2000, the very day of the election, Army ran the following item in his nationally syndicated column that recaps the whole story from beginning to end.

FREEDOM OF THE PRESS? Larry Flynt says his comments about a hush-hush 1970 Houston abortion, on a rumored girlfriend of George W. Bush, have been stifled by the mainstream media. (Flynt claims knowledge of the identity of the girl, the hospital, etc. He never printed it, "because she'd deny it; you'd have egg on your face and you'd face a libel suit.") Still, he's more concerned with the fact that the media is ignoring the rumors. Flynt's comments on the subject were reportedly edited from his "Crossfire" appearance; his appearance on Howard Stern aired only on radio, not TV; and his "Court File" appearance, booked on Friday, was unbooked Monday. I spoke to Flynt, who claims this rumor about Bush was known to "the mainstream media for some time. But they never picked it up to investigate. My whole focus," Flynt said, "was on the lack of investigation by the media—in other words, they never asked Bush."

Blacking Out the World

In a world that gets its news from television, if there's no camera around when it happened, it didn't happen. That's one of the reasons why Americans don't know much about the rest of the world. The media conglomerates that control news organizations have cut back on overseas bureaus. Years ago, they decided that we didn't care about Muslim unrest in the Middle East, for instance. The networks have rooms full of MBAs squeezing the margin to feed the bottom line, and anything they can cut back, they will. That's part of the reason we were blindsided by all the troubles brewing when they exploded on 9/11. Only a few eggheads on National Public Radio were paying attention.

The fact that the public wasn't paying attention is how, in the 1980s, Reagan and Bush the First could arm Osama so he could fight Russians in Afghanistan, and then, when Osama turned those arms against us, Bush II could express simple-minded explanations like "these people hate freedom." Same thing with the

U.S. arming Saddam against the Iranians, ignoring him when he used poison gas against the Kurds, then suddenly deciding that he is the lynch pin on the axis of evil and we have to take him out.

A half-asleep, ill-informed public is the greatest thing that ever happened to politicians who want to manipulate us to get their way. The world is a complicated place, and nobody can really understand what's going on by dozing through Dan Rather or Peter Jennings between commercials for Preparation H. Big media decides what is news and what is hype; what to report and how it should be reported, and what to keep from the American people. And guess what? The crony capitalists pushing for tax cuts for the rich and contracts for Halliburton are the same guys, or kissing cousins of the same guys, who own the media empires.

> **A half-asleep, ill-informed public is the greatest thing that ever happened to politicians who want to manipulate us.**

Gutsy reporters have to check their balls at the door if they want to work for big-time TV. Even the best newspapers, the *New York Times*, the *Washington Post*, and the *L.A. Times*, have so many corporate constraints and legal constraints and constraints based on politeness and decorum and maintaining their prestige, that they still can be used like chumps by the likes of Karl Rove and George W. Bush. Our best hopes are the op-ed columnists like Frank Rich, Tom Friedman, and Maureen Dowd, all with the *New York Times*, and Howard Kurtz with the *Washington Post*, Robin Wright with the *Los Angeles Times*, and Robert Scheer on the occasions he still writes for the *Los Angeles Times*. Although Bob Woodward is not a regular columnist now, when he does write for the *Washington Post*, he does excellent reporting. These are great media watchdogs. I'm sure the more conservative press wishes they would disappear.

The information we had on Bush was certainly enough for a member of the press to publicly question him about whether or

> This was a question that could have changed the outcome of the presidential election.

not he'd ever facilitated an abortion. It was a sad day for real journalism when the media chose not to ask him, because this was a question that could have changed the outcome of the presidential election.

Fortunate Son

In early summer of 2000, shortly before the election, the book *Fortunate Son* by James H. Hatfield was yanked off the shelves in its first week of publication. Despite the fact that the book had already leapt to #8 on Amazon's bestseller list, the publisher, St. Martin's Press, destroyed 70,000 copies.

Was the book suddenly discovered to contain lies and slander? Had its substance been discredited? No, not at all. Then what was wrong? In this country founded on freedom of the press and free expression of ideas, what kind of power could force a book off the shelves like that?

Well, I've read it, and *Fortunate Son* actually paints a fairly sympathetic portrait of the future president. It almost makes him sound human. But that's certainly not why it got vaporized.

The book examines the Bush family's link to the Saudis, to the BCCI scandal, to W's insider trading with his Harken Oil stock, to the way W and his cronies at the Texas Rangers convinced the people of Arlington, Texas, to pay for a baseball stadium, then walked off with a bundle. But the American people seemed to have been sweet-talked out of any concern about W's ethics.

Fortunate Son also explored the fact that Senator Prescott Bush, George W's grandfather, worked for the Nazis from 1936 to 1942, when he was at the Union Bank in New York. But hell, Americans don't understand history. The governor of California's *father* was a Nazi, and nobody seems to care. Actually, I agree with that lack of concern. It's when our *current* politicians are Nazis that I worry!

Other reporters had asserted that W was a drunk for twenty years, and that he was arrested in Maine in 1976 for driving off the road and into a hedge.

The most salacious allegation in *Fortunate Son* was that W was busted for cocaine use in the early seventies, and that, in return for community service in a poor neighborhood, the crime was dropped from his record. Salon.com broke the story at about the same time, and nobody has ever shown that it was not accurate.

Nonetheless, just after the book's publication, the *Dallas Morning News* happened to get a tip that the author of *Fortunate Son* had a criminal past. No question about it, it wasn't pretty. Hatfield had been convicted in 1988 of paying a hit man to murder his former boss with a car bomb.

Hatfield was hardly the only ex-con to ever write a book, so why did his past suddenly disqualify him from having something worth reading? The public seems to love crooks and killers. Just look at all the books by the Watergate crew that hit the bestseller lists, or the ones by Mafia thugs and hitmen that are so popular. Legislators passed the "Son of Sam" laws to prevent criminal psychopaths from profiting from fat publishing contracts, but those laws were later repealed. When Norman Mailer championed Jack Abbott, a convicted murderer, literary types went wild over *In the Belly of the Beast,* Abbott's account of life in prison.

Hatfield did his time—he spent five years in the slammer—and then set about rebuilding his life. He started writing quiet little celebrity biographies that nobody paid much attention to. Then he decided to write about the Texas governor who might someday be a presidential contender. He hit the jackpot on that choice of subject—but then the jackpot exploded in his face.

Hatfield went from being an author with a hit book on his hands to being a pariah with no way to make a living. He got death threats from wing nuts. But more important, criticism of Bush was suddenly discredited along with Hatfield, and for the longest while nobody wanted to go there again.

Theories abound as to why the right wing harpies descended on this one book. Some people think there are lurid details in those pages we don't notice because the shit simply hasn't hit that particular fan yet. Sort of the way that being in bed with the bin Ladens didn't sound quite so bad . . . until 9/11.

The most interesting theory, though, is that Hatfield was a patsy all along. It later came to light that Hatfield had interviewed Bush buddies Clay Johnson and the evil genius himself, Karl Rove. Hatfield didn't know that they had done a check on him and knew all about his past. In August of 1999, when W did some loose talking about his wild past—he dodged a reporter's question about drug use in a way that left no doubt that he had used serious drugs prior to 1974—Rove saw Hatfield as a useful tool. Rove let the book go forward, telling tales that were already out of the bag, then dropped the hammer on him. It was the perfect way to silence the critics and move the national debate away from what a sleaze W really is.

Sometimes, when a negative story passes through the first news cycle, if the guy is still standing, it never happened. There are no consequences. It's like Arnold's sexcapades—the accusations of his groping and otherwise abusing women throughout his career in Hollywood. Now that he's governor, Arnold is "too busy" to investigate his own sex scandal, and the world moves on. That's because, unless there are zealots who keep feeding fuel into the fire to keep the story alive, as there were in the case of the attacks against Clinton, the media moves on. That's why the hustling tactics of a trial lawyer—the tactics Baker used in Florida

> **You do not attempt a reasonable, honest exchange of ideas. You destroy your opponent any way you can.**

and Gingrich and his buddies used against Clinton—win. You simply nuke the other side. You do not attempt a reasonable, honest exchange of ideas. You destroy your opponent any way you can, especially by attacking his credibility. You use PR stink bombs that linger in the air.

Fortunate Son got assassinated. Anytime the powers that be can have a book yanked off the shelf not because its filled with lies, but simply because they don't like it, we're all in trouble. Go back and watch those old black and white newsreels of the Nazis burning books and you'll see what I mean.

A documentary film about James Hatfield called *Horns and Halos* is making the rounds. I suggest you see it, but the ending isn't happy. He was found dead, presumably a suicide, in a Days Inn in Springdale, Arkansas, on July 18, 2001.

Checkbook Journalism

With CNN and all the rest of the cable outlets, we're on a twenty-four-hour news cycle. Reporters have acres of air time to fill, and the competition puts them into a feeding frenzy. All the major networks say they'll never pay for their information, and yet in indirect ways, they already do. Movie stars don't do magazine covers unless the story inside is the way they want it. Top gets like Michael Jackson can write their own interview, then agree to be interviewed.

And then there are slightly more subtle forms of playing ball. Barbara Walters didn't have to pay Monica Lewinsky for an interview, but the interview, worth several million dollars of advertising, aired the day Monica's book went on sale.

Some of the networks will do interviews with personalities with the expressed stipulation that they won't be available to the foreign markets. If you're conducting an interview with a subject in the U.S. market and he doesn't want you to air it in a foreign market, it's because he intends, obviously, to sell those rights to the foreign market. So checkbook journalism is already the order of the day.

How do you separate out the "news" function of a show like "Today" from the entertainment function? All media is going the way of "Entertainment Tonight," "Access Hollywood," and "Inside Edition."

The only drawback to checkbook journalism is the loss of integrity in the information you're getting. People might have a tendency, because they're getting money for their information, to embellish what they have to say. But, on the flip side of that coin, if people are telling the truth and do have something to tell that they wouldn't necessarily say without being paid, where's the harm?

During Clinton's impeachment and subsequent trial in the Senate, I spent a lot of money, not just on the sources relating to Livingston, but also on Bob Barr's ex-wife. We paid her $250,000 to reveal things she never would have under any other circumstances. When I use checkbook journalism, I go public with exactly what I paid and who got the money.

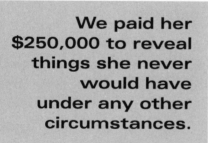

We paid her $250,000 to reveal things she never would have under any other circumstances.

The *National Enquirer,* the *Globe,* the *Sun,* and the *Star* all pay. As a result, they often get some serious and true stories before the mainstream papers have them. These papers all require three sources of verification before they will publish a story. The established media will resist this kind of checkbook journalism for as long as they can, but after they've been scooped enough for it to affect their bottom line, I think they'll cave.

Several years ago, when I was in Cedar Sinai Hospital in Los Angeles, Liz Taylor was in the room next to me. When they brought her in, I said to my nurse, "Hey, do you want to make a couple grand? Call the *National Enquirer* and tell them Liz Taylor's here and what room she's in." She called and they sent her a check for $1500.

What TV Won't Tell You

If you can't figure out the bias in news, you should just go stick your head in the sand, because you're beyond help anyway. Too many Americans buy into the news's propaganda on a nightly basis. Most people watch the news for entertainment value when they should be tuning in for real news and information. We need to learn how to watch it and how to decipher what is really going on.

When you see someone on television being used as a spokesperson to prove one point or another, always think of who you're *not* seeing. Network news stories are tailored by producers who decide who they want on air to make a story go a certain way. I can tell you from experience, they're not taking any chances with who they'll use. They always conduct what they call a "pre-interview" ahead of time, to see what you're going to say on air. Then the producers will try and script the segment to make it as predictable as possible.

Producers love it when their guests argue and yell at one another, and they encourage the high drama. It's good for the ratings, and you can't understand what anyone is saying anyway so you can't get into trouble. What they don't like are soft-spoken experts with well-researched opinions and grounded information, unless it proves a point their station managers want made.

Though my point of view might be unusual and not necessarily popular, that doesn't mean it shouldn't be heard. If I'm suing the Department of Defense because our free press is not allowed to cover a war in which American soldiers are fighting and I seek airtime to voice my opinion and raise the public's awareness, should I not be heard? Court TV was the only network that invited me on a show to discuss my lawsuit against the Defense Department and to open a dialogue with the American people about what was going on.

Most of the information we get is controlled by the source, and television is much more controlled than print. In television, everything comes in a sound bite. When you have a thirty-minute press conference or a three-hour meeting reduced to a ten-second quip, that gives the people selecting the sound bites a lot of power to shape public opinion.

Personally, I often wonder if I should just turn off the television for good and stop thinking that I might actually catch what's going on in the world if I watch it.

Every once in a while, I'm lucky enough to be privy to some piece of information before it breaks, and then it's interesting to see how it gets distilled by the time it hits the airways. I can see how it's been masked, or how the way it's told, or who tells it, can really slant the story and change its meaning. When I'm determined to get the straight story, I'll start surfing channels to see how each network is dealing with that particular issue.

The problem is, most people get all their information from TV. When you're on TV and you try to explain an idea in a thoughtful, in-depth fashion, you get cut off on the way to a commercial.

> **In this country, we've got maybe two million people who read, but nearly three hundred million people with opinions.**

Books are the form of media that allow for the most detailed explanations, but they don't reach a fraction of TV's audience. Even a huge bestseller like *Stupid White Men* reaches maybe a million people. A hit TV show reaches 20 million. Icelanders read more books than Americans do! In this country, we've got maybe two million people who read, but nearly three hundred million people with opinions. How are all those other opinions being formed?

We need more hard-hitting investigative reporters like Greg Palast. Why can the BBC handle him, but the U.S. media can't? He can tell you how, when our president was trying to stay out of Vietnam, and his daddy lined him up for the Texas Air National Guard, he tested at twenty-five out of one hundred—one point above "too-dumb-to-fly" status—yet the Guard slot was his. That position did not go to any of the other hundreds of applicants who tested way better.

Here's another story Palast can tell you, and that no mainstream media source is going to touch. Back in the late sixties, an aide to Ben Barnes—then lieutenant governor of Texas—suggested to Air Guard Chief Brigadier General James Rose that he find a safe spot for Congressman George Bush's son to hide.

Thirty years later, in 1994, the question of using family influence to keep W out of the war became a big issue when W was running fo governor. Funny how not one of the four Bush boys, patriots all, set foot in Vietnam. During that campaign, Bush was asked if daddy had helped him get in the Guard, and Bush, of course, said no. Bush has worked hard for everything all his life, right?

After Bush won the election, a guy named Lawrence Littwin got fired for trying to reform Texas's very crooked lottery system. Bush-appointed directors cancelled Littwin's audit and restored the lottery contract to some cronies from a New Jersey company called GTech.

In 1998, Littwin filed a suit charging that GTech had essentially "bought" themselves a no-bid contract for the lottery job by way of $23 million paid to a very well-connected lobbyist. That lobbyist was the same Ben Barnes who had done the big favor for W thirty years before.

A whistle-blower sent a letter to the Department of Justice saying that "Governor Bush . . . made a deal with Ben Barnes not to rebid (the GTech lottery contract) because Barnes could confirm that Bush had lied during the '94 campaign. Barnes agreed never to confirm the story (of helping W dodge the draft) and the governor talked to the chair of the lottery two days later and she then agreed to support letting GTech keep the contract without a bid."

The whistle-blower remained anonymous, but offered to come forward later to authorities. The letter remained sealed and buried, though Palast claims to have a copy. No investigation followed, and the Feds didn't call Barnes or the letter-writer. But then Littwin subpoenaed Barnes, and in 1999, under oath, Barnes admitted that he was the one who pulled strings to get W into the Guard. Of course, he claimed to have done this out of the kindness of his heart, and without any contact, direct or indirect, from the Bushes. In November 1999, GTech paid a reported $300,000 to settle with Littwin. In return, Littwin agreed to seal forever Barnes's five-hour deposition transcript about the Bush family influence on the lottery and the Air Guard.

Aren't those the kinds of stories of American democracy in action that warm your heart? Trouble is, you don't get to read stories like that in the paper, because they remain covered up. You sure as hell don't see stories like that on the network news because they're too complicated, and there aren't enough visuals to spice them up. It's much easier to run story after story about a bimbo in the Map Room with a presidential cigar up her ass.

The Media vs. Larry Flynt

> **They don't trust me because they're afraid once I'm on the air, I'll tell the truth. I don't trust them because I know they won't.**

The American media doesn't trust me, and I have to say that the feeling's mutual. The difference is, we distrust each other for opposite reasons. They don't trust me because they're afraid once I'm on the air, I'll tell the truth. I don't trust them because I know they won't.

When the media gets a story from me their first thought is "this must be a publicity stunt." When somebody in the White House—and lots of fingers point at Karl Rove—leaked the name of CIA agent Valerie Plame, wife of Ambassador Joseph C. Wilson IV, did the media ask, "Is this a publicity stunt?" When Bush gave them a big juicy photo op by coming in on a fighter plane for a tail-hook landing on a carrier, with a big banner in the background saying "Mission Accomplished," they didn't say, "Ah, that's just a publicity stunt . . . we got better things to do." No. Like good little poodles, they lined up their cameras just where the White House media experts told them to.

Ever since Roger Ailes brought sophisticated television techniques to the Reagan White House, just about everything a president or a candidate does is a media stunt. They go to a "location" to make a speech, and the shot of the location is more important than the words. It's all visual symbols for a public that doesn't read or think. The words that count are pre-selected sound bites, created intentionally because they will be picked up and aired to a public with a limited attention span. Spiro Agnew started it with his "nattering nabobs of negativism," and ever since, screwball phrases have been run over and over again.

To the American media, I'm a publicity stunt, but in Europe, it's a different story. In France, where a man's mistress and her kids can show up at his state funeral alongside his wife and her kids, they never ask me about stunts or pornography. They ask me about politics.

Shortly after I Flynted Congressman Livingston, Erica Jong, the bestselling novelist, came out to write an article about me. Nobody would touch it—which is no reflection on the quality of the piece. She sold it to the *Sunday Times of London Magazine,* not exactly a trashy venue,

> **In the States, I was still considered too hot to handle.**

and they ran it as a cover story. In the U.K., I was big cultural news. In the States, I was still considered too hot to handle.

I asked one anchor from the largest television show in Germany, "How come you're asking me questions that would normally be asked to a political pundit?" He says, "Well, Mr. Flynt, you are very well known throughout Europe, and we are very much interested in your opinions of American politics."

How is it possible that the moment I cross the ocean, I'm perceived totally differently than I am in my own homeland? It's because Europeans are more adult about "adult" matters. Which brings us to a subject very near and dear to my heart—sex.

6

The Moral Majority Minority

Moses freed the Jews, Lincoln freed the slaves, and I'd like to free the neurotics. These are the millions of people being driven crazy by sexual repression. Because they are uptight, they are miserable and bitter, and all too often participate, one way or another, in oppressing the rest of us.

Republicans have managed to exploit our conflicted attitudes about sex in order to create an effective voting block they wouldn't otherwise have on the basis of their policy positions. They're political hypocrites using sexual repression to pander to voters who can be hypocritical themselves. I want to make sure that doesn't continue, and I see sexual liberation as the first step in giving power back to the true majority in this country.

> I see sexual liberation as the first step in giving power back to the true majority in this country.

I want to offer an alternative political philosophy that has no use for hypocrisy. It is based on a deep conviction that drove human history long before the Puritans decided we were "sinners in the hands of an angry God." It is a concept that I see as the last great hope for coming back to more honest and less cynical politics, politics that truly have room for compassion, and that can heal the rifts that divide us. Ultimately, that concept, and my political agenda, is based on the same simple credo that has made me a very rich man:

Relax . . . it's just sex.

Love Sex

For the past thirty years, I've been trying to get us beyond our hang-ups.

Explicit sex is my business, and I'm good at it because I believe in it. To me, good sex and good porn are the perfect antidotes to the hypocrisy that undermines our health as a nation. That's why I see both good sex and good porn as political acts. After all, when you're naked, you've got nowhere to hide the truth.

The big secret that the forces of repression want to keep under wraps is that sex is wonderful and magical, not shameful. It makes us feel good when nothing else can. It's energizing, relaxing, exciting, and it relieves anxiety. A little sex in the middle of the afternoon can clear our heads, help us concentrate, make us work harder. It's one of the few things in life we do for its own sake—like art. It allows anybody to get beyond the mundaneness of life and enjoy something more exciting.

If we could live in a land of sexually healthy people we'd have less crime, less poverty, less divorce, less drug use—and fewer right-wing Republicans. Americans would have better relationships, enjoy their work more, and not be so overweight. There would be less depression, and consumers would spend more money to make themselves desirable, therefore helping the economy.

Sex is completely equal opportunity. There's no reason that Brad Pitt and Jennifer Aniston's sex has to be any better than yours. They're movie stars, they're rich, they're perfect looking, but it doesn't matter. Your enjoyment of sex is up to you, and when you're between the sheets, money and fame, or even having a perfect body, have nothing to do with it.

Despite all the attempts to drive it underground, sex is still the ultimate physiological and psychological goal. We dress a certain way to attract one another. We keep in shape, spend billions of dollars on cosmetics, read books about how to do it best. If we're not having sex, we're thinking about it, and if we're not thinking about it, we will be in a minute. I'm not the only guy who mentally undresses every woman he sees, but I might be the only one who doesn't feel guilty about it.

Trouble is, too many Americans won't allow themselves to be sexually liberated, and if they're not allowed, then damned if they'll let anyone else get there. Instead, they let anger, bitterness, resentment, and envy poison their lives. That poison, in turn, screws up society as a whole. Americans need to come clean about sex—about how much they like it, and about how much it matters—in order to clean up their politics.

The Democratic party and *Hustler* magazine have something in common. They share the support of both the least educated and the most educated people in the country. My marketing studies show that along with the truck drivers and assembly line guys who buy my magazine, far more Ph.D.s buy *Hustler* than either *Playboy* or *Penthouse*. That's because, by and large, neither blue-collar workers nor college professors buy into the uptight middle-class attitude. They like their porn explicit, and their politics progressive.

I'm a hillbilly, and people like me come to sex without all the hang-ups imposed by the hypocritical, "you must maintain proper appearances" morality of the middle class. When good Christian folk tell me that sex is dirty, I say, "Yeah, when it's done right." For me, sex has al-

> **When good Christian folk tell me that sex is dirty, I say, "Yeah, when it's done right."**

ways been a way of saying, "I am outside the reach of your power." Really poor people make their babies with their other kids sleeping in the same room with them because in the houses of really poor people there's only one room. The very poor have never had the luxury of being able to "maintain appearances." The very rich have never had to bother—they've always done what they like and paid people to keep it quiet.

To me, it seems a waste that so many people lead such guarded, repressed, and guilt-ridden lives that they're still afraid to tell their partners what turns them on. As soon as you reveal your fantasy, you form a stronger bond with the person you love.

Thanks to our repressed society, some people actually get turned on when they feel ashamed. It's part of our historical sexual dynamic: keep sex secretive, nasty, in the dark, then feel guilty about it. If being embarrassed is what turns you on, fine. But what's not fine is when that embarrassment results in public and personal accusations and judgments about *other* people's tastes and preferences. Those are nobody's business, least of all the government's.

If relentless brainwashing from right-wingers makes their true believers even more conservative in their sexual attitudes, that's their loss. Trouble is, right-wing agitation not only makes these people more twisted and more miserable, it makes them more judgmental of everyone else. This kind of fanatical insecurity, this fear of losing control, drives radical Islamic men to force Islamic women to dress in those stupid burkas. Because all those uptight preachers can't deal with their *own* sexual impulses, they rail against *anyone* having sex.

John Ashcroft and his ilk believe they are ordained by God to pass judgment on the rest of us. That would make Ashcroft just another crank, but he and his friends now have the power to pass laws enforcing their narrow-minded view of the world.

Imagine being told that you're only allowed to have sex on certain days of the week, and only in the missionary position with all the lights out. Sounds like a law the Taliban would come up with.

But if you're a couple living in Boston and you're receiving or giving oral sex, you could be arrested. In Virginia, if a married couple does it in any position other than missionary and the lights are not off, they could be arrested. Texas and Mississippi have laws against any device "designed or marketed as useful primarily for the stimulation of human genital organs."

You may laugh at some of these blue laws, but as long as they are on the books, they can be used as a pretext for nailing anyone whom John Ashcroft doesn't like. They make a great excuse when law enforcement just wants to shake you down.

America may be the land of the free, but it's certainly not the land of sexual freedom. Not yet, anyway. Not until we live in a country unencumbered by the senseless, insulting laws and damaging criticisms of others. The greatest right the government can afford its people is the right to be left alone, but the American voter will lose that right unless he or she demands it.

> **The greatest right the government can afford its people is the right to be left alone.**

Despite the judgment of an uptight minority, many modern men and women are enjoying sexual openness. It's not putting us on the road to Sodom and Gomorrah. It's putting us on the road to emancipation, and to a better understanding of human sexuality, which will ultimately lead to a better understanding of mankind. If I could accomplish one last thing on this earth, it would be to wipe out all sexual oppression and make it possible for all of us to freely enjoy ourselves as sexual beings.

The American voter needs to rediscover compassion—the quality that our president still seems to be looking for, along with Saddam Hussein's weapons of mass destruction. The human condition is that we all shit, we all fuck, we all die—these are life's realities. The more we can accept them, the more we accept ourselves. And the more self-accepting we are, the more we are in touch with the basic humanity of others. A self-accepting person with compassion for others does not need to ride roughshod over everybody else. That's my prescription for a better democracy, and a better life.

Any Flavor You Like

During my thirty years in porn, I have had the rare opportunity to see directly into the erotic minds and kinky bedrooms of thousands of people. What I know about sex is based on the countless stories I've heard and the intimate sexual details I'm privy to, as well as my own personal experiences with hundreds of women. When it comes to role-playing, even fetishes, I've heard it all, from both sexes. I've participated in or known someone who has tried every scene you can imagine, using as many different props, gadgets, positions, or people you can think of.

Personally, I'm into "vanilla" sex. I like my sex straight and to the point. I have no objections to more than one woman at a time, but I've never much cared for elaborate role-playing or particular fetishes. I'm probably the straightest pornographer you'll ever know, a real meat and potatoes man. There are definitely sexual behaviors and preferences that I may not understand or be into, but I don't judge anyone else's tastes.

Most scientists will now tell you that our sexual preferences are to some extent genetic. You don't just decide to be gay; you're *born* gay. Sexual desires may be formulated in our brains from highly stimulating experiences in childhood that create uncommon associations, such as shoes and sex. It happens in our brain anatomy when the wires get crossed.

One of the congressmen that we exposed in the nineties, for instance, liked to crawl around on all fours, naked, wearing a dog collar, lifting his leg to pee and so on while being hollered at by a naked lady friend of his. If anybody had accused him, he could have repeated what Bill Clinton said, "I never had sex with that woman." He'd be telling the truth. He didn't have sex with her.

But to him, crawling around on the floor naked, in a dog collar, was highly sexual.

Unfortunately, in our repressed society, any sexual behavior that's considered the slightest bit unusual—even when practiced by upstanding Republican politicians—threatens the bluenoses like John Ashcroft whose fetish is controlling other people. What should be a simple matter of choice—chocolate or vanilla—becomes a "moral" issue, and in some cases, and some states, a crime.

> **Any sexual behavior that's considered the slightest bit unusual threatens the bluenoses like John Ashcroft whose fetish is controlling other people.**

We received a letter once from a guy who likes to suck toes, but his problem was that when he actually sucked a woman's toes, he became embarrassed and it lost its excitement for him. The more outside-the-norm our behavior is, the more embarrassing it is. Yet a brain scientist in San Diego has found that the area in the brain that receives stimulation from the genitals is right next door to the area that receives nerve signals from the foot. It's a simple case of anatomy: A few nerve cells from the foot area had slipped over into the genital area. Most likely this guy was born this way. And he has to feel like a pervert? Should our doggie congressman feel like a pervert? I don't care what turns him on, and I don't think he or any of his fellow congressmen should care what turns *us* on.

If sex takes place between consenting adults, no one is being harmed, and you're in the privacy of your own home or hotel room—it's your business. Who knows why your girlfriend likes to be bound and gagged, or someone else's husband likes to do it on top of the washing machine during the spin cycle while his old high school buddy watches?

Unless your preferences are dangerous or are making you unhappy and you *want* to change them, leave them alone and enjoy.

My message to John Ashcroft, Jerry Falwell, and the rest of the radical conservatives is get your own sex life, and stay the hell out of everybody else's.

Good Clean Fun

The papers ran a story not long ago about a mother of three, Joanne Webb, from Burleson, Texas. She was arrested for her work with Passion Parties, a firm that sponsors Tupperware-style events to sell sex toys. This is a perfect example of the hypocrisy that controls us and gives the lie to the Supreme Court's emphasis on community standards. Her small community a few miles from Fort Worth had voted with their dollars that they wanted Mrs. Webb's dildos and tasty sex lotions. She was doing a land office business, helping rebuild the economy like a good American, not to mention helping to support her family. She'd even joined the local Chamber of Commerce. But some uptight prosecutor determined that he knew better than the marketplace, and he tried to prove that her business violated community standards.

Funny, but I thought Texas conservatives always believed in letting the market decide. Hell, at Enron they thought the market was God.

When I developed my own plans for going into the retail business, my vision was not a Tupperware party, but it also wasn't some sleazy adult bookstore with blacked-out windows and guys wearing raincoats sneaking in and out. I wanted to have a place where sex could come clean—an attractive, appealing, bright and open department store for men and women, dedicated to adult merchandise. I went up to Sunset Boulevard in West Hollywood, found the greatest location I could get, put a lot of money into it, and created Hustler Hollywood. I wanted the store's atmosphere to make people feel comfortable, like they were in a Barnes & Noble or Saks Fifth Avenue. And sure enough, everyone came, and the customers leave with shopping bags brimming over with toys, videos, and novelties. The store's success proves to me that Americans are starving for a chance to make sex fun and free from age-old guilt.

Porn Wild

The fast lane to sexual gratification is good old pornography: no waiting, no anticipation, and no disappointment. It gets you right where you're going and where you want to be. According to the rise in our video sales and online subscription base, pornography is helping more people get off today than ever before.

A large part of the rising popularity of porn today, as well as the thriving business in sexual toys, can be attributed to the same force—women. Once women started getting more involved in watching and buying porn, sales really took off and the old-fashioned embarrassment attached to porn started to decrease. Couples can get bored with the same old thing, or perhaps the excitement is still there and couples want to increase it or enhance it. For consenting adults who are both into it,

> Once women started getting more involved in watching and buying porn, sales really took off.

porn is the perfect aphrodisiac. Watching an adult movie or playing around with some sex gadgets can really do the trick. Or, say, you find yourself alone and horny—that's when porn really comes in handy. Masturbation is the safest sex in the world. With all the healthy benefits, you'd think the government would promote smut.

Instead, we have a morass of confusing legislation, intrusive censorship, pointless accusations, resource-wasting arrests meant to intimidate, and legal battles that cost the taxpayer (as well as the porn industry) millions of dollars.

Why all the fuss? To me, and to millions of other people like me, whatever adults want to view or read in the privacy of their own home should be their business. So what is it about pornography that people like Attorney General John Ashcroft find so threatening?

Obscenity or Obsession?

Supreme Court Justice William O. Douglas once wrote: "Obscenity is like the concept of sin: it defies definition. What might be to one is not to another. It is best left in the minds of men."

Nonetheless, the dictionary has to give it a crack. Most definitions of porn usually come down to "any written or pictorial matter intended to arouse sexual feelings." Does that include the Calvin Klein ads I see up on billboards, showing half undressed eighteen-year-olds sprawled out in erotic positions? What about the Victoria's Secret catalog that men swipe out of the mailbox and look at when they choke the chicken before their wives and girlfriends get home? Most ads we see selling clothing, underwear, cars, and music are packed with imagery clearly intended to arouse sexual feelings, but they are not considered pornography. Does that mean it's okay to arouse sexual feelings as long as your real purpose is to sell clothes or cars?

Hugh Hefner is considered a pornographer, but Hefner dressed up his porn by using very high-quality photographs, wrapped around sophisticated articles with socially redeeming value. Only the nuttiest of right-wing nuts will say that the photographs of naked women in *National Geographic* are pornographic, because clearly there is no sexual intent. Just seeing breasts is erotic only to those not accustomed to seeing them. It's the covering up of breasts that makes them sexy when uncovered, and the tribal African women depicted in *National Geographic* don't even know what a bra is. And yet some men, and all little boys, get worked up when they see those images.

Is pornography, in fact, in the eyes of the beholder? If, as the dictionary tells us, material is pornographic when its sole purpose is to arouse sexual feelings, then for straight women, the Victoria's Secret catalog is merely something to shop from, but for some men, unless they're cross-dressers, it's pornography.

Pornography has been around forever, and will continue to be around, because we enjoy it. I knew a couple who didn't want their little boy playing shoot'em up so they took away his play guns, but that didn't cure his itch. He picked up twigs and used them for guns. They took away the twigs, but that still didn't stop him. One night at dinner, he picked up some white bread, wadded it into the right shape, pointed it at his dad, and said, "Bang!"

> **Pornography has been around forever, and will continue to be around, because we enjoy it.**

If Attorney General John Ashcroft ever succeeded in outlawing nude photography, he'd simply up the ante on what was considered erotic. Back when Victorian women were covered up at all times, men found girls' ankles erotic. In the middle ages, a girl's forehead was considered erotic. If you've never seen Victoria's Secret, the underwear ads in the *Dallas Morning News* can look pretty hot.

Some critics of pornography say it's "bad" because it's addictive. If that's true, I can't think of anything better to be hooked on. Who cares if people want to spend hours jerking off to images they find on the Internet? Who is harmed by this? If these people are avoiding their "regular" lives, if they are ignoring their relationships or their partner's needs, chances are something is wrong in the relationship anyway. Couples who break up because one of the partners is spending too much time looking at porn would have broken up over something else. On the other hand, porn can help some couples get through the hard times in a relationship. I'm sure many women would rather have their husbands watching porn than going out and having an affair.

There is no scientific evidence to indicate that exposure to pornography is harmful in any way. A presidential commission on obscenity was set up in the late 1960s by President Lyndon Johnson. Attitudes toward sex were loosening up, and everyone had these 16mm cameras and were using them to make porn. The adult bookstores and the nudist magazines were supplied with fresh material every day. The adult industry was booming—people were getting busted left and right, but which of these cases should the government prosecute? With all the conflicting standards, Johnson did what he thought was the prudent thing. He asked a blue ribbon panel of eighteen experts to study the effects of porn, and to issue a report so that guidelines could be established.

The commission, which included social scientists from all over the world, investigated for eighteen months, and their findings unanimously concluded that exposure to pornographic material is not harmful to adults. But by the time the commission had completed its study, Republican Richard Nixon was in office, and the backlash against the sixties had already set in. The findings hardly supported Nixon's political positions—sort of an early preview of the so-called "Moral Majority"—so he buried the study.

In 1973, not that long after the commission's findings dropped off the radar, the Supreme Court issued its famous *Miller v. California* decision, which ruled that pornography, in itself, is not illegal, but that "obscenity" is. The Supreme Court offered the following guidelines for sorting out one from the other:

> The basic guidelines for the trier of fact must be: (a) whether "the average person, applying contemporary community standards" would find that the work, taken as a whole, appeals to the prurient interest; (b) whether the work depicts or describes, in a patently offensive way, sexual conduct specifically defined by the applicable state law; and (c) whether the work, taken as a whole, lacks serious literary, artistic, political, or scientific value.

They offered some further language about such things as "lewd exhibition of the genitals," but I've never quite been able to figure out what that means. To me, the most erotic part of a female's body is her genitalia. If the human body is obscene, complain to the manufacturer! If Ford Motor Company built a bad car, people would complain to Ford, wouldn't they? From

If the human body is obscene, complain to the manufacturer!

my perspective, however, I've never seen a woman's crotch that I didn't think was a work of art. Then again, I prefer my porn without any serious literary, artistic, political, or scientific value, so I guess what truly interests me will always be considered obscene.

When you push the envelope, as I have over the years, when you become more explicit, you become more prone to prosecution.

That's why now, thirty years after porn got its clean bill of health, the Bush administration, backed up by Christian evangelicals and other conservative radicals, is threatening a crackdown that has the whole industry walking on eggshells. It's really impossible to know ahead of time what a certain prosecutor will decide is obscene, but we do know what pushes those hot buttons of law enforcement, and we wind up censoring ourselves. We pay lawyers to watch porn to make sure the videos don't include any images that might set off some trigger-happy prosecutor.

Here's our list of red flags that police and prosecutors will usually go after.

BOX-COVER GUIDELINES
MOVIE PRODUCTION GUIDELINES

1. No shots with the appearance of pain or degradation
2. No facials (body shots are okay if shot is not nasty)
3. No spitting or saliva mouth to mouth
4. No food used as sex object
5. No peeing unless in a natural setting, e.g., field, roadside
6. No coffins
7. No blindfolds

8. No wax dripping
9. No two dicks in/near one mouth
10. No shot of stretching pussy
11. No fisting
12. No squirting
13. No bondage-type toys or gear unless very light
14. No girls sharing same dildo (in mouth or pussy)
15. Toys are okay if shot is not nasty
16. No hands from two different people fingering same girl
17. No male/male penetration
18. No transsexuals
19. No bi-sex
20. No degrading dialogue, e.g., "Suck this cock, bitch!" while slapping her face with a penis.
21. No menstruation topics
22. No incest topics
23. No forced sex, rape themes, etc.
24. No black men–white women themes

What makes it tricky, of course, is that every district, every state has a different standard. It might be that in Virginia selling a movie that shows mouth to mouth saliva might land you in jail, while in New York it could take two dicks in the same mouth to get a prosecutor angry. And look at number twenty-four. Even though we're supposed to have come so far on race, a blue-eyed blonde woman having sex with a black man is *not* a tape you want to go into court with.

> **When John Ashcroft draped a sheet over the nude breast of a statue holding the scales of justice, did he do that because he himself got turned on by the statue?**

If two people are watching a movie (mainstream or porn), and one gets turned on by a certain scene or image and the other person doesn't, does that mean it's porn to one but not to the other? When John Ashcroft draped a sheet over the nude breast of a statue holding the scales of justice, did he do that because he himself got turned on by the statue?

Politics and Porn

I believe that when the war against terrorism has sufficiently eroded our rights through the Patriot Act and other measures, if Bush and Ashcroft are still in power, they will wage a nice little reign of terror on pornography.

But as I've already suggested, relying on community standards might hit them with a big surprise. Public attitudes have changed. A district attorney can have all the fantasies he wants about prosecuting an obscenity case, but as long as we have trial by jury, he'll still need the consensus of twelve people to get a conviction.

My lawyer recently told me about an obscenity case he tried in St. Louis. He said it was the worst stuff he'd ever tried to defend. Really raunchy. He also said that the jury was made up entirely of women, and all over the age of sixty. Well, he thought he was dead. But then he says they deliberated for two hours and, even after watching all those dirty movies, came back and delivered a verdict of not guilty. He said that these women took the position that, this stuff isn't my cup of tea, but who's it harming? Leave 'em alone.

Americans love their porn and their toys and, as a people, we're hypocrites to say otherwise. The market says it all. A smut peddler like me would not be riding in a Bentley and a private jet if Americans did not have a healthy appetite for the stuff that makes John Ashcroft chew his prayer rug in aggravation.

And yet I have been dragged into court time and time again by prosecutors who were trying to close down one of my stores or magazines. As recently as 1999, I was indicted in Cincinnati, Ohio, on fifteen counts of pandering and obscenity, and I faced up to twenty-four years in jail. Cincinnati—the city where I was first arrested on obscenity charges in 1977—was after me again. The recent charges made by Joe Deters, a Hamilton County prosecutor, and the obvious setup that led to them, made me feel like time had stood still.

My store in Cincinnati is for adults only, and we have the strictest guidelines to assure that is the case. We demand proper identification before any purchase, as we did in this case. But Deters, the prosecutor, sent in a fourteen-year-old kid who looked like he played football for the Bengals to buy armloads of videos with his fake I.D. This was a kid who was making a career of police work, helping the cops try to trick liquor stores into selling to a minor.

Aside from the nuisance, I was almost glad our Hustler store got busted. It gives an opportunity for more dialogue about government encroachment on our freedom of speech and our right to privacy. Also, I've always had a special place in my heart for the people of Cincinnati. I feel they deserve the same right to watch porn that people in other parts of the country do.

Americans like to tell the world that we live in the land of the free. But how free are we when our sexual tastes are being constantly monitored? When we are being told, as if we were children, what we can or cannot purchase, watch, or read? How free are we if our local governments can declare a certain visual image or phrase "obscene" and deny us access to it? I'm *not* talking about underage children. I'm talking about videos produced by consenting adults, starring consenting adults, for the viewing pleasure of consenting adults.

> **How free are we when our sexual tastes are being constantly monitored?**

Our tax dollars are stretched thin. Law enforcement has plenty to do as is. Why on earth is government still obsessed with what adults view in the privacy of their own homes? Aside from being an infringement of our rights, it's a huge waste of *our* money!

Women on Top

One of the things that gives me hope for maintaining our sexual liberties is the outspokenness of women. For centuries, they had to pretend that they had no real interest in sex. Now that they have the hard-won freedom to express themselves sexually, they aren't about to let some fool like Ashcroft put them back in the nunnery.

When we started *Hustler* in the 1970s, only 3 percent of our readership was female. Now it's 30 percent. At our Hustler retail stores over 50 percent of our customers are women. Men are buying most of the X-rated videos, but women are buying them as well, to watch alone, or as gifts for their boyfriends, girlfriends, or husbands. They're into all of it: straight, gay, couple swapping, wherever their imaginations lead them. Women will come into the store and buy a whole assortment of things: a couple of videos, sexy lingerie, a vibrator, an oversized velour pillow, scented candles—everything they'll need to create an erotic evening. Creams and lotions are no longer used just to make a woman's skin soft, and our customers are eating them up—literally. "I'm going out to the store to pick up a few things, honey," has taken on a whole new meaning.

It's not unusual to see a fifty-year-old woman come into our Hustler Hollywood store, choose a deluxe vibrator and some strawberry lube, and plunk it down on the counter for all the world to see. She won't be embarrassed about comparing a couple of different sizes, holding them up, squeezing them, right in front of everyone. We don't have a "try on" room, but I'm convinced if we did, women would be in there checking out the dildos before bringing them home. By contrast, you'll see a guy off in the corner of the store sticking his X-rated video under his coat because he doesn't want anyone to see what he's buying. I think it's fascinating (and refreshing) that the women are so open and the men still so wracked with guilt.

Everything I see, from our *Hustler* magazine subscription base to the people who shop at our boutiques, proves to me that

Women are less ashamed of their desires, more open and less guilt ridden.

American women match men in their interest in sex and desire to participate in sex. Women of all ages are aggressively going after what they want, and they're not afraid to say how they want it. Women are less ashamed of their desires, more open and less guilt ridden, and they're leading the way to sexual freedom.

Men are sometimes taken aback by this. Many of us, particularly men over forty, can't come to grips with so many females asserting themselves sexually in and out of the bedroom. Things are out of whack because men are not emotionally prepared to deal with reality overturning what we've always been taught, which is that women don't really like sex, that they just put up with it for us.

It's ironic that the founders and leaders of the feminist movement, many of whom call themselves my enemies because I publish *Hustler,* have in fact "allowed" women to be turned on by pornography, giving them the right to decide for themselves what they like. While there are plenty of die-hards who stick to their outdated notion that pornography is anti-female, in reality it is women—many of them ardent feminists—who purchase more than 50 percent of the erotic products sold in America.

But there are many young women who are still confused. Can I get turned on by pornography and still be a feminist? Can I be a feminist and only want to be married and have children? The answer should be "yes" to both. Feminism should mean never having to make excuses or feel ashamed for whatever it is you want or like to do. Even if you are turned on by watching a woman perform sex in what some may consider to be degrading positions, no one should tell you that you don't have feminist values.

Thirty years later, the same women who fought for equal pay for equal work, who convinced men to assume more responsibility for child care, and who worked to give women freedom of choice are the very ones who are telling younger women that certain behaviors are politically correct and some are not.

I think it's time to go to the next level of feminism. Feminism should be about empowering women to make their own choices, not about passing judgment on the choices they make. It should be about nondiscrimination in the workplace, breaking through the glass ceiling, not about making women bitter. If a woman wants to be a porn star, that's her business.

Safe and Legal Abortion

Some months back I saw a bumper sticker that said, "Just Say 'No' to Sex with Pro-Lifers." Ironically, the date was January 22, 2003, the thirtieth anniversary of *Roe v. Wade,* the 1973 landmark decision legalizing abortion.

"Just Say No" is a good line, but it's no joke how much a woman's right to choose is in jeopardy. In November of 2003, Bush signed into law an act criminalizing "partial birth abortion." The photograph of W at a table with eleven dopey legislators behind him—all white, and all male—made front pages all over the country. The Bush Administration is obsessed with regaining control over anything

> In hock to the religious right, they have made a political issue out of what should be a deeply personal matter of choice.

having to do with sex. In hock to the religious right, they have made a political issue out of what should be a deeply personal matter of choice.

When our Constitution was written, explicitly saying that no church should have any say in government, England was just coming off two centuries of religious war, torturing and executing people over whether they teamed up with the Archbishop of Canterbury or the Pope in Rome. The American voter needs to understand that once you let one part of the Constitution slide, the whole thing can slip away.

While I personally don't like the idea of abortion, at the same time, I am pro-choice. Just as I defend the First Amendment, I will defend a woman's right to be in control of her reproductive life, and to be able to make whatever choice she needs to make. No one should take this decision lightly, but the decision has to be hers.

When my daughter was born thirty years ago, she came into a world where a woman could decide for herself what to do with her own body. She has never known a time when, if a woman needed to terminate her pregnancy, she would have to go to some back-alley butcher, or struggle to save money to fly to some country that wasn't run by blue-nosed puritans who wanted to punish her for the very idea of having sex.

Laws don't "stop" abortions. They simply make the procedure seedy and difficult and extremely dangerous. None of us should forget that abortion-related deaths are low in countries where the procedure is legal. In places where it's still illegal or highly restricted, abortion mortality is hundreds of times higher.

Health officials estimate that 48 percent of American pregnancies are unintended, and half of those are now being terminated by abortion. What right is it of some judge, or some sex-obsessed preacher, to tell you what to do in this most personal of all decisions? Imagine if the government decided to outlaw treating any medical condition they could say resulted from behavior they disapproved of. If you had lung cancer, they could blame you for smoking. They could say your skin cancer came from too much time out in the sun. You'd been warned, treatment is banned, and you're stuck with a life-threatening condition. Would you settle for that?

The issue is not, as these right-to-lifers would like you to believe, about "killing" a human life. It's about a woman's right to determine what goes on inside her own body. A fertilized egg or a fetus does not have the same rights as a woman. The same right-wingers who claim to care so much about the rights of the unborn don't seem to care nearly as much about the rights, and health and well-being, of those who *are* born. Talk about hypocrisy. They cut spending for prenatal care for mothers, early childhood education, and other programs that strive to give underprivileged kids a chance. Their movement isn't about right to life. It's about power—their power to control other people, especially with regard to sex.

To them, sex is immoral, so if you've had sex, your punishment will be to live with the consequences, and the child will be sentenced to live with a woman or a couple who don't have the resources—emotional or financial—to take care of it. When it comes time to deal with all those unwanted and abused children, the conservatives turn their backs. They can only think in terms of

> **To them, sex is immoral, so if you've had sex, your punishment will be to live with the consequences.**

retribution. Do nothing for people, kick them when they're down, and then if they act up, throw 'em in jail. That's been the conservative mantra for the past thirty years.

Now the jails are overflowing and the costs are helping to drive our cities and states into bankruptcy. You can send a kid to Harvard for what it costs to keep a drug offender in jail. Maybe that's one good result of the financial crisis in government. Conservatives will learn that if you want to lock people up and throw away the key, it costs money. Just like it costs money to have decent roads or decent schools. There's no such thing as a free lunch, especially not when trying to deal with social problems. Ignore them in one place and they pop back up in another.

Of course the pro-lifers never consider just how truly immoral it may be to give birth to a human being you can't take care of, and whom the world may not be able to accommodate. They can only see it in terms of their own narrow-minded view of "morality." The world population is scheduled to double by 2060. Take a look around even in America's richest cities. We already have people living in what amounts to garbage dumps, just like they do in the Third World. Under the brilliant influence of the evangelicals and the Catholic Church, the U.S. denies aid to any organization promoting the use of any form of birth control, even condoms. On November 12, 2003, the National Conference of Bishops met and voted not just to maintain this ban, but to pursue it even more aggressively. Could anything be more stupid? This is, of course, the same Catholic Church that on September 9, 2003, agreed to pay $85 million—and this was just in the archdiocese of Boston!—to settle lawsuits arising from their priests sexually abusing children. Is it any wonder that this church is so afraid of sex? For 2,000 years they have tried to denounce and deny or defuse one of the most powerful forces in the universe, and denial and denunciation just doesn't work. It's only when you accept the *whole* human being that you begin to find solutions that work.

Fourteen- and fifteen-year-old kids are having babies, who will then have their own babies by the time they're fourteen or fifteen. Health care is in the crapper. Schools are a joke. Government is broke. And the Republican response? Build higher walls around those gate-guarded communities. Hire a private security firm. Keep your assault rifle handy. Is that really what they had in mind when they called America "the last best hope for the world," and "a city on a hill"?

Those of us who are pro-choice are well aware of what a horrible decision having an abortion entails. No one "wants" to have an abortion. But each year, two out of every 100 women aged fifteen to forty-four have one. Forty-seven percent of these women have had at least one previous abortion. An estimated 43 percent of women will have at least one abortion by the time they're forty-five.

Women don't have abortions for irresponsible reasons; they have them when they are trying to be responsible and carefully evaluate what they can and can't handle. Maybe they've had all the children they can possibly afford to take care of; they want to delay their next birth because they're not ready to add to the family; they're too young or too poor; or their husband has walked out on them; or maybe they can't raise a child while they're in school or working.

For a teenager especially, having a child can take her entirely off course in terms of education, career, and even her ability to have a stable marriage and a happy family later on, at the appropriate time in her life.

Yet, on his first day of work as president of the United States, George W. Bush re-imposed the insidious global gag rule first instituted by President Reagan, then lifted by President Clinton, barring any health providers receiving American family planning assistance from counseling women about abortion, engaging in political speech on abortion, or providing abortion services, even with their own money. To put it simply, Bush's first order of business as president was to attack the right to terminate a pregnancy.

On a recent Bush administration trip to Bangkok, Assistant Secretary of State Gene Dewey announced to the audience: "The United States supports the sanctity of life from conception to natural death." Those are code words for "we support controlling the sexuality of women." And it's not "the United States" that supports this. It's a vocal minority of religious nuts who have taken over our government.

We have an anti-choice president, an anti-choice Senate, and the Supreme Court majority in favor of *Roe v. Wade* is hanging by a thread. More and more states are requiring teenage girls to have a parent's permission before they can obtain an abortion. Bush is slowly but surely changing the laws whenever and wherever he can get away with it.

With Bush in the driver's seat, we know that the religious right is setting the course. Bush and his supporters want to take us back into the dark ages just as sure as any Taliban mullah

> **With Bush in the driver's seat, we know that the religious right is setting the course.**

does. These self-loathing, self-righteous blowhards are a minority, but a very vocal minority that wields power in Washington far beyond their numbers. Unless those of us opposed to them become equally aggressive, women might not only lose the right of free choice over their own bodies, but the day could come when we could get locked up for having pro-choice slogans on our bumper stickers.

Relax—It's Just Sex Education

The basic distinction between healthy and happy sex on the one hand and twisted repression and neurosis on the other begins when we're kids.

In John Ashcroft's America, hundreds of thousands of children and young adults are being brainwashed every day by ignorant, dangerous and scared religious zealots who teach fear and sexual repression the way it was taught in the dark ages. For them, suppressing the sexual urge is not about "safe sex," or being cautious with one's feelings, it's about control. Just as the church has had its hand on our collective crotches for over two thousand years, the religious right would like to put a lock on each of our individual crotches and throw away the key.

The answer cannot be "just say no to sex." Look at the huge numbers of children and teens suffering from obesity like never before. Do we tell them "just say no to food"? Or, do we teach them healthful eating habits and provide them with nutritious alternatives to fast food? Teens are going to sneak in sex the same way they're going to sneak in French fries. What they need is to learn the proper way. Our obligation as parents, teachers, friends, and counselors is to help them understand that sex can be the best thing in the world, but that it also carries a responsibility. There can be dangerous repercussions when it's engaged in irresponsibly. Casual sex can be great. Irresponsible sex is not. Have sex wisely, and with the proper protection.

I talked to all my kids about birth control, and when my daughter Theresa was a teenager, my wife, Althea, was a lot of help to me in talking to her. Parents who don't communicate with their teenagers are doing them a huge disservice. Open discussion is essential, and not only did I insist that my kids listen to what I had to say, I even had different things to say to each sex.

I said to my teenage daughter something I would hope all parents would say: "I want you to be happy, and I think part of your being happy is to get a good education. I'm not telling you what you should be or what you should study. But I want to remind you that any dreams you have can be destroyed, can literally go up in smoke, if you were to become pregnant, because if you become pregnant, who would take care of the baby? You wouldn't be able to finish your education and be a mom at the same time. And I doubt you really want to go through the psychological turmoil of putting it up for adoption, or going through an abortion. I'm telling you that what you need to do is make sure that you do not have sex with a boy until you're ready, until you know in your heart the moment is right. And, when you're ready, talk to your mother about birth control and make sure that he's using a condom."

I told my son, "If you're with a girl and she becomes pregnant, you ought to share in that responsibility. If you don't share in that responsibility, you're not a man, and you're not someone worthy of being my son. I'm telling you this because I don't want you to take it lightly. If you decide you've reached a point that you want to have sexual intercourse with a girl, first of all, she should be on birth control, and you should be using a condom, taking precautions yourself. Because some girls might not tell you the truth about whether they're using birth control, you should use a condom anyway."

It's good that many middle schools are teaching a legitimate and practical sex education class, where they actually hand out condoms and teach the boys how to put them on (they have the eighth-grade boys slipping them over bananas, in fact). But, something is missing from what they're learning. It's fine to learn the nuts and bolts of getting that condom on, and what sexually transmitted disease is making its way across campus, but the very first thing I would teach young people about is sexual responsibility. I would teach them about what it really means to bring a child into this world. I would explain to them that one quick act of irresponsible and impulsive sexual intercourse could mean that a woman who might have been a doctor would instead become a single mom flipping hamburgers at McDonald's. I wouldn't put a moral value on their desire and their actions, but rather a practical one.

Sex education should be about listening to your kids and answering their questions as honestly as possible without trying to control their actions. But until adults understand and are comfortable with their own sexuality, they will never be able to guide their children and help them to discover what's right for them.

No one needs a group of uptight religious nuts preventing our kids from getting practical sex education. The "just say no to sex" crowd is driven by religious convictions, but a public school is not a church. It is in the state's interest to minimize unwanted pregnancies and the transmission of venereal diseases, and sex education accomplishes those goals. Even the most devoutly religious Americans need to remember that the separation of church and state is a very American idea, and if you are a patriot, you must speak up for it.

> **No one needs a group of uptight religious nuts preventing our kids from getting practical sex education.**

Religious Nuts

There's a T-shirt I want to get that says, "So Many Right-Wing Christians . . . So Few Lions." Religious nuts make me very nervous, and there seem to be more of them every day. It's not just that they're religious, it's that they're aggressively religious, as in cram-it-down-your-throat religious, burn-you-at-the-stake religious.

The polite, live and let live churches seem to be shriveling up and dying. Since 1960, the number of Episcopalians has dropped by half, and in the same period, the number of Pentecostals has quadrupled. This is fire and brimstone, roll-on-the-floor, speak-in-tongues religion that sends people knocking on your door to save your soul.

When I was eight or nine years old growing up in Kentucky, I used to go to revival camp meetings and watch the true believers play with snakes. These preachers would travel from town to town setting up their tents, trying to get crowds to come and join their bizarre world. We'd watch them cast their spells, and even as a kid I thought their behavior was totally nuts. I, personally, was not raised to fear God, but I have witnessed what happens to people who are raised that way. They basically turn against anything in life that is pleasurable. When they themselves indulge in any pleasure, whether it's sex or having a drink, they hypocritically tuck that away, because the guilt they feel is unbearable.

Thirty-five percent of American Christians today describe themselves as "born-again." Fifty-eight percent of Americans say that you have to believe in God to be moral. A staggering 83 percent of Americans believe in the virgin birth of Jesus. Only 28 percent of the American people believe in evolution. Think about that! A lot of born-agains (including George W. Bush) think it was "God's will" to elect Bush as president, and "God's will" for Bush to invade Iraq.

The Pew Research Center says that in 1987, evangelicals were evenly divided between the Democrats and the Republicans. Now, they are twice as likely to be Republicans. These zealots feel no temptation to listen to anyone with a different idea. They're *that* convinced that God is speaking directly to them, and through them. And they are not all just standing on street corners thumping their Bibles.

In October 2003, NBC News and the *Los Angeles Times* created a tempest in Mr. Bush's teapot by reporting on some speeches given by his undersecretary of defense for intelligence, Lt. General William G. Boykin. It seems that this gentleman, the administration official in charge of rounding up our most-wanted list of "evil doers," had been going around to evangelical churches, in uniform, describing his work as a "spiritual battle" against Satan, and saying that, "as a Christian nation," the only way to defeat terrorism was to "come against them in the name of Jesus."

Now that's a surefire way to win the hearts and minds of our brothers and sisters in the Islamic Middle East. It makes about as much sense as referring to your fight against terrorism as a "crusade," which, of course, our president *did*.

George W. Bush, John Ashcroft, and others in the present administration are basing national policy on their belief that they have a direct line to God. The joke, of course, is that we're trying to fight Islamic terrorists who are out to kill us because . . . they have a direct line to God. But the threat from true believers with "God on their side" isn't just from Muslim fundamentalists.

> **The threat from true believers with "God on their side" isn't just from Muslim fundamentalists.**

In 2003, police finally arrested Eric Rudolph, the man from the Army of God and the Christian Identity Movement who is accused of bombing abortion clinics as well as the 1996 Olympics. Police also arrested Matthew Hale, leader of the World Church of the Creator, for soliciting the murder of a federal judge. The same year also saw the conviction of James Kopp, a man affiliated with the Army of God, for killing a doctor who performed abortions in Buffalo, N.Y.

Obviously, not every born-again Christian is going to shoot somebody they disagree with. But despite the meek and forgiving teachings of Jesus, the belief in having a special deal worked out with God seems to make people a hell of a lot less tolerant of others. Societies don't remain open and free without tolerating a wide diversity of opinion. And for far too many people—my old friend Charles Keating comes to mind—religion seems to be nothing more than some kind of E-ZPass to self-justification. As long as they maintain certain pieties—usually involving heavy sexual prudishness—they can justify almost anything. They can swindle, start wars, hate other races, and, in the case of the right-to-life extremists, murder doctors in cold blood.

Religious questioning, or wondering about the ultimate meaning of things, is a very natural human trait. The trouble starts when people become convinced that they *have* the answer—in fact, *all* the answers. Next thing you know, they decide they have to "save" the rest of us by cramming their answers down our throats.

Founding Free-Thinkers

The truly great thing about this country, where the myth lives up to the reality, is the U.S. Constitution, and the tolerant form of government it gave rise to. Fortunately, the rebellion we pulled off against the king of England in 1776 took place at a time when men like Thomas Jefferson, from Virginia, wanted to throw off all the constraints of religious superstition and oppression and warfare and start fresh.

Even though the puritans set up a government run by preachers in Massachusetts, by the time the Constitution was adopted in 1789, that idea had been replaced by something totally new—the idea of complete separation of church and state. Jefferson and Adams and Franklin and Hamilton did not set out to

Jefferson and Adams and Franklin and Hamilton did not set out to create a Christian nation, as the Jerry Falwells of the world would have you believe.

create a Christian nation, as the Jerry Falwells of the world would have you believe. Our founding fathers were free-thinkers, and they created a nation very explicitly without *any* established religion. This is what gave us not only freedom *of* religion, but freedom *from* religion. The Republicans, especially the ones holding their daily prayer breakfasts at the White House, need to be reminded of that.

Religious Fanaticism Can Be Cured

Many people who have born-again experiences—hearing God's voice or seeing signs—are uneducated, working-class people who have nobody to talk to about these experiences except maybe a neighbor, a family member, or the local pastor. They're vulnerable, they go talk to the local pastor, and they get sucked into the program.

I had "religious" experiences like this in the late seventies and I sought counseling. This was right before I was shot and frankly, I would have believed in anything at that time of my life. I was under the spell of wanting so badly to believe in a power greater than myself, greater than *anything*. I saw visions, I heard voices, the same story any born-again Christian will tell you. I had a horrible time reconciling my attitude toward human sexuality with religious teachings. But I knew I had to question any institution that made rules against sex. Luckily, I was taken care of by one of the best psychiatrists in L.A. He diagnosed me as having bipolar disorder, put me on medication, and I've been fine ever since.

If a person having religious visions can afford to get proper medical help, he can be adequately diagnosed as being bipolar or manic-depressive or even schizophrenic, or probably psychotic in the case of snake-handlers. Most often these disorders can be successfully treated by medication, but too many people never get the chance because they can't afford it. Maybe that's one reason right-wingers fight so hard against affordable health care for everyone.

If we had better mental health care in this country, the religious right would disappear. Instead, people with chemical imbalances in their brains say they are born-again, and they become pawns of the church for the rest of their lives.

The Power of Positive Thinking

Positive thinking is what people are seeking through prayer, except that, instead of praying to God, they develop inner skills to help focus the mind on "good thoughts" to get through a crisis, whether it's an illness, or other problems in life. The advantage of positive thinking is that the energy is not assigned to someone larger than life and completely unknown, but to yourself. This gives you a real strength as well as responsibility for your own actions.

There is tremendous power in positive thinking and certainly more of a guarantee for results than hoping that whatever you need is also God's will. Imagine everything in your life starts coming loose at the seams. Your kid's always getting in trouble. Your husband's become a drunk. It feels like the whole world is falling apart, so it's very easy for you to fall apart too. You have to say to yourself, "I won't let that happen to me." You don't say, "Please God, don't let this happen to me." Talk to somebody who can hear you: *yourself*.

If it gives someone a greater sense of meaning to quietly contemplate the existence of God, more power to them. Religion becomes a problem when it becomes *organized* religion. Throughout history, organized religion has been the greatest divisive force in human existence. Through wars, persecution, and torture, it has caused more harm than any other idea since the beginning of time.

W. C. Fields said he was an atheist, but when he was dying, he sat in his hospital room reading the Bible. Someone said, "Fields, I didn't know you read the Bible!" He replied, "I'm just lookin' for a loophole!"

I've heard my friend Bill Maher say he doesn't believe in God, but he considers himself a spiritual person. What does this mean? I think he simply doesn't want all the baggage that goes along with organized religion, but he doesn't want to come out and say he's an atheist. So, like Fields, he tries to hedge his bets. That's what millions of people do. They're trying to be socially acceptable. They want to keep a foot in the door, just in case.

When somebody says, "I don't believe in God, I'm an atheist," now that hits like a sledgehammer.

I have not had any belief in the concept of God since 1978. I am not a spiritual person and yet, I love my family, I love my friends. I will go out of my way to help anybody that I can, within reason. I consider myself to be beyond corruption, simply because that's how I live my life. People who know me know they can always take my word for anything. So when I try to compare myself to all of these other CEOs that are going away to jail, awaiting trial for all the funky stuff they did to their stockholders and employees, I realize I'm a decent person, *and* an atheist.

> **I am not a spiritual person and yet, I love my family, I love my friends.**

Once I had accepted my core belief that after you're dead, you're dead, and no one will be up there judging you, for the first time in my life I became truly happy. I never had to take ulcer medication again. I'm not out to convert anybody, I'm just saying that the way I believe works for me, and there's no sense of hypocrisy or shame involved. I'm fine with not believing and don't think I'm a lesser person for it. If the way other people are living their lives works for them, then great. But in my view, the real deal is that when you're gone, you're gone, so you had better do the right thing while you're here.

The only situation where I have seen positive results from people giving themselves to a power greater than they are is in the twelve-step program, Alcoholics Anonymous. The fundamental way that AA asks their members to try to accept God before they can get off drugs and alcohol has a way of working, and I don't know how effective that same program would be if you told these people, "You have to think positively. Positive thinking is the answer to your problems." I don't know if that would carry as much weight for them as the Big Guy Upstairs.

When you're suffering from something so powerful as drug addiction, perhaps you have to find something greater than the force that addicts you. But the power you feel when you accept that there is no God might be even greater. That knowledge removes a huge burden from your shoulders, because you no longer have to protect an ideal you can never be absolutely sure of. It removes a tremendous amount of what could be called "neurotic feelings" from your psyche.

People organize into religious groups to reinforce group behavior. It's as if they don't trust their faith enough to let it stand on its own. So they band together to make and enforce rules, and to put people on a guilt trip, particularly about sex. The net effect is to divide people into different camps—"us" and "them"—so they can have one more reason to hate.

> **People organize into religious groups to reinforce group behavior.**

Of course morality is important, but in my view, morality has no necessary connection to religion. In fact, if you look at the history of religion and all the suffering it has caused, how can you ever associate the two? Given the amount of bloodshed caused in the name of religion, and the amount of theft it has been used to justify, you might come to the conclusion that religion is the enemy of morality.

Morality is what feels good after. Unless you're a sociopath, that definition rules out actions that harm other people. We have a legal system based on that kind of common sense. The problem is, when religious people start discussing morality, they base it not on common sense, but on some teaching laid down 800 or 2,000 or 5,000 years ago by some guy out in the desert with a strange gleam in his eye. And those guys came up with some pretty weird rules. According to one of these great prophets, you can't shave your face, but you have to shave your pubic area. If you're an orthodox Jew, you can't eat pork or shellfish.

Now, admittedly, before refrigeration this did have a certain logic to it. But it was not a question of *morality*—it was a question of self-preservation. And guess what? Before modern medicine and modern birth control, sexual prudence was a question of self-preservation too. Syphilis and gonorrhea would cause insanity or death, and sex resulted pretty reliably in pregnancy. But now we have refrigeration, medicine, and birth control, and it makes no sense to hold on to our old fears and attitudes.

One Nation, Under God

In 1892, when the Pledge of Allegiance was first drafted, the phrase "under God" was not in it. It was added over sixty years later, when we were involved in the Cold War and fighting the Communists. It was during the McCarthy era and super patriotism had skipped the rails and was blurring into paranoia. According to the emerging right-wing, where there's patriotism, there has to be God.

But what about all the very loyal and patriotic Americans who don't believe in God? What about loyal and patriotic Americans who are Hindus or Muslims and believe in a different god? We all have to recite "under God" as part of our oath. I don't say the Pledge of Allegiance whether the phrase "under God" is there or not. I just don't get into any of this ceremonial crap. I'm a

> **I served in two branches of the military, but I think that patriotism is more than saying a few words.**

patriotic American, I served in two branches of the military, but I think that patriotism is more than saying a few words. I'm deeply offended whenever religion raises its head in any aspect of our public lives.

I not only don't pledge allegiance to the flag, I also don't sing the "Star-Spangled Banner"—and thank your lucky stars you don't have to hear me try. Wars are unjustly glorified, and it's fine that Old Glory is flying, and that she still stands and so on and so forth, but just leave me out of it. I did my bit in both the army and the navy, and I consider myself to be just as patriotic as the next guy.

Anybody who wants to volunteer for some type of ceremony should be able to do it. Sing the national anthem, pledge to the flag. I just don't think that people should be put in a position where they have to participate when they don't want to. And they shouldn't be made to feel any less patriotic for not wanting to participate. It's a personal thing, just like all these matters should be. At least for now, and with John Ashcroft you never know, we are not breaking the law by not pledging or by not singing. We are exercising our rights *as Americans* to do what we feel is right for ourselves. I feel the same about this as I do about gays. Do what you want, just don't make me do it. Be married to a tree if that's what you want.

Unfortunately, the people in power today see it just the opposite. They are pushing to erase the distinction between church and state so that our government will be a party to the church's game, which is to repress any expression of individuality and free thought, especially when it comes to sex.

Except for a few very liberal places like San Francisco or Madison, Wisconsin, you'll never see anyone, male or female, elected as a member of the United States Congress who doesn't have a religious affiliation attached to his or her name. There are plenty of sinners in Congress, and probably more than a few atheists, but you better believe they belong to a church somewhere.

Religion that insists on conformity is at the heart of the Big

Hustle. A great many religious people aren't spiritual, they're just hung-up and controlling, and belonging to an organized religion allows them to feel superior.

The hardcore, extra chromosome, evangelical crowd may believe what they're pitching, but more often than not, the politicians they elect—and a lot of the preachers they support—are as phony as a three-dollar bill. I was delighted to see that when Jimmy Swaggart fell from grace, and they found him with that hooker in a Baton Rouge motel room, he had a copy of *Hustler* with him. He had been preaching against us for years.

The sham of religion as a marker of decency is so strong that politicians are forced into a certain amount of hypocrisy just to get elected. Good ol' boy Bill Clinton never missed a photo-op at church, and just like back in Arkansas, he always carried a big fat floppy Bible.

I believe that, compared to most politicians, Bill Clinton is a decent guy, but he was still going to do what was politically expedient. Back in the early nineties, there was an inmate on Death Row in Arkansas who had an IQ below 70—basically someone who was mentally retarded and should never have been sentenced to death. During his first presidential campaign, Clinton made sure he was back in Arkansas to preside over that execution to show that he was no wimp when it came to crime. When asked what he wanted for his last meal, the condemned man said he wanted pumpkin pie for dessert. When he got finished with his dinner, the guard was about to take him to the electric chair and he asked him, "Well, aren't you going to eat your pumpkin pie?" And the poor guy said, "Oh, that's okay. I'll eat it when I get back." As far as I'm concerned, Clinton can have all the interns he wants. What was obscene was executing a guy with the IQ of a three-year-old.

Some people are so easily threatened that they can't tolerate nonconformity of any kind.

If you're a free thinker, and don't believe in God, the popular feeling is that you can't be trusted. Some people are so easily threatened that they can't tolerate nonconformity of any kind. That's why Bush surrounds himself with yes-people and never tests ideas in a healthy way—because he's so intellectually insecure.

I have always challenged everything all my life: authority, religion, government. Today, I don't believe in anybody but myself. I don't talk about "God's will" or use the expression "it was meant to be." Sometimes people ask me questions about being in a wheelchair, and I tell them I don't think about it. And you know why I don't think about it? Because I have been self-programmed all my life to tackle

> **I have always challenged everything all my life: authority, religion, government.**

the things I can change, but not to dwell on things I can't do anything about. I just charge ahead and live my life.

God Is Love

Baptists don't tolerate drinking or dancing, but they don't make such a big deal about contraception, maybe because they're too afraid to talk about it. Catholics will drink and dance until the cows come home, but God forbid a married couple with nine kids should decide to use a diaphragm. Do you see the logic here yet?

From my admittedly limited reading of the Bible, I seem to recall that Jesus was okay with drinking (water into wine, I do remember), took no position on dancing, and really didn't have that much to say about sex, one way or the other. One of his inner circle was a prostitute, as the story goes. He also made a big deal out of siding with the so-called "sinners," because they were the ones who needed his help.

Among some of the whackos who followed him, things got out of control. The fanatics believed that the world was going to end in about twenty minutes. Leaving their jobs and families behind and wandering around in the desert was very popular, as was fasting in order to induce visions. Some went off by themselves to await the Second Coming in caves. Others sat up in high towers to avoid the temptations of the world. Self-flagellation was encouraged in some circles. Some took it as far as self-castration. And we're expected to follow church teachings on sexuality derived from these same traditions? Give me a break.

> **If sexuality is so evil, why did "God" create it in the first place?**

If sexuality is so evil, why did "God" create it in the first place? Was it really just to tempt us into sin—to mess with our heads? I don't know about you, but I think that's a pretty sick concept of a supreme being.

The absurd rules about celibacy for priests didn't even enter the picture until the medieval church had managed to amass considerable land holdings, which they worried might slip away. Priests continued to screw whoever they were going to screw. The church simply decided that they couldn't get *married* so that they couldn't bequeath church real estate to any legitimate offspring.

In my opinion, the Catholic Church is the most reprehensible of all religions, because it has spread sexual repression throughout the ages, never recognizing that human sexuality is one of the most divine gifts we have. They condemn birth control while, except in very few cases, supporting right-wing dictatorships that offer nothing to help the millions of unwanted children that are brought into the world.

In my view, the Catholic Church is not much more than a haven for homosexual pedophiles and a key part of the power structure that keeps the peasants quiet while a few rich families live off the fat of the land. I wouldn't take their sexual advice any more than I would the advice of an inmate in a mental institution.

Even though Christians say that "God is love," the sexual part of loving got locked in the basement.

There are other religious traditions in which good sex is seen as a step on the path to spiritual growth. A Hindu scholar in the fourth century wrote the Kama Sutra as a kind of marriage manual, to keep couples together and on the path to God. Tantric sex comes out of that same tradition. The Tantra sees sex as a sacred ritual, and instead of sitting on a hard bench and singing hymns, couples work together in a discipline sort of like yoga and meditation to prolong and enhance pleasure. To these people, sex is holy.

All I can say to that is "Amen."

7

We the People

Two hundred years ago, some free-thinking guys in three-cornered hats launched an experiment in self-rule that had never been tried before on this planet. The highest authority in their new government would not be God, or God's supposed representative sitting on a throne, but a body of laws based on a written constitution. It was based, in part, on English common law, but mostly, it was made up from scratch. Their constitution began with the words:

> We the people of the United States, in order to form a more perfect union, establish justice, insure domestic tranquility, provide for the common defense, promote the general welfare, and secure the blessings of liberty to ourselves and our posterity, do ordain and establish this Constitution for the United States of America.

Today, I wonder just who the radical conservatives running the government think "we the people" are. If they knew, certainly they would also know that their policies are not serving to help "form a more perfect union, establish justice, [or] insure domestic tranquility." So I have provided the following reminder of the true nature of "we the people" and what we really want:

WE THE PEOPLE want to be left alone
We work hard
We want to have families
We want to know our children are safe when they leave the house
We are saving for retirement
We want to live long enough to know our grandchildren
We look forward to our weekends
We want clean air and safe schools

WE THE PEOPLE love sex
We fantasize about the girl next door, or the UPS man
We have smut hidden somewhere in our homes
We love our sex toys and keep them in our bottom drawers

WE THE PEOPLE want honest leadership
We want to trust our government
We want to believe our democracy works
We are fed up with career politicians
We crave better and less expensive medical care
We wish there were no threat of war
We want to believe what we see and hear in the media
We long for heroes
We want to go about our business without anyone *in* our business
WE THE PEOPLE cherish our privacy

WE THE PEOPLE of the United States, contrary to what the media would like us to believe, are *not* for the most part conservative.

Fifty-eight percent of us support labor unions
Sixty-three percent of us are pro-choice
Over eighty percent of us support equal pay for women
Almost ninety percent of us favor laws that protect the environment

The majority of us are liberal to middle of the road when it comes to the "issues." The problem is, there aren't enough liberal-to-middle-of-the-road leaders with the guts and courage of their convictions to stand up for what we the people want. So the majority of Americans end up either not voting, or voting for someone they consider the lesser of two evils.

But ever increasingly, we the people are under constant surveillance. We the people are being monitored with video cameras. We the people can't go to the library and take out a book without taking a chance that a record of the transaction will turn up on John Ashcroft's desk. Our "personal records," including our medical and financial information, are no longer personal, but are available to the government for scrutiny. That's why the ACLU is filing an amicus brief in support of fat-ass Rush Limbaugh's right to medical privacy. He trashes us up one side and down the other; we support his freedoms.

> **We cannot allow a vocal minority of right-wing cranks to get away with rampant intrusion in our lives.**

We the people, who cherish freedom for everyone, individual rights for everyone, and civil liberties for everyone, must fight to protect these things. We cannot allow a vocal minority of right-wing cranks to get away with rampant intrusion in our lives.

We the people need to look beyond the deliberate smokescreen of religion and "family values," to see if our elected officials are truly serving us, or if they're hustling us while serving corporate interests instead.

I served my country with great pride in both the army and the navy, but I'm also aware that the most important part of being a loyal and patriotic American is to participate in the democratic process, which includes exercising my right to criticize our foreign policy when I don't agree with what our government is doing. We have to speak up and remind the radical conservatives that we don't show love of our country by keeping our mouths shut while a leader takes us down the wrong path. Silence in the face of military disaster does not "support our troops."

Giving Them Something to Steal

Unfortunately, many of the things Europeans admired about America have been overshadowed by the way America has misused its status as a world power. The arrogance of George W. Bush, made apparent by his disregard for world opinion in his Iraq attack, was disgraceful enough. When he was forced to go back before the U.N. and ask for help in Iraq, it became pathetic.

Don't get me wrong—European leaders are hardly models of perfection. The messed-up world that the U.S. now leads was inherited from Europeans who had run it into the ground for hundreds of years. Their screw-ups—especially in the Middle East— have landed in our laps. Vietnam was a French fiasco before it was our fiasco. There would have been no wide support for a Jewish state sitting on top of all those Arabs had it not been for German atrocities against the Jews. The colonial arrogance of the French, and especially the British, carved up the traditional lands in the Middle East, creating patched-together states like Iraq composed of feuding tribes with no interest in each other except hatred. British arrogance took land from Islamic Palestinians and gave it to Jewish refugees, leading to fifty-plus years of bloodshed. But we don't have to repeat their mistakes.

Years ago, a sixties radical told me, "Man you don't have to cram democracy down people's throats. If it's so great, they'll come over here and *steal* it."

He was right. The trick is to maintain a nation that is a model of openness, fairness, and prosperity for all. When you're offering people something that's really good, they don't have to be coerced and manipulated.

There's a Reason It's the First Amendment

The First Amendment is the cornerstone of our democracy.

The most important thing I've ever done is to defend freedom of speech. I've been at it all my life, but it's taken me years to understand and appreciate the seriousness of what I've been defending. Every day I see more reasons why this is a freedom we cannot take for granted. The First Amendment is the cornerstone of our democracy.

The one question regarding free speech that everyone always asks me is, do I defend it in the most extreme cases? The answer is always yes. I am a purist when it comes to free speech and the First Amendment. I don't cut any corners. I'm absolute, unequivocal, and I don't think free speech or free expression should ever be compromised. Free speech starts with a thought. If you stifle that thought, you are censoring free speech.

Supreme Court Justice Brandeis said that free speech is not absolute, citing as an example that you can't scream fire! in a crowded theater, because someone might get hurt. That's the worst decision the Supreme Court ever made. To me, screaming "Fire!" in a crowded theater is not a crime. The crime occurs when someone gets hurt as a result of your action.

If you ask people if they believe in free speech, 97 percent of Americans will tell you yes, they do. However, when you start qualifying it and ask them, "What about hate speech? What about flag burning? What about pornography?" they will tell you, "Well I didn't know that's what you meant," and all of a sudden, the 97 percent in favor of free speech has now dropped to under 50 percent. There's the inconsistency, and there's the threat.

The American voter pays a price to live in a free society and that price is tolerance. We have to allow others to do things that we don't necessarily like, so that we all can remain free. People who want to build up their own walls of "decency" have to realize what would happen if their rule were extended. We would all be bound by the strictures not only of the most conservative among us, but by everybody else's peculiar little obsessions as well.

> **The American voter pays a price to live in a free society and that price is tolerance.**

What most confuses people in their acceptance of the idea of truly free speech is a tolerance for hate speech. If I kill you because I don't like you, or because you're gay, what's the difference—you're dead either way. I committed murder, and I should be punished for that.

But as for calling each other names? I feel very strongly that hate speech is protected by the First Amendment, and I am against any legislation that tries to criminalize the mere expression of hateful thoughts. That may be the only issue on which I agree with Republicans.

If someone knowingly says something false about you that causes you harm, you can sue them for libel and collect damages in court. You have the right to express yourself, but if what you say causes material damage to someone else, you can be held responsible for it.

If someone's standing on the corner yelling hateful things at a group of gay people or blacks or Jews, and a riot breaks out as a result, unless the person who was yelling also got involved in fighting, I do not see how he has committed an infraction. There are many things people can do to incite others, but trying to control the expression of any idea is a slippery slope. Where do you draw the line?

Many states are enacting hate speech laws now. It all began on these politically correct college campuses, and it's a mistake. We have laws on the books in every state in the Union that allow us to prosecute any type of crime committed against another person. I don't participate in hate speech and I don't advocate it, but what you say and what you actually do have to be kept separate.

Speak Up!

The danger of being born into a free society is that too many of us are not aware of the significance of our rights. When we come into a free world, we take everything like free speech, abortion rights, equal opportunity, and civil rights for granted. We forget how hard won they were. Today's generation has never had to fight for any significant rights.

Too many American voters say "all politicians are alike." Meanwhile, they don't pay enough attention to the details to see the big differences. Too many American voters say "government's hopeless." But instead of voting on the issues that might change things, they vote on the basis of gut feelings like "I don't think he's man enough," or "He seems more likable." Complete psychopaths are often highly likable, that's why people fall for their hustles. What about the issues?

Way too many American voters get hoodwinked into voting on the basis of symbolic issues. You may not like the idea of gay marriage, for instance. But unless you're gay, it isn't going to make a *damn bit* of difference in your day-to-day life. What matters is picking leaders who are going to improve life for more Americans—jobs, education, and keeping the big corporations from running roughshod over everyone else.

When I talk to students on college campuses around the country about apathy, I'm trying to jolt them awake. I want them to be concerned, informed, and to believe that they can make a difference. But to make a difference, you have to know what's going on.

If we want a more moderate, humane form of government, the way it can be attained is to get non-voters to the polls. It's a simply question of arithmetic: There are a lot more of us than there are of them. Democracy is not a spectator sport, and even the seemingly trivial stuff can matter. All those dumb little elections for school board or state rep—these people are making the decisions that affect your

> **You can't just leave the decision-making to the people with some deeply vested interest.**

kids' education, the value of your property, the economic vitality of where you live, and the quality of your life. Guess who runs for those positions on the local planning board? Real estate people and developers. And the school board? The teachers' unions and religious nuts who want to teach the Bible in science class. You can't just leave the decision-making to the people with some deeply vested interest, or a few screws loose. If only just to protect yourself, you might actually have to drag your butt out to some meetings and participate.

Republicans do a great job at getting all the right-wing fanatics to the polls. They throw them "red meat" issues like prayer and abortion to ensure turnout, then dupe them into voting against their own economic self-interest. The right-wingers win only because less than 50 percent of the people vote. Sad to say, the people with the lowest voter turnout are the poor and the minorities, the very people who are getting screwed the most.

Dissent, a Fine American Tradition

To protect freedom of speech, and freedom of thought, and even freedom of religion (which includes freedom *from* religion) the American voter needs to understand and appreciate what he has, and he needs to kick up a fuss when he sees those freedoms being trampled on. That means we all have to exercise our most basic freedom as Americans—the freedom to *dissent.*

This country was founded by colonists expressing their objec-

> **To keep our democracy on its toes, I believe that we all need to throw a little tea over the side from time to time.**

tions to an oppressive government—and another George, by the way, King George III. Occasionally, their dissent meant breaking the rules, as with the Boston Tea Party. To keep our democracy on its toes, I believe that we all need to throw a little tea over the side from time to time.

My own acts of dissent have usually taken place in a court of law. That's part of the reason I've spent more quality time in front of a judge than most people have spent with their children. One thing I've learned is that justice isn't just handed to you. You don't get justice just because you deserve it, just like being innocent won't necessarily keep you out of jail. To have any hope of victory, you have to keep fighting. It never ends.

Back in the seventies and eighties, I was a target for the fundamentalist preachers and politicians who believed I represented the downfall of everything American. In those days, when I was a guest on a radio show, four out of five of the callers wanted to crucify me. They called me every name in the book. And people would sue my ass for whatever they could come up with. I was in court so often, I got to know all the bailiffs. When director Milos Forman was filming *The People vs. Larry Flynt,* he hired a bailiff as a consultant, and he turned out to be one of the same guys who'd cuffed me and taken me away once years before.

I probably shouldn't admit that I'm proud of all my behavior in the courtroom, but I am. My antics were conceived in self-defense. But if I were to give you Larry Flynt's Rules for How to Behave in a Court of Law, the most important one would be: *Don't be like me.*

I had been shot and paralyzed, and I was in constant pain. I figured if they were going to treat me like a joke, I was going to act like one, and that's why I behaved like an asshole every time I went to court. It finally got to the point where judges just didn't want to see me anymore.

Once I was watching Court TV and this guy in Connecticut went up for sentencing for armed robbery before a female judge. She asked him if he had anything to say before she passed sentence, and he whipped it out and started pissing right on the bench. I thought, "Man, why didn't I think of that? That was a great one!"

When they took me in front of the federal magistrate to arraign me for disrupting the Supreme Court, I was wearing a T-shirt that said "Fuck this court." The marshal tried to make me take it off, and he and I got in a fight, and of course, I'm in a wheelchair, and this guy is trying to rip this shirt off me. The judge had to rein him in with the gavel, and ultimately they were forced to deal with me while staring at "Fuck this court."

When Milos Foreman came up with the idea of having me play the movie role of the judge in the obscenity trial, I thought it was totally brilliant. I would never have dreamed of that. I said, "But, Milos, I'm not an actor. I don't think I could do it," and he said, "I think you'd be perfect."

It took twenty-six takes to get it right. Woody Harrelson, who played me, was a great help, and so was Edward Norton, who played my lawyer. I forced myself to get into that role, and to feel what the judge was feeling when he sentenced me to a quarter century in prison—that absolute hatred and resolve I knew he had. It was satisfying in a strange way. To get into the role, I bought myself a pair of black-framed reading glasses just like the ones I remember the real judge wore. I'll never forget the way they sat on the tip of his nose, and the way he glared over them to look straight into my eyes. I still wear them sometimes today, just to remind me what it feels like to be under a judge's thumb.

As the scene was being filmed, as I pounded my gavel and sentenced "Larry Flynt," it brought back memories of sitting in one stuffy courtroom after another, always nervous as hell about what some judge's ruling would be. The fake jury sitting there on that movie set looked more real than I was comfortable with, just like the jury that convicted me in Ohio. It was so realistic that I almost felt sorry for Woody.

I've seen American justice from both sides. It makes me appreciate what we have, and it makes me realize how hard we have to work to keep it. Personal liberty and a decent society do not come for free, especially not when so many other people are out to trash it all, often while wrapped in the flag and saying how much they are fighting to defend the very freedoms they are bringing down.

Whatever Happened to Compassion?

> **Americans have turned their backs on any sense of responsibility for the country as a whole.**

Somehow, over the past twenty years, too many Americans have turned their backs on any sense of responsibility for the country as a whole—especially for those who aren't getting stock options, but are just barely getting by. Too many of today's corporate executives, whether they built the company themselves or took over from daddy, act like they have no regard for anything but their quarterly stock price—and their own compensation, of course.

A recent Towers Perrin study showed that the salary spread between the average CEO and the average worker in Japan is 10 to 1. Between the average German CEO and the average German worker it's 11 to 1. In Canada, it's 21 to 1; in England, 25 to 1. But in the land of the free and the home of the brave—that would be the United States—the average CEO makes a whopping 531 times what the average worker does.

That's just not right.

We're creating a perpetual aristocracy in this country with huge salaries and tax benefits for the top dogs, trust funds and private education for their kids, and everybody else can go die. Money allows the wealthy to buy politicians who have no principles other than staying in office, so we get congressmen blathering on about morality while setting up tax breaks and off-shore favors for the rich.

The trouble is, the Republicans have perfected their scam. When we talk about gross unfairness, they start chanting "class warfare." They've all lashed themselves to the same

> **When we talk about gross unfairness, they start chanting "class warfare."**

mast: punishment rather than assistance or rehabilitation, self-reliance (as long as they keep getting those fat government contracts, that is), and lower taxes.

Democrats, on the other hand, are all over the place. We've got unions, blacks, Hispanics, gays, tree-huggers—the list goes on and on. And each group cares most about their particular issue. We never come together with a united message, or a real program. These days, we just get blamed for everything because the conservatives have mastered the blame game and the average person can't see through it.

The Democratic Leadership Council tried to solve the problem by being more pro-business, which means more Republican without all the lies. But the white working class still goes for "Morning in America," "Honor and Integrity," and "Mission Accomplished." They buy the Republican images, even though they're fake. And with the DLC continually trying to meet the Republicans halfway, the center keeps shifting to the right.

There was a cartoon in *The New Yorker* not long ago that showed a geezer on his deathbed, surrounded by his grieving family. Waxing philosophical at the end of his life, he looked up into his wife's eyes and said, "I should have bought more crap."

Funny, but in a reverse sort of way, that cartoon reminded me of the deathbed conversion of the infamous conservative hitman, Lee Atwater. Dying of cancer, Atwater, the junkyard dog of politics for the elder George Bush, called up all the people he'd stabbed in the back, poked in the eye, and kicked in the balls, and asked for their forgiveness. George Wallace, the last segregationist to make a major play for the presidency, was the same way; if not "coming to Jesus," then at least coming to Jesse Jackson and asking to be let off the hook for a career built on racism and opportunism.

You don't hear about too many deathbed apologies coming from people with progressive political ideas. No more than you hear of people who took good care of their friends and families wishing they'd spent their time buying more crap. Liberals may change their minds in their bitter old age—that's the textbook definition of a neoconservative. But generally speaking, I think those who devote themselves to trying to make the world a better place end their lives without that kind of afraid-to-meet-their-maker turnaround.

As I have argued throughout this book, the radical conservatives who have taken over this country are, by and large, damaged people. How else can you explain someone like Dick Cheney? He's got a bad heart, he's not going to be with us too terribly much longer. He's got all the money anybody could use. And yet, he seems to have no purpose in life except helping the rich build the walls higher around their gated communities.

There's nothing wrong with being rich. I enjoy it. But making some money has not deprived me of compassion. I don't think it's a crime for me to have to pay taxes to help us sustain a civil society. The conservatives like Rush Limbaugh demand tough laws to put first-time drug offenders in jail for years, then howl about the tax money it takes to pay for prisons. You don't get government services for nothing, and clearly there are government services that we all want and need.

The State of Our Union

If you're ever tempted to believe that the Democrats and the Republicans are all alike, that there's no difference, that one's as bad as the other, I hope you'll remember some of what you've read in this book. The question, fundamentally, is who's giving you a reasonably truthful presentation of their ideas? Certainly in terms of domestic policy, the Democrats have no need to lie. They are by no means immune to pressure from special interests, but generally speaking, what they have to say can be argued on the merits. They don't have a comprehensive, hidden agenda like

> **Most Americans favor Democratic positions on the issues.**

"starve the beast" or "no millionaire left behind" that requires them to wrap themselves in the flag, sing hymns, or pretend that they are fundamentally something they are not in order to get elected. In fact, polls have shown that personalities and images aside, and even while the number of registered Democrats is slipping badly, most Americans favor Democratic positions on the issues.

It takes political courage to maintain democracy. I was sorry to see that Senator Robert Bryd of Virginia, eighty-six years old, was the only member of the Senate with the guts to vote against the $87 billion Bush managed to coerce out of Congress for Iraq. He shouted out his "nay" vote loud and clear. There were only six senators in the chamber at the time, but none of the others had the guts to stand up and be counted.

Bush's war has never been discussed honestly. We've never committed enough soldiers even to protect our own troops, and now Bush is cutting back for purely political reasons. He got to make his macho statement, and his radical advisors got to try out their screwball ideas about remaking the Middle East. But he also knows that American support for this war, to the extent that it exists at all, is paper thin, and he wants to be able to wash his hands of it by Election Day. That's why we've never had more than 28,000 troops on patrol at any one time in the entire country. For comparison's sake, there are 39,000 police officers in New York City alone (which has 8 million people). There are six million people in Baghdad. Mosul has 1.7 million. Kirkuk has 800,000. Bush is trying to run his war the same way he runs domestic policy—all politics, all the time—and it is killing our young men and women in uniform.

Beyond being in harm's way, our men and women who do serve are all grossly underpaid. A third of the military is on relief. You talk to somebody who's an E-6, which is equivalent to a Master Sergeant, and makes $32,000 a year, and some of those guys have four or five kids to support. We are just not paying the military what we should be, and yet we expect them to take the risks, endure the hardships, and do our dirty work for us. I think people should protest *that* in a big way. We need to support our troops by paying them a living wage. And we need to ensure that the corporations and their Republican gofers don't get away with turning America into a banana republic, with fat cats on top and peasants on the bottom and nobody left in the middle.

Bush is trying to undermine the most precious and distinctive qualities of life in the United States—our tradition of tolerance, the freedom to dissent, and the freedom from having anyone else cramming his religious ideas down our throats. After all its centuries of religious wars, fear, and bloodshed that made relocating to a half-frozen wilderness in North America seem attractive, Europe has now moved ahead of us in terms of tolerance. They now have a progressive, secular society, and we have government threatening to be run by preachers. Immigrants fled Europe to get away from societies built around priests and aristocratic privileges, and now we're worse off over here.

On January 1, 2004, Pat Robertson announced to viewers of his "700 Club" TV show that God's already told him that George W. Bush is going to be reelected in a "blowout." I guess another way of looking at Pat's insight is that God was issuing the rest of us a warning. Certainly, unless we do something about it, Pat's little prophecy is going to come true.

Born-againers like Pat Robertson, and George W. Bush for that matter, may think they're getting their political ideas from God,

but I think we need to recon-
nect with the ideas of another
George, George Washington. In
1790, he ended his State of the
Union address with what still
stands as the best mission statement for all Americans, govern-

> **We need to reconnect with the ideas of another George, George Washington.**

ment leaders and average citizens alike: "The welfare of our
country is the great object to which our cares and efforts ought to
be directed—and I shall derive great satisfaction from a cooperation with you, in the pleasing though arduous task of ensuring to
our fellow citizens the blessings which they have a right to expect,
from a free and equal government."

I couldn't have said it better myself.

A NOTE ON SOURCES

Information is like money. There's plenty available—it's just not evenly distributed. In this book, I've tried to bring together what I think everybody ought to know about the current political scene, then spread that information around. But I didn't have to reinvent the wheel when it came to research. So many damning accounts of George W. Bush and his cronies already exist that all it takes is Internet access or a library card to be up to your eyeballs in outrage. Unfortunately, the message—scattered in bits and pieces, here and there—still hasn't gotten through. After all, forty percent of Americans still consider themselves Republicans!

I've been doing investigative journalism for thirty years, and of course, I've drawn on my own gumshoe work and that of my staff. But I've also had the benefit of solid investigative work already done by a number of fine reporters.

I read the *New York Times* every day, and there's a reason it is considered the newspaper of record for the whole world. Aside from an in-depth presentation of all the facts, they provide columnists like Maureen Dowd, Paul Krugman, and Frank Rich, who are national treasures.

Most of the facts and figures in this book are drawn from the *Times,* but I've also made use of reporting in the *Los Angeles Times,* the *Washington Post, Vanity Fair,* and from Reuters.

I've also relied on a number of books, articles, and Web sites.

Here is a listing of those I have drawn upon most heavily, primarily in Chapters 2 through 5, which deal with the Bush administration and the right-wing conspiracy that brought it to power:

David Brock, *Blinded by the Right* (Crown, 2002). I believe this guy is a major asshole for what he did to Anita Hill, Bill Clinton, and others, but the book gives a unique, insider's view of the entire right-wing disinformation machinery and the nutcases who run it.

Joe Conason's *Big Lies* (St. Martin's, 2003). Conason covers the years from Reagan to Bush II, focusing on the right wing's nasty little habit of providing deliberate misinformation.

David Corn, *The Lies of George W. Bush* (Crown, 2003). Corn, Washington editor for the *Nation,* has a narrower focus for his study of deliberate disinformation, but he still had plenty of material to work with.

Al Franken, *Lies and the Lying Liars Who Tell Them* (Dutton, 2003). Franken, with his team of 14 Harvard student-researchers digging up the dirt, provided a handy reference for juicy facts and figures on the Bush administration.

J. H. Hatfield, *Fortunate Son* (Soft Skull Press, 2001). The book they tried to suppress in 2000 is available in paperback. It's actually a pretty fair-minded appraisal of Bush as a man, but one who used cocaine, drove while drunk, whose grandfather made a fortune helping Nazis move their money, and whose father may have tried to subvert democracy through the "October Surprise" that helped bring Reagan to the White House. W comes across as a guy who was probably a lot of fun to hang out with as a college sophomore . . . but President? Are you joking?

Molly Ivins and Lou Dubose, *Bushwacked* (Random House, 2003). These two Texans tell the back story of what it means to have George W. Bush in charge. They were on the scene while he was governor and lived to tell about it. By any measure except the number of obnoxious, self-serving millionaires, Texas has always been one of our most backward states. After Bush, it is a backward state awash in red ink.

Paul Krugman, *The Great Unraveling* **(Norton, 2003).** This collection of columns about economics from the *New York Times* could make a grown man weep. Krugman shows not only what's really going on, but what it's really costing us, now, and into the future.

Jane Meyer, "Contract Sport," *The New Yorker,* **February 16 & 23, 2004, pp. 80–91.** An in-depth study of crony capitalism as played out at Halliburton, and in the person of their former CEO, and our current number two, Dick Cheney.

Michael Moore, *Stupid White Men* **(Regan Books, 2001); and** *Dude, Where's My Country?* **(Warner Books, 2003).** Michael provides background on the Bush–bin Laden connection among other things, along with his distinctive style of outrage.

Greg Palast, *The Best Democracy Money Can Buy* **(Plume, 2003).** This book should be taught in high school civics classes—if they still have them after all the budget cuts the conservatives have foisted on us. Of all reporters, Palast, who works mostly for *The Guardian* and the BBC, has dug deepest into the dirt of what really went on during the 2000 election in Florida.

Kevin Phillips, *American Dynasty* **(Viking, 2004).** Phillips likes the Bush boys about as much as I do, but he takes the story back four generations to the roots of their particularly obnoxious behavior. The joke is, Phillips was until about four years ago a Republican (he said the 2000 election made him "ashamed"). In 1969, he wrote *The Emerging Republican Majority,* the book that

explained—in advance—how the radical conservatives consoli-
dated their power over the past thirty-five years.

**David Reiff, "Blueprint for a Mess," *The New York Times Sun-
day Magazine*, November 2, 2003.** The long and pathetic story of
how Ahmed Chabali played into the geopolitical fantasies of Paul
Wolfowitz, Richard Perle, and Donald Rumsfeld to get us a war in
Iraq.

**Christopher Scheer, Lakshmi Chaudry, and Robert Scheer, *The
Five Biggest Lies Bush Told Us About Iraq* (Seven Stories, 2004).**
Robert Scheer, contributing editor for the *Los Angeles Times*, and
his colleagues expand on the whole Iraq mess, showing that we
are well on our way to having another Vietnam.

David Stockman, *The Triumph of Politics* (Harper, 1986). Reagan's budget director not only gives the lie to "supply side" economics, he makes you wonder why the Gipper ever became such a
saint to right-wingers.

Ron Suskind, *The Price of Loyalty* (Simon and Schuster, 2004).
Somehow this reporter got Paul O'Neill, first secretary of the treasury under Bush II, to spill the beans. The book shows you just
how out of control things can get when you have an empty suit sitting at the head of the table and lightweight lackeys and extremist
ideologues gathered around everywhere else.

www. aclu.org If you want the latest on how the Patriot Act will
soon be climbing in your window—with a video camera—this is
the place to go. I am proud to be a "card-carrying member" of the
American Civil Liberties Union, the people who will defend even
Rush Limbaugh's right to privacy and due process.

www.Buzzflash.com This is today's electronic version of one of
the great underground newspapers that were everywhere in the

sixties. Aside from its own compilation of the outrage du jour, it has links to just about every other news source on the planet.

www. geocities.com/the Reagan years   A vast collection of out-takes from the "Teflon presidency" of Ronald Reagan. You get everything from Nancy's astrology to the word from angry Reagan children to the whole story of Iran-Contra to clueless quotes from the Gipper himself. And they named an airport after this guy?

www.robertscheer.com   This contributing editor for the *Los Angeles Times* regularly skewers those who deserve it, such as former secretary of the interior James G. Watt.

I have given credit in the text where it seemed appropriate, and to all these sources, I offer my thanks.

INDEX